WHO'S TAMPERING
WITH THE
TRINITY?

WHO'S TAMPERING
WITH THE
TRINITY?

AN ASSESSMENT OF THE
SUBORDINATION DEBATE

MILLARD J. ERICKSON

Kregel
Academic & Professional

Who's Tampering with the Trinity? An Assessment of the Subordination Debate

© 2009 by Millard J. Erickson

Published by Kregel Publications, a division of Kregel, Inc., P.O. Box 2607, Grand Rapids, MI 49501.

The Greek font used in this book is SymbolGreekU and is available from http://www.linguistsoftware.com/lgku.htm, +1-425-775-1130.

ISBN 978-0-8254-2589-9

Printed in the United States of America

09 10 11 12 13 / 5 4 3 2 1

To Linnea and Malaya
"Children's children are a crown to the aged."
(PROV. 17:6)

Contents

Preface

In my experience, books come into existence for various reasons. In some cases, publishers request a book on a particular subject. In other cases, series of lectures lend themselves to publication in book form. Often, a burning issue ignites discussion and convinces an individual that a book is needed to deal with the matter. This book, however, came into being in a manner a bit different from all others I have mentioned.

Since 1992 I have written two books on the doctrine of the Trinity and also dealt more briefly with the subject in a chapter in my *Christian Theology*, which I wrote in 1982. I was aware of the issue of the relative authority of the three persons, and discussed this briefly. I also know that my own view has been criticized on this point in the writings of one or two evangelical theologians, but I chose not to respond, since in my judgment defensiveness is not a particularly desirable quality in a theologian or any other type of scholar.

More recently I was drawn into the discussion rather indirectly when the Gender Studies study group of the Evangelical Theological Society asked me to present a paper on the Trinity at their meeting in November 2006. Since a well-known "complementarian" was presenting a paper at that same session, I asked that my presentation follow his, and outline some of the issues that I thought needed to be addressed by those of his persuasion. The ensuing discussion proved very interesting to me, and one person's comment especially piqued my interest. He said, "It seems to me that the major difference between the view that the Son is eternally subordinated to the Father and the view that the subordination is only temporary is that we have biblical support for our view, and our opponents do not."

Being by nature a curious person, I decided to investigate that assertion, simply for my own interest. Others, however, urged me to share my findings. That led to a paper at the next meeting of the society on the topic, "Is Eternal Intratrinitarian Equality of Authority Biblical?" By this time I had concluded that issues of great importance for the doctrine of the Trinity were involved in this discussion, and having now in hand the makings of two chapters of a book, I decided to pursue my investigations further. Editors at two publishing houses that had recently published volumes on the subject assured me that there was still more to be said on the subject and encouraged me to write on it. This volume is the result of that effort.

As in my past books, my aim here has been to investigate as thoroughly and fairly as possible the alternative positions on the subject before attempting to decide which is the more adequate theory. This procedure was insisted upon in my studies at the University of Minnesota, the University of Chicago, and Northwestern University. It is also something I have learned from reading the work of scholars in other fields, such as the noted late economist Milton Friedman, who said, "You cannot be sure that you are right, unless you understand the arguments against your view better than your opponents do."[1]

This experience has been especially satisfying because it required me to draw upon several fields of study from my past education: not only systematic theology, my major in the Ph.D. program; but also historical theology, a minor in that program of study; biblical languages, which constituted the concentration in my seminary studies; and philosophy, my major in the B.A. and M.A. programs and a minor in the Ph.D. All of these have contributed to the method I have sought to develop in doing systematic theology and confirmed for me the value of these disciplines for theological methodology. Beyond that, the practical dimensions of Christian doctrine that have informed my pastoral ministry over the years have proven essential to examine.

---

1. Mary Ruth Yoe, "Market Force," *University of Chicago Magazine* 99, no. 3 (January–February 2007): 30.

I especially wish to thank Jim Weaver, director of academic publishing at Kregel Publications, who enabled me to bring this manuscript to published form. It has been a pleasure to collaborate with him again as we have done on so many publishing projects in the past. I also want to thank my colleagues in the Evangelical Theological Society, who read and listened to my papers, asked probing questions, and encouraged me to share my findings in a larger context.

What's All This Chatter About the Trinity?

The speaker stepped to the podium to deliver his remarks. Short and dark-haired, with a beard, he spoke rapidly because of the large amount of information he wanted to impart. With clarity and certainty, he argued that the Father and the Son, though both properly called God, must be understood in their proper relationship to one another. The Father, he said, is the supreme member of the Godhead, the one with authority over the Son. The Father has planned all that the deity has accomplished and has carried it out through the Son. The Father commands, and the Son obeys. That is what the very terms "Father" and "Son" convey.

The speaker contended that this is the correct understanding of the Holy Scriptures, which the earlier theologians of the church had believed and taught. He cited abundant references to establish his point. The certainty with which he held these convictions was underscored by his repeated use of words like *clearly* and *obvious*. Those who differed from this point of view, who argued that the Son's obedience to the Father was only during the period of his earthly ministry and for the purpose of carrying out the work of redemption of the human race, were departing from the clear teaching of the Scripture and the tradition. Although he did not use the terms *heresy* or *heretics* to describe his opponents, it was clear that he considered their errors serious in nature. They obliterated any real basis for distinguishing between the Father and the Son. And, because they denied that the Father and the Son had any inherent difference of function, they had no basis for answering the question of why it was that the Son came to earth in the Incarnation, rather than the Father or the Holy Spirit.

Because the speaker had so much to say, his remarks occupied almost the entire time allotted to him, leaving little time for questions, remarks, and discussion. Following the session, however, in the meeting room and in the hallways of the meeting place, debate raged among delegates to the meeting, some strongly agreeing with the first speaker and others criticizing his position. Other speakers gave their scheduled speeches, varying in emphasis but all relating in one way or another to the issue of the relationship of the Father and the Son, for that was the topic for which the meeting of these delegates had been convened.

Later that same day, another speaker gave his carefully prepared presentation. Taller and older than the first man, and with an accent that indicated that he came from a different locale, he developed his view in opposition to that of the first speaker. The Father and the Son must be understood as possessing equal authority, he insisted, if they are to be considered fully divine. Like the earlier speaker, he supported his contention with documentation from the Scriptures and earlier church theologians. It was not he, but the other speaker and those who held that view, who had departed from the church's established doctrine. While he also was loath to use terms like *heresy*, he did liken his opponents' views to those of an earlier heretic and expressed concern lest they and their students should slip toward that deviant view. This speaker left adequate time for interaction, and it followed swiftly. The earlier speaker and others who held his view rose to express their strong disagreement, and others joined in on both sides of the argument. It was apparent that consensus would not be reached any time soon.

To the reader familiar with church history, this may sound like an abbreviated account of some of the proceedings of the ecumenical council that met at Nicea in 325. The topic debated on that occasion was the divine Trinity and specifically the relationship between God the Father and God the Son. The primary proponents of the two major views were Arius and Athanasius. In reality, what you have read here is a brief synopsis of the proceedings of one study group of the Evangelical

Theological Society, meeting in Washington, D.C., on November 16, 2006. Although the specifics of the debate were quite different from that which took place 1,681 years earlier, there are some interesting parallels. While the doctrine of the Trinity has been discussed throughout the history of the church, controversy on the subject has broken out anew—and among persons who hold the same basic view of the Bible's authority.

As the early church grew and spread, it increasingly reflected upon what it believed. Some of its beliefs were quite easy to understand, although in some cases, such as the resurrection, they were difficult for some to believe. Other beliefs, such as salvation purely by the grace of Christ, ran contrary to some deeply ingrained tendencies of human nature but were conceptually not too difficult to understand. At one point, however, the believers found an unusual tension between two beliefs that were both of great importance to them. On the one hand, they held to the absolute uniqueness and exclusivity of the God of Abraham, Isaac, and Jacob, whom they referred to as Yahweh or Jehovah. This belief, monotheism, inherited from Hebrew belief and taught in the Hebrew Scriptures, also was enunciated in the books that came to be known as the New Testament. On the other hand, they believed that Jesus is Lord, which, as they understood from the revelation he brought, entailed belief in his deity, for here was one who claimed the right to forgive sins, asserted that he would preside at the final judgment, and set forth his teachings as going beyond the writings of Moses. In short, he claimed prerogatives proper only to God.

Here was an apparent contradiction: that God is one, and yet, in addition to Jehovah, Jesus also should be understood as being God. Complicating the dilemma further was the status of the Holy Spirit, who also seemed to be revealed as fully divine. It was, however, the relationship of Jesus to Jehovah that constituted the real dilemma; and if it could be solved, the additional question of the Holy Spirit's status probably could be treated in a similar fashion.

A number of solutions to this dilemma were proposed. One of the most vigorous was attributed to Arius and his followers. On this model,

Jesus was not God in quite the same sense as the Father. He was a created being, the highest of the creatures, and perhaps entitled to be called a god but not *the* God, in the same sense or to the same degree as the Father.

The church struggled mightily with the question of whether to allow this view and in the end, at the Council of Nicea in 325, decided that Arianism was contrary to the correct understanding of the biblical revelation and therefore heresy.

The true view was declared to be that Jesus was God the Son, *homoousios* with God the Father. They were of the same nature. The Son was as fully God as was the Father. A modified form of Arianism, which has been termed Semi-Arianism, claimed that the Son was similar in nature (*homoiousios*) but not identical. The church, however, rejected this as well. For the most part, Arianism ended with the fourth century, although small pockets lived on; and in our time the Jehovah's Witnesses vigorously continue to proclaim this view and zealously seek to convert others, including Christians, to belief in it.

With the settlement reached at the Council of Nicea and extended at the Council of Chalcedon (451), the official position of the church became that the Father, Son, and Holy Spirit are all divine and are divine in the same sense and to the same degree as one another. There is no difference in what they are or in their being or essence. Yet these are not three gods but one God. Precisely how these three were to be understood in their relationship to one another continued to be a problem, but the formula was definite.

Through many centuries this basic doctrine continued to be held, and the questions raised in those first centuries were considered to have been answered. From time to time, there were Christian groups that denied this doctrine. Some of these, such as the sixteenth-century Socinians, maintained that Jesus was not in any sense to be thought of as God. That designation was reserved for the Father. Their intellectual and spiritual descendents came to be known as Unitarians, those who believe that only one is God. For the most part they were found in a denomination known today as the Unitarian-Universalist Church.

The liberal theology that arose in the nineteenth and twentieth centuries did not think of Jesus as God in quite the same sense as in earlier times. In some cases he was thought of as merely the most profound prophet or teacher whom religion had produced, or even as the one who had discovered more about God than anyone else, before or since. Some theologians saw him as the human in whom God had dwelt and worked to the greatest extent of any human who had ever lived. The difference between Jesus and other humans was one of degree, but the difference between Jesus and God was one of kind. Rather consistently, however, these views were seen as falling outside the mainstream of orthodoxy. Those who held them also ordinarily held views in other areas of doctrine, such as the doctrine of Scripture or the doctrine of salvation, that represented modifications of the classical views.

In the late twentieth and early twenty-first centuries, a new debate has arisen. It is interesting that those who stand on opposite sides of the discussion agree quite closely in most other doctrines and even in most aspects of the doctrine of the Trinity. In this case, the disputants are evangelicals and even conservative evangelicals. Both parties hold to the supreme authority, divine inspiration, and the inerrancy of the Bible. They hold to the full deity of Christ, his bodily resurrection and second coming, and salvation by grace. They believe there is one God existing in three persons, and these three—Father, Son, and Holy Spirit—are, as to their nature or their being, fully and equally God. There is one point of understanding of the Trinity on which the two parties disagree quite strongly, however; namely, the relative authority of the three persons.

We may term the one view the gradational view, because its proponents maintain that there is an eternal hierarchy of authority among the three persons. According to this view, the Father is the supreme member of the Trinity, possessing the highest authority, and the Son and the Spirit are subordinate to him and submit to his authority. This is how the three have been related in eternity past, during the earthly ministry of Jesus, and the present ministry of the Holy Spirit in the life of believers, and it will also be true throughout eternity future. The Son came in the Incarnation because the Father sent him, which he had the authority to do. The Son rightly obeyed the Father. This is of the very nature of the relationship and is believed to be of the very essence of the Trinity. Yet, this view maintains, there is absolute equality of being or essence among the three persons.

The other view can be called the equivalence view, for it holds that the Father, Son, and Holy Spirit are eternally equal in authority. A temporary functional subordination of the Son and the Holy Spirit to the Father has been established for the purpose of carrying out a particular mission. But when that mission is completed, the three persons' full equality of authority will resume. References to the Father's superiority to the Son, or to the Son doing the Father's will, are to be referred to this temporary functional and missional subordination.

These two views can be clearly contrasted by juxtaposing quotations from representatives of each:

> First, the Father is, in his position and authority, supreme among the Persons of the Godhead. . . .
>
> The Father who is above all the nations, is also above the king whom he sets over the nations. The father's supremacy is both over the nations themselves and over the king whom he places over the nations. . . . Here, then, is evidence that the Father's role is supreme over that of the Son, for it is the Father who sends the Son, and who puts the Son in his place as king over the nations; and this is fulfilled as the Son of God, who is the Son of David, comes to reign and bring all things into subjection under his feet (Heb. 2:8). Yes, the Father is supreme in the Godhead, as Psalm 2 makes clear. . . .
>
> Further, this attitude of bowing to the authority and position of the Father marked Jesus' own life and ministry over and over.[1]

By way of contrast, note the following statement: "Because there was no order of subordination within the Trinity prior to the Second Person's

---

1. Bruce A. Ware, *Father, Son, and Holy Spirit: Relationships, Roles, and Relevance* (Wheaton, IL: Crossway, 2005), 46–47.

incarnation, there will remain no such thing after its completion. If we must talk of subordination it is only a functional or economic subordination that pertains exclusively to Christ's role in relation to human history. Christ's *kenosis* affected neither his essence nor his status in eternity."[2]

Here then are two quite diametrically opposed positions on one basic issue: the eternal authority relationship of the Father and the Son (and for that matter, the Holy Spirit as well). The former position maintains that eternally the Trinity is characterized by a hierarchical authority structure: the Father is supreme, possessing supreme authority, and the Son and the Holy Spirit obey his commands, or submit themselves to them. The latter position contends that eternally the Trinity is characterized by an equal authority structure in which the Father, Son, and Holy Spirit possess equal authority with one another and the submission or obedience of the Son and the Spirit to the Father is a temporary functional submission, for the purpose of executing a specific mission of the triune God.

In some other ways, these two views are mirror images of one another. Each group contends that its view is the true biblical one, and can be shown to be so by a careful study of the Scriptures. Each also claims that it has the support of history—indeed that it is the view that has always been held by the church. Each also holds that the advocates of the opposing view have adopted the view they have on this issue because of a prior commitment on another issue—the relationship of men and women in the church and in the family—and in order to justify that prior commitment. They believe the other theology has distorted the traditional formulation of the doctrine of the Trinity. Note, for instance, the terms they use in titles of significant treatises. Ware has entitled an article, "Tampering with the Trinity,"[3] Bilezikian also wrote of "tampering with the doctrine of the Trinity,"[4] and Giles refers

---

2. Gilbert Bilezikian, "Hermeneutical Bungee-Jumping: Subordination in the Godhead," *Journal of the Evangelical Theological Society* 40, no. 1 (March 1997): 60.

3. Bruce Ware, "Tampering with the Trinity: Does the Son Submit to His Father?" *Journal for Biblical Manhood and Womanhood* 6, no. 1 (Spring 2001): 4–12.

4. Bilezikian, "Hermeneutical Bungee-Jumping," 58, 66.

to those who are "reinventing the doctrine of the Trinity."[5] At least one of the equal-authority theologians, Kevin Giles, has suggested that the hierarchical view has tendencies toward Arianism, thus implying that it is in danger of slipping into heresy.[6]

The advocates of each of these views believe they can identify the motivation of the other party in holding the view of the Trinity that it does. Each believes that this is in order to justify a particular view of the relative roles of male and female. Gradationists have suggested that their opponents are egalitarians and are unwilling to accept eternal subordination of the Son to the Father because that would mean that women are to be subject to men; that is, wives should be subject to their husbands, and women should not hold positions of authority, of ruling, and of preaching or teaching in the church. The proponents of the equal-authority view, on the other hand, believe that the gradationists are using the idea of God's eternal authority over the Son to justify the permanent authority of men over women.

I have long wrestled with the question of what titles to assign to these two views. To some extent, the titles that have been used reflect titles assigned to corresponding views of the relationship of men and women. The former group prefers to label their view the "complementarian" view and the other group's the "egalitarian" view. Some in the latter group have objected to the first group taking the name "complementarian," contending that their own view is that men and women may have complementary roles but that the real issue is whether either is in a position of supremacy over the other.

The second group prefers to refer to the two positions as the "hierarchical" and the "egalitarian" views, respectively. The former theologians, however, have generally tended to avoid or even disavow the use of the term *hierarchical*. It seems that the issue probably could be more profitably and objectively discussed if this terminology were avoided. Further, to separate the issue of the respective roles of Father and Son

---

5. Kevin Giles, *Jesus and the Father: Modern Evangelicals Reinvent the Doctrine of the Trinity* (Grand Rapids: Zondervan, 2006).

6. Ibid., 306–9.

from those of men and women, a pair of terms not used of the two views for the latter relationship may be desirable for denominating the two views of the former relationship.

I therefore propose to use the term *gradational authority* for the view of those who hold that the Father eternally has supreme authority over the Son and the term *equivalent authority* for the view that eternally the Father and the Son have equal authority, although the Son took a position of subordinate authority for a particular time and purpose. This would then yield the names "gradational view" and "equivalence view." Although the resulting terms, *gradationists* and *equivalentists,* are admittedly rather awkward, they do have the advantage of being descriptive and of preventing either party from attempting to gain a rhetorical advantage by stipulative definition.

This issue is not merely an unimportant hairsplitting exercise among ivory-tower thinkers. Potentially it has far-reaching implications for other areas of theology and for the practical life of Christians and of the church. Indeed, if theological conclusions are being driven by what may be primarily nonbiblical considerations, then the doctrine of biblical authority has been compromised, and one may expect to see modifications of other doctrines as well. Further, if the view held on this doctrine represents a tendency to depart from the orthodox position in this area, one may expect the departure to increase, as a second generation of theologians in that movement takes the position to its next logical step.

Beyond that, however, there are definite practical issues. How do we worship, and how do we pray? Should praise and prayer be directed only to the Father, through the Son and by the Spirit, as at least some gradationists insist; or should these activities be directed to each member of the Trinity, in relationship to particular areas of their work, as the equivalentists claim? The distinctions of authority have other, practical distinctions. Should our understanding of the human relations we have mentioned be governed by our conclusion on this doctrine, and if so, what should that conclusion be?

The aim of this book, therefore, will be to seek to determine which of these views is true. The author frankly acknowledges that he is working from the perspective that the Bible is the supreme and final authority for the believer in matters of faith and practice. Indeed, in terms of giving us the content of that belief and practice, it is the only authority, to be distinguished from such instrumental authorities as exegetical methods and logical analysis, which assist us in understanding what that content means.[7] The views and insights of theologians in the history of the church, like the commentaries of biblical scholars, are means to assist us in understanding the supreme authority, the Bible. This presupposition of biblical authority is one that I believe I share with the advocates of each of these two positions.

The plan for achieving this aim of choosing between these two views is as follows. In the next two chapters, the two views will be examined in greater detail, giving something of the historical development of each of these in the past 140 years or so, with special emphasis on developments since 1970. This description and analysis will be as balanced and fair as I can make it and will seek, not to be the arbiter between the two, but rather to determine just what are the exact issues that separate them.

Before we can decide which of these two alternatives is the stronger, however, we will need to self-consciously review just how to go about evaluating such alternatives. While we wish we could simply look in the Bible for a direct answer, the issue is considerably more complex than that. We will therefore ask just what sorts of criteria are appropriate for a choice of this type. What are the characteristics of a stronger versus a weaker theory in any area of inquiry that we may apply to the decision before us? This will constitute chapter 3.

In chapter 4, we will carefully examine the biblical texts cited by the proponents of each view, as well as texts that have not been appealed to by either one. Each side advances a number of biblical passages and arguments in support of its view and believes that the texts cited by the opponents do not really support their view because they have either

---

7. I have developed at greater length this distinction between what I term the "legislative authority" and the "judicial authority," respectively, in my *Christian Theology* (Grand Rapids: Baker, 1998), 282–85.

assumed certain interpretations or have omitted crucial texts that do not support their view. The question we will ask is, which view can better account for more of the relevant biblical evidence with less distortion of the data?

Chapter 5 will deal with the historical tradition. Here we will examine what theologians prior to the nineteenth century have said on this subject. Since each party claims to be upholding the historic position of the church, this will enable us to evaluate that claim. One underlying question here will be the status and authority of these sources for the current issues. It will be necessary to ask to what extent the ancient theologians were addressing the questions being dealt with today and, where they are not, what principles underlie their statements and how those may be applied to the current questions.

Chapter 6 will examine philosophical questions. While some may feel that such issues should not be considered, there actually are a number of these intricately attached to the discussion. For example, the gradationists contend that while the Father occupies a superior role and performs superior functions to those of the Son, they are actually equal in being. There is no differentiation there. That distinction will need close examination to determine the relationship of function to essence. This chapter also will ask about logical arguments, analyzing the structure of the arguments advanced, assessing whether the deductive conclusions drawn follow from the premises, and in the case of inductive arguments, whether there is a sufficient amount of evidence to conclude that the hypothesis has been established.

Chapter 7 will explore theological issues. By this I mean the extent to which the positions taken on an issue depend upon theological conclusions in other areas of doctrine. Conversely, the two positions also will be examined in terms of the ways in which their conclusions affect other areas of doctrine.

In chapter 8 we will examine the practical implications of the positions taken on this issue. This will relate to how such practices as worship and prayer are affected by one's position on this issue and how the logical outcome in those areas conforms to what the Bible teaches about those practices. There is potential here as well for verification or rebuttal of one or the other views. To the extent that a given doctrinal stance on this issue implies a particular practice, negative biblical support for such a practice would also constitute negative evidence for the doctrinal position. There will also be concern here for how the understanding of the relationship between the three members of the Trinity may affect our understanding of relationships among humans, and particularly among members of the church, since according to Scripture humans bear the image of God and in some sense reflect his triune nature.

In the final chapter, we will attempt to draw together the conclusions from the previous chapters and determine which of these two views is the more adequate and therefore is the one we should adopt and support.

I noted earlier that the two sides frequently use the conclusion regarding the relative authority of the Father and the Son as a basis for a conclusion on the relative roles of men and women, whether within the church or the family structure. Each contends that the other side has allowed its view of the intratrinitarian relationships of authority to be governed by a desire to justify a preconceived view of these interhuman relationships. While we will ask what implications the view of the Trinity might have for these questions, we will not attempt to judge the theological conclusions held by the possibility that they have been adopted to justify these practical commitments.

In our postmodern age, it is not uncommon to hear arguments of this type advanced to discredit the view of one's opponent. These are essentially ad hominem arguments. While interesting and potentially informative, they do not necessarily bear on the question of the truth of the doctrinal view. They are essentially explanations of the motivation of the person doing the questioning. However, it is possible to hold a correct conclusion for the wrong reason. I would suggest that motivation is to argumentation as understanding is to evaluation. The question is not why the person holds this view but whether there is a basis for concluding that the view is true. For example, during the impeachment proceedings against President Clinton, his counsel sought to rebut the charges brought by the special counsel by saying, "Mr. Starr has a personal vendetta against Mr. Clinton." My response was, "Perhaps that is true, but how does that bear on the guilt or innocence of the president? The question is not, 'What is the special counsel's motive for pressing these charges?' Rather, the question is, 'Did the defendant do it?'"

We may well conclude that one or both parties have been influenced in their argumentation by a desire to justify a conclusion on another matter, and we may feel it important to exhort those parties to try to be more objective in their treatment of this issue. As a clue to the relative truth of the two positions, however, such questions of motive must be considered quite irrelevant. The question still must be, which position is better supported by the arguments mustered in support of it?

CHAPTER I

The Gradational-Authority View

The modern discussion of the relative authority of the persons of the Trinity has moved through two general phases. The transitions were gradual and not necessarily in a direct line, but development can nonetheless be discerned.

The Early Period: 1870 to 1970

Charles Hodge

Perhaps the strongest influence on American evangelical theology in the late nineteenth and early twentieth centuries was the "Princeton theology," emanating from Princeton Seminary. For an extended period of time, systematic theology there was taught by Hodge and two of his sons. Of these, Charles Hodge produced the most extensive written systematic theology. He states that the Bible is clear in its teaching on the Trinity. While all three persons are equally divine and the titles and attributes of God apply equally to the Father, the Son, and the Holy Spirit, nonetheless, "In the Holy Trinity there is a subordination of the Persons as to the mode of subsistence and operation."[1] Hodge elaborates:

> (a.) That the Father is first, the Son second, and the Spirit third. (b.) The Son is of the Father (ἐκ θεοῦ, the λόγος, εἰκὼν, ἀπαύγασμα, τοῦ θεοῦ); and the Spirit is of the Father and of the Son. (c.) The Father sends the Son and the Father and the Son send the Spirit. (d.) The Father operates through the Son, and the Father and the Son operate through the Spirit. The converse of these statements is never found. The Son is never said to send the

---

1. Charles Hodge, *Systematic Theology* (Grand Rapids: Eerdmans, 1952), 1:445.

Father, nor to operate through Him; nor is the Spirit ever said to send the Father, or the Son, or to operate through them.[2]

Later, in discussing the Nicene Creed, he states what he means by this subordination:

The principle of subordination of the Son to the Father, and of the Spirit to the Father and the Son. But this subordination does not imply inferiority. For as the same divine essence with all its infinite perfections is common to the Father, Son, and Spirit, there can be no inferiority of one person to the other in the Trinity. Neither does it imply posteriority; for the divine essence common to the several persons is self-existent and eternal. The subordination intended is only that which concerns the mode of subsistence and operation, implied in the Scriptural facts that the Son is of the Father, and the Spirit is of the Father and the Son, and that the Father operates through the Son, and the Father and the Son through the Spirit.[3]

Hodge does not elaborate very fully upon this definition. The basic concept is that this is a subordination of subsistence (the existence of the several persons) and working, not of essence. He distinguishes between the content of the Nicene Creed, which he believes to be simply a reflection of the biblical teaching, and the attempts made by the Nicene fathers to explain what was meant by this title. While he states much of their explanation, he does not really elaborate his own. Although this idea of subordination is declared by Hodge to be a biblical teaching, he does not give a single text where it is taught. He simply states that it is implied by certain teachings of Scripture.[4]

It is significant that beyond these statements, he does not speak of the authority of the Father over the Son and of the Father and the Son over the Spirit, or of the obedience of the Son. He says of the subordination of the Son to the Father and what is meant by generation,

---

2. Ibid.
3. Ibid., 460–61.
4. Ibid., 462.

or the relation between the two, "These two points are so intimately related that they cannot be considered separately."[5] In examining the Nicene fathers' explanation of their statement, he considers the idea that the Father communicates the essence of the parent to the child and rejects this idea, since it is not true even of human parents and children. Such an idea assumes the Traducian view of the origin of the soul, which has never been generally accepted by the church. He concludes, "As, therefore, it is, to say the least, doubtful, whether there is any communication of the essence of the soul in human paternity, it is unreasonable to assume that such communication is essential to the relation of Father and Son in the Trinity."[6] Further, however, "while it is admitted that the terms Father and Son are used to give us some idea of the mutual relation of the First and Second persons of the Trinity, yet they do not definitely determine what that relation is. It may be equality and likeness."[7] The Nicene fathers had cited John 5:26 in support of the idea that "the First Person of the Trinity communicated life, and therefore the essence in which that life inheres, to the Second Person," but Hodge believes that in its context the text should be understood as applying to the theanthropos, the historical person, Jesus of Nazareth, and therefore it does not teach such communication of essence.[8]

Regarding the eternal Fatherhood and Sonship, Hodge agrees that because the terms *Father*, *Son*, and *Holy Spirit* have been part of God's revelation of himself, it is incumbent upon us to use them. There are numerous passages of Scripture in which it is clear that they speak of an eternal relationship among the members of the Trinity, because, for example, they can be seen to apply to the persons before the Incarnation.[9] The use of expressions such as "only-begotten Son of God" also are evidence of this eternal relationship.[10]

---

5. Ibid.
6. Ibid., 469.
7. Ibid.
8. Ibid., 470.
9. Ibid., 472.
10. Ibid., 473.

Hodge considers the objections to this doctrine of the eternal Sonship. A primary one is that the texts, such as Psalm 2:7; Acts 13:32–33; and Luke 1:35, refer to events within the earthly life of Jesus, the Godman. He replies that they need not be so understood. For example, the reference, "today I have begotten you" is to be understood of the date of the decree itself, or the statements may refer, not to the Father becoming the Father of the Son at that time, but rather to that being the time in which the existing relationship is manifested.[11]

Augustus Strong

Strong, a Baptist, wrote his *Systematic Theology* about a generation after Hodge's. His treatment of the Trinity is somewhat briefer than Hodge's but follows much the same pattern. While insisting that all three members of the Trinity possess equally the full divine essence, he describes the relations between them in terms of direction and movement: "The Trinity, as the organism of Deity, secures a life-movement of the Godhead, a process in which God evermore objectifies himself and in the Son gives forth of his fullness. Christ represents the centrifugal action of the deity. But there must be centripetal action also. In the Holy Spirit the movement is completed, and the divine activity and thought returns into itself."[12]

Because of this oneness of essence and what Strong describes as "an intercommunion of persons and an immanence of one divine person in another," there is a definite implication for God's work.[13] This oneness "permits the peculiar work of one to be ascribed with a single limitation, to either of the others, and the manifestation of one to be recognized in the manifestation of another."[14] That lone limitation is that "although the Son was sent by the Father, and the Spirit by the Father and the Son, it cannot be said *vice versa* that the Father is sent either by the Son, or by the Spirit."[15]

---

11. Ibid., 474–77.
12. Augustus Hopkins Strong, *Systematic Theology: A Compendium* (Westwood, NJ: Revell, 1907), 336.
13. Ibid., 332–33.
14. Ibid., 333.
15. Ibid.

This opens the discussion to the topics of generation and procession, which Strong regards as eternal. He bases the generation of the Son on texts that speak of the begetting of the Son, as Psalm 2:7, and seems to attribute the word *Son* to a period before his Incarnation.[16] The eternal generation of the Son should not be thought of as a creation or a beginning of existence, or as "an act of the Father's will, but an internal necessity of the divine nature."[17] This in turn leads to the concept of the Son's subordination. Strong says,

> The subordination of the *person* of the Son to the *person* of the Father, or in other words an order of personality, office, and operation which permits the Father to be officially first, the Son second, and the Spirit third, is perfectly consistent with equality. Priority is not necessarily superiority. The possibility of an order, which yet involves no inequality, may be illustrated by the relation between man and woman. In office man is first and woman second, but woman's soul is worth as much as man's; see 1 Corinthians 11:3—"the head of every man is Christ and the head of the woman is the man; and the head of Christ is God."[18]

Here is an anticipation of the use made of this text later in the twentieth century. Strong, however, does not emphasize the ideas of authority and obedience or submission, either with respect to the Father-Son relationship or the man-woman relationship. Rather, he introduces the man-woman relationship as a parallel to the Father-Son relationship to show that there can be order without inequality.

Louis Berkhof

To a large extent, Berkhof was the successor to Hodge. Although he did not teach at the same institution, he formulated the basic Reformed doctrine for another generation, and his textbook supplanted Hodge's. In many ways, his treatment of the Trinity parallels that of Hodge. Thus,

---

16. Ibid., 340.
17. Ibid., 341–42.
18. Ibid., 342.

while the whole divine essence belongs to each member of the Trinity equally, there is a definite order of their subsistence and working:

> There is a certain order in the ontological Trinity. In personal subsistence the Father is first, the Son second, and the Holy Spirit third. It need hardly be said that this order does not pertain to any priority of time or of essential dignity, but only to the logical order of derivation. The Father is neither begotten by, nor proceeds from any other person: the Son is eternally begotten of the Father, and the Spirit proceeds from the Father and the Son from all eternity. Generation and procession take place within the Divine Being, and imply a certain subordination as far as the manner of personal subsistence, but no subordination as far as the possession of the divine essence is concerned. This ontological Trinity and its inherent order is the metaphysical basis of the economical Trinity.[19]

This order means that the subsistence of the Son is derived from the Father and that of the Spirit from the Father and the Son. Beyond that, because of the connection between the ontological and the economic Trinity, the order is reflected in different works of each of the persons: "Scripture clearly indicates this order in the so-called *praepositiones dictionales*, *ek*, *dia*, and *en*, which are used in expressing the idea that all things are out of the Father, through the Son, and in the Holy Spirit."[20] While Berkhof insists that all of the works of God are works of the triune God, nonetheless each person is in the foreground of certain works. So, for example, the Father is the primary person in designing the work of redemption (i.e., election), as well as in creation.[21]

Further, in light of this order, generation is properly ascribed only to the Father, filiation to the Son, and procession only to the Holy Spirit.[22] Berkhof describes more fully this eternal generation of the Son by the

---

19. Louis Berkhof, *Systematic Theology*, rev. ed. (Grand Rapids: Eerdmans, 1953), 88–89.
20. Ibid., 89.
21. Ibid., 91.
22. Ibid., 89.

Father. It is a necessary act, an eternal act, of the personal subsistence rather than the divine essence, and is a spiritual and divine generation.[23] So he summarizes his understanding of divine generation as follows: "*It is that eternal and necessary act of the first person of the Trinity, whereby He, within the divine Being, is the ground of a second personal subsistence like His own, and puts this second person in possession of the whole divine essence, without any division, alienation, or change.*"[24] While this summary seems to take back what he has said about this not being a generation of the divine essence, that appears not to be his intent. He claims that the biblical basis for this teaching is the use of the terms *Father* and *Son*, especially those that apply to the preincarnate existence of the Son, as well as the references to the preexistence of the Son and his equality with the Father, and the statements such as the Son being "begotten" or "only-begotten."[25] He also contends that John 5:26 supports this doctrine.[26]

Berkhof does not emphasize the authority of the Father or the obedience of the Son the way some later subordinationists have. He does, however, allude to this when he says of the Son, "In the Counsel of Redemption, He takes upon Himself to be Surety for His people, and to *execute the Father's plan of redemption.*"[27]

The Later Period: 1970 to the Present

George Knight

In 1977 George Knight introduced a new development into the discussion when he published a small book with a definite purpose. He describes his book as "an attempt to set forth the New Testament teaching concerning the relationship of men and women in the teaching and ruling offices and functions in the church, in public worship, and in the marriage and family relationship."[28] In the very title of the

---

23. Ibid., 93–94.

24. Ibid., 94.

25. Ibid., 93.

26. Ibid., 94.

27. Ibid., 95 (emphasis added).

28. George W. Knight III, *The New Testament Teaching on the Role Relationship of Men and Women* (Grand Rapids: Baker, 1977), 9.

book, he introduced a concept that has become crucial both to the discussion of the relationship of men and women and that regarding the relationship of the Father and the Son: "I have chosen to speak of this relationship as a *role relationship* where the question of authority, headship, or leadership is in view."[29]

Some have contended that the Bible is concerned simply with preserving stability in government and marriage, and not with specifically who it is that rules in these institutions. In response Knight offers some evidence that the specific form of the leadership being discussed (e.g., men over women) is based upon some permanent or transcultural consideration. One of these has become very significant in discussions of the Trinity: "For the basis of man's headship and woman's submission, the apostle Paul appeals to the analogy of God the Father's headship over Jesus Christ, His incarnate Son (I Cor. 11:3); . . . With full authority and with absolute and permanent reasons, Paul argues for the form of this relationship between man and woman."[30] Although he refers to another passage he has cited in the same sentence as 1 Corinthians 11:3, Knight apparently indicates the basis of the strength of his argument from this text as well by saying, "One would have to deny Paul's argument or his explanation and application of Genesis 2 to overturn the fact that this is the teaching of the apostles which they intended to be believed and obeyed."[31]

In other words, the teaching regarding God's headship over Christ is to be taken as teaching that the Father has authority over the Son, and this implies that the man has similar authority over the woman. Knight takes pains to explain that the Father's authority over the Son does not mean that the Son is inferior to the Father:

> The headship of God the Father in relation to the incarnate Christ in no way detracts from or is detrimental to Christ's person as incarnate deity. His full deity, His being of the same essence as the Father, is not at all denied, or must His deity be

---

29. Ibid.
30. Ibid., 26.
31. Ibid.

affirmed in such a way that the Father's headship must be denied
to maintain it. The headship of God in reference to Christ can
be readily seen and affirmed with no threat to Christ's identity.
This chain of subordination with its implications is apparently
given to answer the objection some bring to the headship of man
in reference to woman. Just as Christ is not a second-class person
or deity because the Father is His head, so the woman is not a
second-class person or human being because man is her head.[32]

From this quotation and the previous one, where Knight refers to
the Father's headship as being "over Jesus Christ, His *incarnate* Son,"[33]
one might infer that he is not necessarily claiming that the authority is
true prior to and after Jesus' earthly ministry, but he makes clear in a
later statement that this is an eternal authority and subordination relationship. Responding to a contention by Paul Jewett that if women are
permanently subjected to men they must be inferior to them, he again
appeals to the relationship of the Father and Son in such a way as to
indicate that the relationship is eternal and permanent:

> The apostle Paul in his appeal to the relation of God the Father
> to God the Son does not regard Christ's Sonship and resultant
> incarnation as implying His inferiority to the Father. Although
> Christ the Son's submission is expressed in the areas of action and
> of incarnation (the areas of service and the accomplishment of
> salvation; cf. also I Cor. 15:24–28), it is also an expression of the
> ontological relationship of preincarnate, submissive Sonship (cf.,
> e.g., John 5:18–23, 30).[34]

Knight does not really explain what he means either by "ontological"
or by "inferior," but he continues to use the terms, underscoring that by
virtue of some definite structure of relationship, both the Son submits to
the Father and the woman submits to the man, but without this involv-

---

32. Ibid., 33.
33. Ibid., 26 (emphasis added).
34. Ibid., 55–56.

ing inferiority. He says, "The ontological relationship analogous to that between man and woman, writes Paul, is that between Father and Son (I Cor. 11:3). That Christ submits as Son and as incarnate, i.e., because of certain ontological aspects, does not mean therefore that He is inferior to the Father, nor does it cast doubt upon His deity."[35] As with the Father and the Son, so also with the man and the woman, no inequality is implied: "In both cases, it is equals in relationship to one another. In both cases, one, because of His or her 'ontological' and ordained role in relation to the other, acknowledges headship and submits."[36]

Bruce Ware

The most extended treatment thus far from the gradational-authority view of the Trinity has been given by Bruce Ware of Southern Baptist Theological Seminary. In several articles as well as a full-length book, he has developed the important doctrine of the Trinity. He considers it crucial, both because it is central to the Christian faith, distinguishing it from other religions, and also because it has far-reaching practical implications for the spiritual life of the Christian.[37]

Ware states the traditional view of the Trinity, that "there is one and only one God, eternally existing and fully expressed in three Persons, the Father, the Son, and the Holy Spirit."[38] It is important to remember, however, that "each member of the Godhead is equally God, each is eternally God, and each is fully God—not three gods but three Persons of the one Godhead."[39] He emphasizes that each is equal in essence; in fact, "each possesses fully the identically same, eternal divine nature, yet each is also an eternal and distinct personal expression of the one undivided divine nature."[40]

Having said this, however, Ware is concerned to emphasize an important feature of the Trinity:

---

35. Ibid., 56.

36. Ibid.

37. Bruce A. Ware, *Father, Son, and Holy Spirit: Relationships, Roles, and Relevance* (Wheaton, IL: Crossway, 2005), 15–22.

38. Ibid., 43.

39. Ibid.

40. Ibid.

An authority-submission structure marks the very nature of the eternal Being of the one who is three. In this authority-submission structure, the three Persons understand the rightful place each has. The Father possesses the place of supreme authority, and the Son is the eternal Son of the eternal Father. As such, the Son submits to the Father, just as the Father, as eternal Father of the eternal Son, exercises authority over the Son. And the Spirit submits to both the Father and the Son. This hierarchical structure of authority exists in the eternal Godhead even though it is also eternally true that each Person is fully equal to each other in their commonly possessed essence.[41]

Each also possesses all of the attributes of deity. So omnipotence, for example, is not just an attribute of the Father, but of each of the persons.[42] While equal in their deity, the three persons are not equal in their authority: "The Father is, in his position and authority, supreme among the Persons of the Godhead."[43] The corollary of this supreme authority of the Father is the Son's *submission* to the Father, a term that Ware prefers to *subordination*.

It is important to notice that this differentiation in which the Father is eternally supreme and the Son and the Spirit eternally submit to the Father is described as a structure that "marks the very nature" of God.[44] It is therefore intrinsic to that divine nature. Things could not have been otherwise.

This means that each of the three persons has roles that are unique to him and that these roles are eternal. Consequently, the relationships among the three differ. The relationship of the Son to the Father is different from that of the Father to the Son and also different from his relationship to the Holy Spirit.

Ware makes much of the differing roles of the three persons. With respect to creation, for example, he says of the Father, "He is the Grand

---

41. Ibid., 21.
42. Ibid., 45.
43. Ibid., 46.
44. Ibid., 21.

Architect and Wise Designer of everything in the created order."[45]
More generally, "From initial creation through ultimate consummation
and everything that happens in between, it is God the Father who is
the Architect, the Designer, the one who stands behind all that occurs
as the one who plans and implements what he has chosen to do."[46]
Thus, the Father is preeminent in foreordination, creation, providence,
and many associated doctrines. He is also the giver of every gift.[47] Yet,
"though the Father is supreme, he often provides and works through
his Son and Spirit to accomplish his work and fulfill his will."[48]

The Son, on the other hand, is characterized by doing the Father's
will: "Without question, the whole framework of the earthly life,
work, ministry, and mission of the Son was one in which the Son
sought to do the will of the Father. Hence, the Son's submission to
the leadership, authority, and headship of his Father must be given
careful consideration if we are to understand how the Father and the
Son relate."[49] Not only do authority and obedience characterize the
relationship, but so also does love: "The Father loves his Son dearly,
and the Son loves his Father with equal fervor. We'll see and marvel at
the fact that while the Father and the Son are in a relationship marked
by eternal authority and submission, yet they exhibit unqualified love
for each other."[50]

Ware spends considerable time on the topic of taxis, or ordering,
within the Trinity. Because the Father, Son, and Holy Spirit are distinct persons and this distinction is not in terms of any difference in
essence or attributes, it must be found in this ordering. Ware describes
it: "The order is not random or arbitrary; it is not the Spirit first, the
Son second, and Father third, nor is it any way other than the one way
that the early church, reflecting Scripture itself (Matt. 28:19), insisted

---

45. Ibid., 59.
46. Ibid., 51.
47. Ibid., 53–55.
48. Ibid., 55.
49. Ibid., 71.
50. Ibid.

on: Father, Son, and Holy Spirit."[51] So the Son obeyed the Father in all things, not only during his earthly ministry, but also in eternity past, just as he will do so in eternity to come. Similarly, Ware traces the role of the Holy Spirit, who submits himself to both the Father and the Son. He acknowledges that the Spirit directed the Son at certain points in the Son's life and ministry, but he regards that apparent submission of the Son to the Spirit as being restricted to the Son's earthly ministry.[52]

Like other gradationists, Ware sees a number of practical applications of this doctrinal understanding, although he extends the application somewhat further than do others. That means that the model of the functioning of the Trinity gives us an example for human authority-submission structures. The first application is a familiar one:

> Who is in a position of authority, with responsibility to pattern his manner of leadership after the Father? Clearly, every married man is in this category. Husbands have rightful authority in their homes with their wives, and if God has blessed them with children, their authority extends also to these precious gifts from the Lord. Husbands should exercise their authority with wisdom, goodness, carefulness, and thoroughness in order to seek the well being of those under their charge. Husbands should seek to be like their heavenly Father in increasing measure.[53]

This admonition is extended to others with responsibility, including mothers with their children, elders of a local church, employers, or anyone with authority over others in any aspect of life.[54] Conversely, wives and children, church members, employees, and citizens should all seek to emulate Jesus' godliness in submitting to authority.

Ware makes one other application, with respect to prayer. Because of the distinct roles that each member of the Trinity plays, we should pray in a definite way. While some may have been encouraged to pray

---

51. Ibid., 72.
52. Ibid., 88–94.
53. Ibid., 59–60.
54. Ibid., 60.

to Jesus, Ware seems to indicate that the correct understanding of the Trinity has a definite implication for prayer: "The Christian's life of *prayer* must rightly acknowledge the roles of Father, Son, and Spirit as we pray to the Father, through the Son, in the power of the Spirit."[55] This principle also is extended to the practice of worship and praise, although not so exclusively. Based especially on Philippians 2:11, Ware indicates the ultimate object of our worship: "Worship of the Son, while right and true and glorious, must also recognize the one whom the Son himself acknowledges as supreme over all, even over himself. The ultimate object of our honor, glory, praise, and worship is the Father of our Lord Jesus Christ, who himself alone is over all."[56]

What support does Ware offer for this vigorously stated theory? We need to note that he makes much of the terminology of Father. He quotes Geoffrey Wainwright's statement that "*there must be . . . something* about human fatherhood that makes father a suitable way for Jesus to designate the one who sent him. In Trinitarian terms, the crucial point is that Father was the address Jesus characteristically used in this connection."[57] While Wainwright does not indicate what this "something" is, Ware is not similarly hesitant: "But is it not obvious? Jesus said over and again throughout his ministry that he came to do the *will* of his *Father.* Clearly, a central part of the notion of 'Father' is that of fatherly authority. Certainly this is not all there is to being a father, but while there is more, there certainly is not less or other."[58] To Ware, the repeated use of this name for the first person of the Trinity is definite evidence of the authority structure inherent in the Trinity.

Ware of course draws heavily on specific Scripture references to support his thesis. Those texts that speak of God planning and originating what happens in the world, such as Ephesians 1:9–12, and those that

---

55. Ibid., 18.

56. Ibid., 154.

57. Geoffrey Wainwright, "The Doctrine of the Trinity: Where the Church Stands or Falls," *Interpretation* 45 (1991): 120; quoted in Bruce A. Ware, "Tampering with the Trinity: Does the Son Submit to His Father?" *Journal for Biblical Manhood and Womanhood* 6, no. 1 (Spring 2001): 8.

58. Ware, "Tampering with the Trinity," 8.

speak of him as the giver of gifts testify to the Father's supremacy.[59] Ware cites Jesus' statements about having come to do the Father's will (John 6:38) and the Father having sent his Son (John 3:16) as evidence of the eternal authority-submission structure.[60]

One passage receives special attention from Ware. Following Wayne Grudem's research, Ware uses 1 Corinthians 11:3 as proof that the Father, as "head," is supreme over the Son, and as well, that man is head of woman.[61]

Ware also appeals to the history of doctrine to support his view. It is not entirely clear just how the use of these sources relates to his view of the authority of Scripture, but it appears that he is largely attempting to rebut the claims of some equivalentists that their view is what the church has always held. He especially cites Augustine's statement that "he [the Son] was *not sent in virtue of some disparity of power or substance or anything in him that was not equal to the Father*, but in virtue of the Son being from the Father, not the Father being from the Son."[62] Ware believes that this establishes that Augustine held to the eternal authority of the Father and the eternal submission of the Son, while maintaining the complete equality and even identity of being of the three.

Ware differs from the tradition at one point. The Nicene Creed spoke of the Holy Spirit proceeding from the Father and from the Son, the latter phrase being ultimately the cause of the separation of the Eastern and Western churches. While agreeing with the additional language, Ware believes that it refers, not to some eternal procession of the Spirit, but to his being sent at Pentecost. He says, "The conceptions of both the 'eternal begetting of the Son' and 'eternal procession of the Spirit' seem to me highly speculative and not grounded in biblical teaching. Both the Son as only-begotten and the Spirit as proceeding from the Father (and the Son) refer, in my judgment, to the historical realities of the incarnation and Pentecost, respectively."[63]

---

59. Ware, *Father, Son, and Holy Spirit*, 51–54.
60. Ibid., 77–78.
61. Ibid., 72.
62. Cited in ibid., 80 (emphasis added by Ware).
63. Ibid., 162n. 3.

Finally, we should note some theological principles that Ware utilizes to sustain this doctrinal point. One is the analogy between the triune God and the creation. This is seen in his strong reliance on the parallel between the divine Father and human fatherhood. It also appears, in connection with 1 Corinthians 11:3, in the parallel between God being the head of Christ and man being the head of woman. More broadly, it appears in the nature of human authority-submission patterns in reflection of the divine authority-submission structure, which he believes he has demonstrated as being eternal.

The last theological point emerges in connection with Ware's criticism of the view that the Father, Son, and Holy Spirit are not to be understood in the hierarchical authority structure he has described. He believes that the egalitarians have a problem here in terms of their inability to answer an important theological question: "It appears that contemporary egalitarianism is vulnerable also to this criticism. Since nothing *in God* grounds the Son being the Son of the Father, and since every aspect of the Son's earthly submission to the Father is divorced altogether from any *eternal relation* that exists between the Father and Son, there simply is no reason why the *Father* should send the *Son*."[64]

Wayne Grudem

A vigorous contemporary exponent of the gradational-authority view is Wayne Grudem, professor of theology at Phoenix Seminary. While much of his writing has been in reaction to what he sees as the egalitarian agenda of contemporary evangelical feminism,[65] here we will be developing his positive statement and argument.

---

64. Ware, "Tampering with the Trinity," 9.

65. Wayne Grudem and John Piper, ed., *Recovering Biblical Manhood and Womanhood* (Wheaton, IL: Crossway, 1991); Wayne Grudem, ed., *Biblical Foundations for Manhood and Womanhood* (Wheaton, IL: Crossway, 2002); Wayne Grudem and Dennis Rainey, eds., *Pastoral Leadership for Manhood and Womanhood* (Wheaton, IL: Crossway, 2002); Wayne Grudem, *Evangelical Feminism and Biblical Truth: An Analysis of More Than One Hundred Disputed Questions* (Sisters, OR: Multnomah, 2004); idem, *Evangelical Feminism: A New Path to Liberalism* (Wheaton, IL: Crossway, 2006); and idem, *Countering the Claims of Evangelical Feminism* (Colorado Springs: Multnomah, 2006).

A central tenet of Grudem's view of the Trinity is the equal deity of the three persons. Each is fully God, and in the same sense as each of the other two: "First, it is important to affirm that each person is completely and fully God; that is, that each person has the whole fullness of God's being in himself. The Son is not partly God or just one-third of God, but the Son is wholly and fully God, and so is the Father and the Holy Spirit."[66] He is clearly distancing himself from any historical form of Arianism or semi-Arianism. It is not just that each possesses a part of the same divine being. Each possesses "the *whole being* of God in himself." The terminology goes beyond mere possession, however: "The Father is *all* of God's being. The Son also is *all* of God's being. And the Holy Spirit is *all* of God's being."[67]

What differentiates the three persons from each other, then, is not a difference of being, but of function. As Grudem states it, "When Scripture discusses the way in which God relates to the world, both in creation and in redemption, the persons of the Trinity are said to have different functions or primary activities."[68] This is what has sometimes been referred to as the economy of the Trinity.[69] With respect to the act of creation, God the Father was the originative force who "spoke the creative words to bring the universe into being," while God the Son was the executor "who carried out these creative decrees."[70] Similarly, in the work of redemption, "God the Father planned redemption and sent his Son into the world," while the Son "obeyed the Father and accomplished redemption for us," and "the Holy Spirit was sent by the Father and the Son to apply redemption to us."[71]

Grudem sums up this scheme of distinct functions as follows:

So we may say that the role of the Father in creation and redemption has been to plan and direct and send the Son and Holy Spirit. This

---

66. Wayne Grudem, *Systematic Theology: An Introduction to Biblical Doctrine* (Grand Rapids: Zondervan, 1994), 252.

67. Ibid.

68. Ibid., 248.

69. Ibid.

70. Ibid., 249.

71. Ibid.

is not surprising, for it shows that the Father and the Son relate to one another as a father and son relate to one another in a human family: the father directs and has authority over the son, and the son obeys and is responsive to the directions of the father. The Holy Spirit is obedient to the directives of both the Father and the Son.

Thus, while the persons of the Trinity are equal in all their attributes, they nonetheless differ in their relationships to the creation. The Son and Holy Spirit are equal in deity to God the Father, but they are subordinate in their roles.[72]

One might think that this relationship of commanding and obeying or of sending and going is only temporary and arbitrary or accidental. Grudem is clear that such is not the case. He poses the question of whether the Father, rather than the Son, might have come to die an atoning death, or whether the Holy Spirit might have been the one doing the sending, and emphatically rejects such ideas. The role of commanding is "appropriate to the position of the Father, after whom all human fatherhood is patterned (Eph. 3:14–15)."[73] Similarly the role of obeying is "appropriate to the role of the Son."[74]

Not only are these roles not arbitrary or accidental; they are also eternal, not temporary: "for all eternity the Father has been the Father, the Son has been the Son, and the Holy Spirit has been the Holy Spirit. These relationships are eternal, not something that occurred only in time."[75] The conclusion to be drawn is that "the different functions that we see the Father, Son, and Holy Spirit performing are simply outworkings of an eternal relationship between the three persons, one that has always existed and will exist for eternity." Further, "These distinctions are essential to the very nature of God himself, and they could not be otherwise."[76]

---

72. Ibid.
73. Ibid., 250.
74. Ibid.
75. Ibid.
76. Ibid., 251.

Grudem presents a vigorous argument for his view, on the basis of several different considerations. The first, naturally, is the biblical evidence. He appeals to those passages that speak of the Father planning and sending the Son (John 3:16; Gal. 4:4; Eph. 1:9–10) and the Son obeying and going (John 6:38; Heb. 10:5–7). These include not only those passages that speak of the Father and Son during the Son's earthly ministry, but also references such as Ephesians 1:3–4, which speak of the Father choosing us in Christ before the foundation of the world. These indicate that before the creation the Father was the Father and the Son was the Son. So "the fact that the Father 'gave his only Son' (John 3:16) and 'sent the Son into the world' (John 3:17) indicate [*sic*] that there was a Father-Son relationship before Christ came into the world. The Son did not become the Son when the Father sent him into the world."[77] Not only did this relationship of commanding and obeying exist from eternity past, but it will also continue into the future, as indicated by 1 Corinthians 15:28, where in the end the Son will turn all things over to the Father and be subject to him. Thus, the relationship of superiority of the Father and subordination of the Son (and of the Holy Spirit) are not merely temporal, restricted to the special soteriological missions of the latter two members of the Trinity, but are eternally true of the relationships among the members.

Grudem also appeals to the history of the church, contending that the church has always held this doctrine of the eternal subordination of the Son and that views that deny that relationship are rejecting the whole of orthodox Christian theology. In response to Gilbert Bilezikian's claim that the church's historic position has been that the subordination of the Son is a temporary functional subordination, limited to Christ's redemptive mission, Grudem appeals to both the creeds of the church and a number of significant theologians from earlier periods of church history. Such expressions as "eternal generation (or eternal begetting) of the Son," "begotten of the Father before all worlds," and "The Son is of the Father alone: not made, nor created, but begotten,"

---

77. Ibid., 250.

are found in the Nicene Creed, the Chalcedonian Creed, and the Athanasian Creed.[78] Similar statements of the Father's priority are found in
the Thirty-nine Articles of the Church of England and the Westminster Confession of Faith, as well as in the writings of individual theologians like Charles Hodge, Augustine, Thomas Aquinas, John Calvin,
B. B. Warfield, Augustus H. Strong, and Louis Berkhof, and church
historians Philip Schaff, J. N. D. Kelley, and Geoffrey Bromiley.[79]

Grudem sums up his findings from this survey as follows:

> This then has been the historic doctrine of the church. Egalitarians
> may differ with this doctrine today if they wish, and they may
> attempt to persuade us that they are right if they wish, but they
> must do so on the basis of arguments from Scripture, and they
> should also have the honesty and courtesy to explain to readers
> why they now feel it necessary to differ with the historic doctrine
> of the church as expressed in its major creeds.[80]

Grudem also uses several theological arguments. By that I mean
that he appeals to some other doctrine or doctrinal principle within
evangelical theology and shows how it impacts this doctrinal consideration, or he shows the doctrinal implications of the two options on this
doctrine. Some of these issues and concepts are actually philosophical
in nature.

The first of these is the effect of the immutability of God, which
is a factor at two points. One is in his contention that if the Father is
now the Father and the Son is now the Son, they must have been this
eternally. He says, "We may conclude this first from the unchangeableness of God . . . if God now exists as Father, Son, and Holy Spirit,
then he has always existed as Father, Son, and Holy Spirit."[81] The other
place where this enters is with respect to the question of the continuing
Incarnation of Jesus Christ. Grudem believes that Gilbert Bilezikian's

---

78. Grudem, *Evangelical Feminism and Biblical Truth*, 415–16.
79. Ibid., 417–22.
80. Ibid., 422.
81. Grudem, *Systematic Theology*, 250.

statement that there will be no continuing subordination of the Son to the Father "after [the Incarnation's] completion" suggests that Jesus ceases to be the God-man. As a support for a continuing Incarnation, he quotes Hebrews 13:8, "Jesus Christ is the same yesterday and today and forever."[82]

The other major area of doctrine that comes into play is in terms of the differentiation of the three persons from one another, so that there are three persons, not just one. Grudem asks what the basis of such a distinction is. It cannot be based on their being or essence, since the three all possess the whole of the divine nature entirely. Similarly, it cannot be that one person possesses some attribute(s) not possessed by the others. The only way in which they can be distinguished is by each having a unique relationship to each of the others, which in turn is revealed in their different roles. He says, "But if there are no differences among them eternally, *then how does one person differ from the other?* They would no longer be Father, Son, and Holy Spirit, but rather Person A, Person A, and Person A, each identical to the other not only in being but also in role and in the way they relate to one another."[83]

This has two consequences that Grudem finds very troubling. The first is that "this would mean that the Trinity has not eternally existed."[84] Making his point even more strongly, Grudem states, "If we did not have such differences in authority in the relationships among the members of the Trinity, then we would not know of any differences at all, and it would be unclear whether there *are* any differences among the persons of the Trinity."[85] The consequences of this situation would be very serious indeed: "If the Father also submitted to the authority of the Son, it would destroy the Trinity, because there would be no Father, Son, and Holy Spirit, but only Person A, Person A, and Person A."[86]

---

82. Grudem, *Evangelical Feminism and Biblical Truth*, 410.
83. Ibid., 433.
84. Grudem, *Systematic Theology*, 251.
85. Grudem, *Evangelical Feminism and Biblical Truth*, 433.
86. Ibid.

The other consequence pertains to the future of individual humans: "Once we lose personal distinctions among the members of the Trinity, we sacrifice the very idea that personal differences are eternally and fundamentally good, and we no longer have in the being of God a guarantee that God will eternally preserve our own individual, personal distinctiveness either."[87]

We should not fail to note also what I would term a sociological consideration, but which Grudem considers to be a theological argument. Some of what constitutes the argument for the authority of the Father over the Son is the parallel and resemblance between divine and human fatherhood and sonship. This is what is sometimes termed the analogy of being between the Creator and the creation, or what might more specifically be considered the analogical character of the image of God in the human, reflecting the triune God. Beyond that, however, the fact of human fathers having continued authority over their human sons, paralleling a permanent authority of God the Father over God the Son, reveals a particular anthropological concept not necessarily shared by all societies.

One place where Grudem's view differs from Ware's is in the matter of prayer. Grudem does not discuss prayer in the immediate context of the doctrine of the Trinity, but he does say that while there is a clear biblical pattern of praying to the Father through the Son, that is not exclusive. Rather, "there are indications that prayer spoken directly to Jesus is also appropriate. . . . There is therefore clear enough scriptural warrant to encourage us to pray not only to God the Father . . . but also to pray directly to God the Son, our Lord Jesus Christ."[88] There are no instances in the New Testament of prayers directly to the Holy Spirit, but there are also no prohibitions of doing so. Grudem infers from the nature of the believer's relationship to the Holy Spirit that such prayers are legitimate: "Therefore, it does not seem wrong to pray directly to the Holy Spirit at times, particularly when we are asking

---

87. Ibid.
88. Grudem, *Systematic Theology*, 380–81.

him to do something that relates to his special areas of ministry or responsibility."[89] Such a practice also can be found in the history of the church, reflected in commonly used hymns. "But," Grudem says, "this is not the New Testament pattern, and it should not become the dominant emphasis in our prayer life."[90]

Robert Letham

A more extensive treatment of the Trinity than that given by either Ware or Grudem is Robert Letham's *The Holy Trinity*, which comprises more than five hundred pages. The work is primarily historical, treating the views of various theologians, but Letham does develop his own views. In many ways, his is the most moderate of the current gradational views.

We should note immediately that Letham rejects both the terms *hierarchy* and *subordination*. In response to Gilbert Bilezikian's treatment of his earlier article, Letham says, "Following this, without citing any evidence (for which there is none), he attributes the term *subordination* to me—a term I never use and steadfastly deny. I never use *subordination* or *hierarchy* or their functional equivalents—indeed, I sedulously avoid them."[91] While acknowledging that some conservative evangelicals have espoused "the eternal subordination of the Son," he comments that "at best, language like this is misleading."[92]

Yet, having rejected some of the more extreme concepts, he insists upon the idea of an order, or *taxis*, within the Trinity. He explains that this term can be understood in various ways, and he seems to prefer the idea of what is suitable or fitting, rather than a hierarchy. It suggests orderliness or organization, and Letham clearly rejects the idea that it involves gradation or rank. He agrees with T. F. Torrance, "This inner-Trinitarian order is distinguished 'by position and not status, by

---

89. Ibid., 381.

90. Ibid.

91. Robert Letham, *The Holy Trinity: In Scripture, History, Theology, and Worship* (Phillipsburg, NJ: P & R, 2004), 480.

92. Ibid., 399.

form and not being, by sequence and not power, for they are fully and perfectly equal.'"[93]

The only place where Letham mentions divine authority is in his discussions of the thought of Moltmann and Pannenberg, and there the context is divine authority in relation to humans, rather than of the Father in relation to the Son.[94] Clearly, to Letham, it is eternally the case that the Father is first, the Son is second, and the Spirit is third. The Son is from the Father.[95]

Letham uses the term *eternal generation* of the relationship of the Father to the Son. He defines it as "the unique property of the Son in relationship to the Father. Since God is eternal, the relation between the Father and the Son is eternal. This is not to be understood on the basis of human generation or begetting, since God is spiritual. It is beyond our capacity to understand."[96] While he is aware of both biblical and theological objections to the idea of divine begetting, he is not willing to surrender the term, so long as it is not misunderstood.[97] In an earlier article, he had spoken of "the ontological relations of the persons of the Trinity,"[98] but in his later book he regards this wording as "unfortunate."[99]

Letham emphasizes the Son's obedience or submission to the Father.[100] However, this is not to be understood as in any fashion compromising the full equality of being and deity of the two.[101] It involves neither subordinationism nor inferiority.[102] Nor is it to be understood only as applying to the time of the Son's earthly ministry. He cites with approval Barth's contention that the Son's obedience is a matter of eternity.[103]

---

93. Ibid., 400.
94. Ibid., 309–18.
95. Ibid., 399.
96. Ibid., 499.
97. Ibid., 383–89.
98. Robert Letham, "The Man-Woman Debate: Theological Comment," *Westminster Theological Journal* 52 (1990): 68.
99. Letham, *The Holy Trinity*, 490, 493.
100. Ibid., 394–404.
101. Ibid., 402–4.
102. Ibid., 399.
103. Ibid., 94–97.

Other Later Gradationists

Several other contributors to this view deserve mention.

Peter Schemm has written several articles defending the gradational view and criticizing the "egalitarian" view. He has especially cited theologians from the earlier history of the church to establish that the former view is the orthodox one.[104]

John Dahms also has written several articles contending for the gradational view. He has spoken of the Son's eternal, functional subordination being based on ontological subordination.[105]

J. Scott Horrell, professor of theology at Dallas Theological Seminary, has endeavored to distinguish clearly between ontological equality and difference of role. He cites the several texts that speak of the Father sending and giving and the views of several theologians of the past. He seems to endorse the formula of praying to the Father, through the Son, in the power of the Spirit.[106]

Institutionally, in the United States this teaching has been most vigorously expounded in certain Southern Baptist seminaries, perhaps because of the perceived connection between this issue and that of the respective roles of men and women, on which the Southern Baptist Convention has taken a definite stand in its 2000 Baptist Faith and Message. Much of the advocacy of the gradational view of the Trinity has come from certain faculty at Southeastern Baptist Theological Seminary, as well as Southern Baptist Theological Seminary

---

104. Peter Schemm, "Kevin Giles's *The Trinity and Subordinationism*: A Review Article," *Journal of Biblical Manhood and Womanhood* 7, no. 2 (Fall 2002): 67–78; idem, "Trinitarian Perspectives on Gender Roles," *Journal of Biblical Manhood and Womanhood* 6, no. 1 (Spring 2001): 13–20; and Peter Schemm and Steven Kovach, "A Defense of the Doctrine of the Eternal Subordination of the Son," *Journal of the Evangelical Theological Society* 42, no. 3 (September 1999): 461–76.

105. John Dahms, "The Generation of the Son," *Journal of the Evangelical Theological Society* 32, no. 4 (December 1989): 493–501; and idem, "The Subordination of the Son," *Journal of the Evangelical Theological Society* 37, no. 3 (September 1994): 351–64.

106. J. Scott Horrell, "Toward a Biblical Model of the Social Trinity: Avoiding Equivocation of Nature and Order," *Journal of the Evangelical Theological Society* 47, no. 3 (Fall 2004): 399–421.

and Southwestern Baptist Theological Seminary. This view is not held by all faculty at these institutions, however, although all of them are required to hold the "complementarian" view of the relationship between men and women in the home and in the church.

Special mention should be made of the stand taken by the Sydney Diocese of the Anglican Church of Australia. A study was commissioned and a document prepared and adopted.[107] While cautious and carefully nuanced, the document takes a definite stand that the historic view of the church is the gradational view. While rejecting subordinationism of being, it endorses the idea that the Son is subordinate to and obedient to the Father. This obedience stems from the very nature of the Son's being.[108] The error of the Arians was in overemphasizing the subordinationist elements in the Scriptures, but there is evidence in Scripture of a relational subordination of the Son.[109] While the creeds teach the equality of the three persons, in the case of the Son and the Spirit, this is a derived equality.[110]

Summary and Analysis of the Gradational View

After this rather extended examination of the view I have identified as the gradational view, it is possible to note both common elements and some variation and development:

1. All of these gradationists agree that the three persons are equally and in the same sense God. This is expressed in terms of their being equal in essence or being or all possessing equally all of the attributes of deity.

---

107. "The 1999 Sydney Anglican Diocesan Doctrine Commission Report: The Doctrine of the Trinity and Its Bearing on the Relationship of Men and Women"; reprinted in Kevin Giles, *The Trinity and Subordinationism: The Doctrine of God and the Contemporary Gender Debate* (Downers Grove, IL: InterVarsity Press, 2002), 122–37.

108. Ibid., par. 18.

109. Ibid., par. 22.

110. Ibid., par. 25.

2. All gradationists agree that the terms *Father, Son,* and *Holy Spirit* apply eternally to the three persons of the Trinity, rather than merely to the period of the Son's and Holy Spirit's special missions. All agree that there is a fixed and invariable "order" among the three, although some seem to regard this as a matter of position, not of rank. Eternally, the Father is first, the Son is second, and the Holy Spirit is third. All also agree that the relationships among the three are eternal, not merely temporary, are fixed, and are of the very nature of the Trinity. This is true of eternity past and will be true in eternity to come.

3. Out of these differing relationships stem the different roles or functions of each member of the Trinity. Some later gradationists insist that without the differing roles, there would be no difference between the three members and the Trinity would not exist.

4. In the earlier period, this relationship was often spoken of as the Father eternally generating or begetting the Son. By this was meant that the Father was the cause or source, not of the Son's essence, but rather of his subsistence, or his personhood. While citing these expressions as evidence of the view held earlier, more recent gradationists tend to avoid these terms and particularly regard the term *monogenēs* as meaning "one and only" rather than "only begotten." Citations of Psalm 2:7, including the claimed fulfillment of this promise in Acts, are regarded as later manifestations of an eternal truth.

5. Later gradationists argue from the nature of human father-son relationships to the divine Father-Son relationship. In some cases, the terms are regarded as applying quite literally in the same sense to the two relationships, as regards relative authority.

6. Later gradationists make much of the Father's authority over the Son and the Son's obedience. Some even speak of the Father as the supreme member of the Trinity. They speak of the Son as subordinate to the Father, or as submitting to him.

Earlier gradationists spoke very little of this authority-obedience structure.

7. This view of the structural relationships among the members of the Trinity is believed by later gradationists to be taught by the texts that speak of the Father as sending his Son and predestinating, and the Son as having come to do the Father's will. More recent gradationists also make much of 1 Corinthians 11:3, and see a parallel between God's headship (authority) over the Son and man's headship over woman. They also claim that orthodox Christians have held this view throughout the church's history, as reflected in the great creeds and in the writings of the church's greatest theologians.

8. Some recent gradationists speak of an "ontological" dimension to the relationship but without specifying what this means, while others avoid such terminology.

9. All gradationists reject the term *inferiority* as applied to the Son and Spirit in relationship to the Father. Without explicitly stating so, it appears that they regard such a term as referring to the essence or being of the Son, thus making him less than fully God. Special care is taken to distinguish subordination of function, when that expression is used, from the heresy of subordinationism, which refers to the Son as a lesser being or less fully divine than the Father.

10. Some later gradationists, notably Ware and, to a lesser extent, Horrell, maintain that prayer is to be directed only to the Father, in the name of the Son and in the power of the Spirit. Others, such as Grudem, teach that prayer may appropriately be directed to any of the members of the Trinity, as well as to the triune God. Ware suggests that while praise and worship may be directed to the Son, the Father is the ultimate object of such practice, the one who is to be glorified.

CHAPTER 2

The Equivalent-Authority View

As vigorously as the gradationist view has been advocated, so also has the strongly contrasting view of the eternal, equal authority of the three persons of the Trinity. As in the previous chapter, we may divide the modern discussion into roughly two periods.

The Early Period: 1870 to 1970

Benjamin B. Warfield

We noted in the previous chapter the clear stance taken by Charles Hodge, as a leading spokesman for the "Princeton theology." Benjamin B. Warfield, who succeeded Hodge's son in the chair of theology at Princeton Seminary, took a rather different stance on the relative positions of the members of the Trinity. In a noted article on the Trinity, which appeared in the original edition of the *International Standard Bible Encyclopedia*, he detailed the biblical basis of the doctrine and then discussed more specific issues. Three of these were of particular importance to his position:

1. The word *Son* speaks of equality. While some naturally assume that the relationship between earthly fathers and sons also applies to the heavenly Father and Son, Warfield points out that this is not the case. Warfield contends that rather than indicating some sort of dependence of the Son upon the Father, the primary meaning of "son" is likeness. This can be seen, for example, in the Jews' interpretation of Jesus' self-designation as the Son of God as a claim to deity or equality with God, in John 5:18. Warfield's statement is clear-cut: "What underlies the conception of sonship in Scriptural speech is just 'likeness': whatever

the father is that the son is also. The emphatic application of the term 'Son' to one of the Trinitarian Persons, accordingly asserts rather His equality with the Father than His subordination to the Father; and if there is any implication of derivation in it, it appears to be very distant."[1] He believes that the adjective "only begotten" adds only the idea of uniqueness, not derivation.

2. The terms *Father, Son,* and *Holy Spirit* are not the exclusive names for the members of the Trinity. While these are used almost invariably by Jesus and in John's writings, there is considerable variability in other biblical authors. This is especially true of Paul, who frequently uses instead the names, God, Lord, and Spirit, even more often than the Father-Son terminology. Warfield, always measured in his statements, puts it thus: "It remains remarkable, nevertheless, if the very essence of the Trinity were thought of by him [Paul] as resident in the terms 'Father,' 'Son,' that in his numerous allusions to the Trinity in the Godhead, he never betrays any sense of this."[2]

3. The common order in which Christians usually express the names of the members of the Trinity is Father, Son, and Spirit, and this is supported by the order in the baptismal formula in Matthew 28. However, Warfield points out that this order is by no means invariable in the New Testament. In the benediction in 2 Corinthians 13:14, the order is Lord, God, and Holy Spirit. In 1 Peter 1:2, the order is Father, Spirit, and Jesus Christ. In Jude 20–21, it is Holy Spirit, God, and Lord Jesus Christ. Sometimes, as in 1 Corinthians 12:3–6, the order is actually reversed completely, which may be a rhetorical device. Again, Warfield's statement is cautious: "If in their conviction the very essence of the doctrine of the Trinity was embodied in this order, should we not anticipate that there should appear

---

1. Benjamin B. Warfield, "Trinity," *The International Standard Bible Encyclopedia*, ed. James Orr (Grand Rapids: Eerdmans, 1952), 5:3020.
2. Ibid.

in their numerous allusions to the Trinity some suggestion of this conviction?"[3]

Warfield recognizes a type of subordination among the members of the Trinity with respect to the modes of operation of their work in the world. From this some have drawn conclusions about a more permanent subordination. Warfield, however, draws a crucial distinction:

But it is not so clear that the principle of subordination rules also in "modes of subsistence," as it is technically phrased: that is to say, in the necessary relation of the Persons of the Trinity to one another. The very richness and variety of the expression of their subordination, the one to the other, in modes of operation, create a difficulty in attaining certainty whether they are represented as also subordinate the one to the other in modes of subsistence. Question is raised in each case of apparent intimation of subordination in modes of subsistence, whether it may not, after all, be explicable as only another expression of subordination in modes of operation. It may be natural to assume that a subordination in modes of operation rests on a subordination in modes of subsistence; that the reason why it is the Father that sends the Son and the Son that sends the Spirit is that the Son is subordinate to the Father and the Spirit to the Son. But we are bound to bear in mind that these references to subordination in modes of operation may just as well be due to a convention, an agreement, between the Persons of the Trinity—a "Covenant" as it is technically called—by virtue of which a distinct function in the work of redemption is voluntarily assumed by each. It is eminently desirable, therefore, at the least, that some definite evidence of subordination in modes of subsistence should be discoverable before it is assumed. In the case of the relation of the Son to the Father, there is the added difficulty of the incarnation, in which the Son, by the assumption of a creaturely nature into

---

3. Ibid.

union with Himself, enters into new relations with the Father of a definitely subordinate character.[4]

Warfield does not go so far as to restrict the very designations of Father and Son to the new relations arising from the Incarnation. Although these terms may apply eternally, they do not carry the connotation of supremacy and subordination. Of the attempt to derive eternal relations of subordination from the terms, he says,

> It must at least be said that in the presence of the great NT doctrines of the Covenant of Redemption on the one hand, and of the Humiliation of the Son of God for His work's sake and of the Two Natures in the constitution of His Person as incarnation, on the other, the difficulty of interpreting subordinationist passages of eternal relations between the Father and Son becomes extreme. The question continually obtrudes itself, whether they do not rather find their full explanation in the facts embodied in the doctrines of the Covenant, the humiliation of Christ, and the Two natures of his incarnated Person. Certainly in such circumstances it were thoroughly illegitimate to press such passages to suggest any subordination for the Son or the Spirit which would in any manner impair that complete identity with the Father in Being and that complete equality with the Father in powers which are constantly presupposed, and frequently emphatically, though only incidentally, asserted for them throughout the whole fabric of the NT.[5]

Loraine Boettner

One twentieth-century Reformed theologian who followed Warfield rather than Hodge, even though he had specialized in systematic theology at Princeton Seminary with Hodge's son, Caspar Wistar Hodge, was Loraine Boettner. He states his position clearly and directly:

---

4. Ibid., 3021.
5. Ibid.

"The Father is, and always has been, as much dependent on the Son as the Son is on the Father, for, as we need to keep in mind, self-existence and independence are properties, not of the Persons within the Godhead, but of the Triune God."[6]

He follows Warfield's understanding of the meaning of the terms *Father* and *Son*, which he says "carry with them, on the one hand, the ideas of source of being and superiority, and on the other, subordination and dependence. In theological language, however, they are used in the Semitic or Oriental sense of *sameness of nature*. It is, of course, the Semitic consciousness which underlies the phraseology of Scripture."[7] Boettner recognizes and emphasizes that the terms must not be taken literally but rather should be understood in light of the fact that much of the scriptural teaching is given in figurative language. While not perfect, these terms are the best we have in our language to express the relationships between the three persons of the Godhead. He cites the idea, emphasized by Calvin, that God adjusts himself to human language the way parents often talk down to children.[8] So, for example, "When we are told that God 'gave' His Son for the redemption of the world we are led to understand that the situation was in some ways analogous to that of a human father who gives his son for missionary service or for the defense of his country."[9]

Boettner makes much of the unity of the three persons, so that "each of the Persons participates to some extent in the work of the others. . . . Hence we say that while the spheres and functions of the three persons of the Trinity are different, they are not exclusive. That which is done by one is participated in by the others with varying degrees of prominence."[10] Each of the persons has a special role that is primarily his, yet this is not based on some inherent structure of superiority.

---

6. Loraine Boettner, *Studies in Theology* (Philadelphia: Presbyterian and Reformed, 1964), 112.

7. Ibid.

8. Ibid., 115.

9. Ibid., 114.

10. Ibid., 118.

Rather, following Warfield's suggestion, Boettner asserts, "In the Scriptures we find that the plan of redemption takes the form of a covenant, not merely between God and His people but between the different Persons of the Trinity, so that there is, as it were, a division of labour, each Person voluntarily assuming a particular part of the work."[11]

This division of labor involves a temporary submission of the Son to the Father and of the Spirit to the Father and the Son, but not in such a way as to involve superiority or inferiority: "This subordination of the Son to the Father, and of the Spirit to the Father and the Son, is not in any way inconsistent with true equality."[12] He likens this to a situation in which persons who are of equal rank in private life may, for a time, have different ranks in the military:

> Officially, and for a limited time, one becomes subordinate to the other, yet during that time they may be equals in the sight of God. In the work of redemption the situation is somewhat analogous to this,—through a covenant voluntarily entered into, the Father, Son and Holy Spirit each undertake a specific work in such a manner that, during the time this work is in progress, the Father becomes officially first, the Son officially second, and the Spirit officially third. Yet within the essential and inherent life of the Trinity the full equality of the persons is preserved.[13]

Boettner also considers briefly the questions of the generation of the Son and the procession of the Spirit. He examines the biblical texts usually cited in support of these teachings and concludes, "The present writer feels constrained to say, however, that in his opinion the verses quoted do not teach the doctrine in question."[14] He rejects even Augustine's teaching on this subject, insisting that if the Father "is the *Fons Trinitatis*—the fountain or source of the Trinity—from whom both the Son and the Spirit are derived, it seems that in spite of all

---

11. Ibid., 117.
12. Ibid., 119.
13. Ibid., 120–21.
14. Ibid., 121.

else we may say we have made the Son and the Spirit dependent upon another as their principal cause, and have destroyed the true and essential equality between the Persons of the Trinity."[15] He believes he is following the lead of Calvin in this matter.[16]

J. Oliver Buswell Jr.

Even Wayne Grudem identifies Buswell as one (of the very few, he would add) theologian who did not hold to the eternal functional subordination of the Son. Buswell, at one time president of Wheaton College, wrote a two-volume theology that was virtually the only conservative evangelical theological textbook between Berkhof's and the outburst of several such theologies in the last quarter of the twentieth century. He is quite clear on two points. The first is that any subordination of the Son to the Father is to be understood as functional only, not a subordinate essence. The second is that this functional subordination was temporary and for the purpose of accomplishing Christ's redemptive work. He says, "When we discuss the person and work of Christ we shall show that all references to the subordination of the Son to the Father signify a *functional subordination* in the economy of the divine redemptive program. It is of the utmost importance that we distinguish between *economic*, or *functional subordination*, and *essential equality*."[17] Referring to Jesus' statements in John 14:28 ("The Father is greater than I") and John 5:30 ("By myself I can do nothing"), he says, "We must understand these statements as referring to His economic subordination in 'the days of his flesh.'"[18]

Beyond that, Buswell examines at some length the concepts of "begotten," "only begotten," and the eternal generation of the Son by the Father. While acknowledging that these concepts were endorsed by the councils, but in distinction to the Son being created, he seems to hold that the idea of "begotten but not made" is a meaningless concept,

---

15. Ibid., 122.

16. Ibid.

17. James Oliver Buswell Jr., *A Systematic Theology of the Christian Religion* (Grand Rapids: Zondervan, 1962), 1:106.

18. Ibid.

for he says this "is reducing the word begotten to absolute zero."[19] He adds, "Yet I do believe that the 'eternal generation' doctrine should be dropped."[20] By this action, he also abandons the basis that such earlier theologians as Hodge give for any sort of functional subordination, but without replacing it with some other basis.

Although Buswell promised to develop this theme at greater length in his later treatment of the person and work of Christ, when he comes to those topics in his second volume, he does not elaborate further but rather refers the reader back to what he had written here. Nothing he says in the Christology discussion, however, contradicts these statements on the doctrine of the Trinity. The position he described earlier is also reinforced by some illustrations he gives of the Incarnation. He speaks of Peter the Great, who became a carpenter in a shipyard but did not thereby cease to be the emperor of Russia. Another illustration he cites is that of the Prince of Wales, who during the First World War served in the British military at a relatively low rank but did not thereby surrender his royalty. These illustrations are offered as "a partial analogy to the incarnation," terminology that indicates that the functional subordination of which he speaks was temporary, not eternal.[21]

The Later Period: 1970 to the Present

Paul King Jewett

Like George Knight on the gradationist side, Jewett, professor of theology at Fuller Seminary, addressed the passage in 1 Corinthians 11:3 and saw there the Pauline idea of a hierarchy. He says, "As God is the head of Christ, so Christ is the head of the man and so the man is the head of the woman (vv. 2, 3). The word 'head' is used by Paul to denote the one next above one in the hierarchy of divinely constituted authority."[22] Although he seems to accept the definition of "head"

---

19. Ibid., 1:112.

20. Ibid.

21. Ibid., 2:31–32.

22. Paul K. Jewett, *Man as Male and Female: A Study in Sexual Relationships from a Theological Point of View* (Grand Rapids: Eerdmans, 1975), 54–55.

promoted by the later gradationists, a closer examination of his thought reveals that it is more complex than this. In a footnote to this passage, he says, "Probably the Greek κεφαλή, as here used, is virtually synonymous with ἀρχῇ, meaning 'origin' or 'first cause.' The female's ontological inferiority, in the apostle's thought, is grounded in the male's priority of creation. The woman is *of* the man; he is her 'first cause.'"[23]

The distinctiveness of Jewett's view is seen in two respects: he virtually equates the two disputed senses of "head" as authority over and as source, and he sees this male priority in creation as leading to the ontological inferiority of the female. Similarly, when he discusses Karl Barth's view, he observes that the idea of woman's subordination to man can be derived only from the idea of the difference between them if the additional premise of woman's inferiority to man is true.

Although Jewett's purpose in the book is primarily to define the relationship of male and female human beings, in the process he also discusses the relationship of the Son to the Father and emphasizes that the Son voluntarily assumed a subordinate role and that this was part of the redemptive work of the Son, not the expression of some eternal relationship: "The subordination of the Son to the Father is not an ontological subordination in the eternal Godhead, but a voluntary act of self-humiliation on the part of the Son in the economy of redemption. As God, the Son is equal with his Father, though as Messiah he has assumed a servant role and become subordinate to his Father."[24]

Nor does Jewett accept the idea of generation: "While the fellowship of the Father, the Son, and the Spirit may be reflected in our male/female fellowship at the human level (Barth's *analogia relationis*), such trinitarian terms as 'generation' and 'spiration' are too obscure to bear the theological freight of the distinction between the Eternal Masculine and the Eternal Feminine."[25] As with Knight, Jewett's thoughts are not carried through in detail, but the elements therein became the basis of the more fully elaborated theologies that followed.

---

23. Ibid., 55n. 3.
24. Ibid., 133n. 105.
25. Ibid., 187n. 19.

Gilbert Bilezikian

The first strong argument for the equivalentist view in the late twentieth century came from Gilbert Bilezikian, a longtime New Testament professor at Wheaton College. His major contribution was an article inspired by his concern over what he viewed as a dangerous development within evangelical theological scholarship regarding the crucial doctrine of the Trinity. While he is not terming this a heresy, he does believe that it is a hermeneutical approach that "stretches our tolerance for theological innovation beyond the limits of orthodoxy."[26] He thinks that just as other hermeneutic deviations from orthodox doctrine are not "the result of premeditated conspiracies to create new heresies," this is not either.[27] Since the formulation of the orthodox doctrine of the Trinity at the councils of Nicea and Chalcedon, "Biblical Christians have been quick to rise to its defense and to guard it against redefinitions and new interpretations."[28] He notes that the Evangelical Theological Society has embodied this "conservative reflex" as well, by adding to the single sentence on biblical authority and inerrancy that had formed its entire doctrinal basis for decades an additional statement: "God is a Trinity, Father, Son, and Holy Spirit, each an uncreated person, one in essence, equal in power and glory."

Bilezikian believes that "with this addendum the ETS resoundingly affirmed the historic view of the Trinity. It recognized the oneness of the Godhead along with the eternity, the ontological identity and the equality in authority or sovereignty ('power') and honor or status ('glory') among the three persons of the Trinity."[29] It appears that he is identifying authority or sovereignty with power.

But should not this addendum be sufficient to assure Bilezikian that all is well with the doctrine of the Trinity within evangelical circles? He is emphatic in his expression of concern: "From within our

---

26. Gilbert Bilezikian, "Hermeneutical Bungee-Jumping: Subordination in the Godhead," *Journal of the Evangelical Theological Society* 40, no. 1 (March 1997): 57.

27. Ibid.

28. Ibid.

29. Ibid.

own ranks a potentially destructive redefinition of the doctrine is being developed that threatens its integrity at what has historically proven to be its most vulnerable point: the definition of the relationship between the Father and the Son."[30] He does not consider those who are promoting this redefinition of the doctrine of the Trinity to be heretics, who are intentionally attempting to undermine the traditional belief. Rather, they have ventured into this area only "obliquely," as a result of their concern over other matters: "It is possible that, in their eagerness to prove their point, they do not even realize that they may be found tampering with the Church's historic commitment to trinitarian doctrine."[31]

The specific issue that Bilezikian believes has led these evangelicals to such a misunderstanding of the Trinity is their commitment to a hierarchical order between male and female, both in the church and in the family. The idea that wives are to be subject to their husbands and that women are not to exercise teaching and ruling roles in the church has been justified by drawing a parallel between this subjection and one of "alleged relationship of authority/subordination between Father and Son."[32]

Bilezikian spells out his own view both directly and in reaction to what he views as this new and distorted view of the relationships among the members of the Trinity. He is emphatic in insisting that the Son is fully equal with the Father, not only in essence but also in authority, and that this equality is eternal. Together with this emphasis upon the greatness of the Son, however, the creed equally emphasizes the Incarnation and the incarnate work of the Son. The accomplishment of the divine mission of mercy was accomplished only by "an unprecedented and unrepeatable dislocation within the Trinity. In order to minister to humans out of love, and in characteristic servanthood, God in Christ became man."[33] This involved the Son taking on a very different status

---

30. Ibid., 57–58.
31. Ibid., 58.
32. Ibid.
33. Ibid.

from that which he had eternally with the Father: "From the position of equality with the Father, at the pinnacle of divine glory, the Son descended to the most degrading experience of debasement known among humans by suffering the humiliation of a public execution as a criminal. While in this state of humiliation the Son's divine nature was not affected."[34]

Yet while remaining fully God, it could be said of the Son that "paradoxically he also made himself subject to the Father when he assumed human personhood."[35] Bilezikian proposes to examine more closely this subjection of the Son to the Father in relation to the version proposed by the complementarians.

Two important scriptural qualifications of this subjection need to be noted. First, it was voluntary. He was not forced to become a servant; he chose to do so. It was not because he was "number two in the Trinity and his boss told him to do so or because he was demoted to a subordinate rank so that he could accomplish a job that no one else wanted to touch" that he came to achieve redemption for the human race.[36] It appears that Bilezikian believes this truth cannot be overemphasized: "He was not forced to become a servant; he was not compelled to be obedient; he was not dragged to death against his will. The Bible puts it tersely: 'He humbled himself.' Therefore it is much more appropriate, and theologically accurate, to speak of Christ's self-humiliation rather than his subordination. Nobody subordinated him and he was originally subordinated to no one."[37]

The second qualification is equally important and relates to Christ's humiliation. Bilezikian emphasizes that this was "an interim or temporary state. It was not, nor shall it be, an eternal condition."[38] For the sake of the task of redemption, the Son took on the condition of humiliation, including obedience to the Father, but only for the time in which

---

34. Ibid., 58–59.
35. Ibid., 59.
36. Ibid.
37. Ibid.
38. Ibid.

that task was to be fulfilled. "From all eternity, and in the beginning, Christ . . . was equal with God, but the time came when he did not consider his equality with God a privilege to clutch as his own."[39] The novelty of this situation is crucial to understanding the real relationship with the Father: "It [the form of a servant] was something new for him. Being in the form of a servant was not an eternal condition. He took it up. He became obedient unto death. Prior to the incarnation there had been no need for him to be obedient since he was equal with God. But despite the fact that he had the dignity of sonship he learned obedience through what he suffered (Heb. 5:8). Obedience was a new experience for him, something he had to learn. It was not an eternal state."[40]

Bilezikian affirms the important hermeneutical function of understanding this principle correctly: "The frame of reference for every term that is found in Scripture to describe Christ's humiliation pertains to his ministry and not to his eternal state."[41] Just as the Son's obedience to the Father began with his coming to earth, it will cease when that task has been accomplished: "Because there was no order of subordination within the Trinity prior to the Second Person's incarnation, there will remain no such thing after its completion."[42] As hesitant as Bilezikian is to use the term *subordination*, he says, "If we must talk of subordination it is only a functional or economic subordination that pertains exclusively to Christ's role in relation to human history. Christ's *kenosis* affected neither his essence nor his status in eternity."[43]

Thus we may summarize Bilezikian's view of the subordination of the Son to the Father, or the Son's obedience to the Father, by saying that it was voluntary, functional, and temporary. This is in contrast to the view of those evangelicals Bilezikian is opposing. They would agree that the subordination of the Son to the Father was indeed functional, not a subordination of essence or being, but they would insist that it

---

39. Ibid., 59–60.
40. Ibid., 60.
41. Ibid.
42. Ibid.
43. Ibid.

was eternal and inherent in the nature of the Trinity and that it never was otherwise, nor could it have been.

Bilezikian offers several types of arguments or types of evidence. One is the church's tradition. He frequently refers to the church's formulation and adherence to a definite statement. This is seen most pointedly in his declaration following the statement above of his view of temporary functional subordination: "Except for occasional and predictable deviations, this is the historical Biblical trinitarian doctrine that has been defined in the creeds and generally defended by the Church, at least the western Church, throughout the centuries."[44] Unfortunately, he does not offer specific documentation for this assertion and even quotes from a creed without identifying it.

Bilezikian deals in considerably greater detail with the biblical data. We have noted above his use of Philippians 2:5–11 and Hebrews 5:8. One of his most emphatic statements is in connection with the Greek term *kephalē*, which is usually rendered "head" in most translations, especially in Paul's uses in 1 Corinthians, Ephesians, and Colossians.

It is important to deal with this term because the complementarians, especially Wayne Grudem, have contended that it means "authority over" or "leader" in each of its occurrences. Bilezikian, on the other hand, says that "in each of the contexts where it is used 'head' in Greek naturally yields the meaning of servant-provider of life, of growth and fullness' (1 Cor 11:3, cf. 8, 12; Eph 1:22–23; 4:15–16; 5:23; Col 2:19, etc.)."[45] He does not here offer lexicographic documentation for this assertion, but he does present two objections to the complementarians' use of it in 1 Corinthians 11:3 to argue for the eternal subordination of the Son to the Father, and thus of the wife to the husband. One is a literary argument: "they have no satisfactory answer for the fact that Paul's ordering of the three clauses rules out a hierarchical sequence (BCA instead of ABC)."[46] The other argument is contextual: "But even if 'head' in this passage were to mean authority, neither the passage nor

---

44. Ibid.
45. Ibid., 61.
46. Ibid.

its context contains any indication that this headship describes an eternal state. In this text Paul is referring to the relationship that prevails between God and Christ in the context of Christ's ministry to men and women within human history."[47]

Bilezikian also contests Grudem's appeal to Hebrews 1:3, that when Christ made "purification for sins, he sat down at the right hand of the Majesty on high." Grudem contends that while Jesus is on the right hand, the Father is still on the throne, indicating the Father's superior authority over the Son. Bilezikian replies that there is no mention of a throne in connection with the right hand of God in this verse, although such is found in 8:1 and 12:2. On the contrary, says Bilezikian, in this same verse (1:3), one finds some of the strongest assertions regarding the deity of Christ: "the radiance of God's glory, the exact representation of his being, sustaining all things by his powerful word."[48] Whereas Grudem assumes that sitting at the right hand of the throne symbolizes subordination, Bilezikian affirms that "it can be cogently argued from Scripture that it is a position of exaltation to supreme glory."[49]

Beyond that, Bilezikian claims that in Scripture we find "not only that Christ is sitting at the right hand of God but also that he is sitting at the center of God's throne. This is not an incidental reference but a heavy emphasis made especially in the book of Revelation."[50] Citing Revelation 3:21, 7:17, 12:5, and 22:3, he summarizes: "Contrary to Grudem's suggestion, God is not on the throne with the Son apart from him or below the throne in a position of subordination. According to the Scripture, both God the Father and God the Son occupy the same throne for eternity. They are 'equal in power and glory.'"[51]

Bilezikian also objects to Grudem's use of biblical references to the "only begotten" Son to justify the doctrine of eternal generation, and thus also the concept of an eternal subordination process "otherwise

---

47. Ibid.
48. Ibid., 63.
49. Ibid.
50. Ibid.
51. Ibid.

not attested in Scripture (John 1:14, 18; 3:16, 18; 1 John 4:9)."[52] He contends instead that "these would be better understood as referring to the necessity of the incarnation, just as 'the Lamb that was slain from the creation of the world' (Rev 13:8) refers to the crucifixion rather than to a theory of Christ's eternal passion."[53]

Bilezikian returns to the treatment of Hebrews 5:8 in connection with his discussion of Robert Letham, who cites it as one of several biblical texts supporting the idea of the Son's obedience to the Father. Bilezikian describes Letham's citation of this verse in support of his view as "careless" and offers three remarks of his own about this text:

> (1) The fact that he learned obedience "although" he was a Son indicates that the nature of his Sonship excluded the necessity of obedience. He learned obedience despite the fact that he was a Son. (2) The fact that he "learned" obedience indicates that it was something new in his experience as Son. Obedience was not a mark of his eternal relation to the Father. He learned it for the purpose of ministry. (3) The fact that he learned obedience "through" what he suffered indicates that obedience was required in relation to his suffering and that it was not an eternal condition. Christ's experience of obedience was confined to his redemptive ministry as suffering servant.[54]

Although not identifying it as such, Bilezikian also appeals to philosophical argumentation. This emerges first in his discussion of the eternal generation of the Son, which Grudem holds and insists implies an eternal relationship of subordination of the Son to the Father in role but not in essence. While characterizing this concept as "a creedal construction subject to aleatory interpretations rather than a strong attested Biblical motif,"[55] Bilezikian points out that it and the terminology of Father and Son have sometimes led to "simplistic anthro-

---

52. Ibid., 62.
53. Ibid.
54. Ibid., 65.
55. Ibid., 62.

pomorphic projections not warranted by Scripture."[56] He points out significant differences between earthly father-son relationships and the divine Father-Son relationship. God, although a Father, had no wife; and Christ, as the eternal Son, has no mother. Christ is eternal, rather than being born in time, and the Father and Son are both eternal, rather than the Father being born before the Son.[57]

Bilezikian also presses the philosophical question of the tenability of separating eternal functional subordination from subordination of essence. In his discussion of Letham's view, Bilezikian says that "a subordination that extends into eternity cannot remain only functional . . . it also becomes *ipso facto* an ontological reality."[58] Observing that Letham seems to see the implications of his view, Bilezikian adds, "Since the attribute of eternity inheres in the divine essence, any reality that is eternal is by necessity ontologically grounded. Eternity is a quality of existence. Therefore if Christ's subordination is eternal, as both Grudem and Letham claim, it is also ontological."[59]

Finally, Bilezikian also argues theologically. By that I mean that he draws implications for other doctrines from the doctrinal conception of eternal subordination in the Trinity. So he contends that Grudem's idea of the Son being obedient to the Father prior to the Incarnation has "devastating consequences" for Christology: "Since according to Grudem there was no functional parity to begin with, the only structure of equality left for the Son's 'emptying' [in Phil. 2:6] was his ontological equality with the Father. Inevitably Grudem's theory of the Son's eternal functional subordination leads to an incarnate Christ who was fully divine neither in function nor in essence."[60]

Bilezikian is emphatic in rejecting this view: "In his incarnation the Son remained equal with the Father. But he temporarily forfeited his functional equality to assume the 'form of a servant.' This was a

56. Ibid.
57. Ibid.
58. Ibid., 63–64.
59. Ibid., 64.
60. Ibid., 62.

new mode of being for the Son in relation to the Father, not an eternal state (v. 7)."[61] He makes a similar criticism of Letham: "One wonders where the equality came from that the Son let go in the *kenosis*. Eternal subordination precludes equality. The Biblical definition of the *kenosis* as the Son's refusal to exploit the status of equality he had with the Father attests to the fact that there was no subordination prior to the *kenosis*."[62]

Stanley Grenz

Grenz, together with coauthor Denise Kjesbo, gave the major exposition of his view of the relationship between the Father and the Son in a book on women in the church, even more so than in his more extensive treatment of the Trinity. He seems to accept unchallenged a number of traditional concepts, but he develops his case for equivalent authority on a different basis than the others we are examining in this chapter. Note in the following quotation the juxtaposition of what seem to be two competitive ideas: "Our model of the trinitarian structure arises from the historical life of Jesus. It consists of the voluntary submission of one specific person (the Son) to another specific person (the Father) on the basis of the personal mission and for the sake of accomplishing the goals of both. This salvation-historical subordination, in turn, points to an eternal ground, namely, in the eternal generation of the Son (and the eternal spiration of the Spirit), to use the terminology of the patristic church."[63]

Here we have, on the one hand, the idea that the submission of the Son to the Father was voluntary, for a specific mission that involved accomplishing goals common to the two. On the other hand, this subordination is seen as pointing to "an eternal ground," here denominated in the very traditional concepts of eternal generation and eternal spiration. Grenz and Kjesbo elaborate by noting "that Christ's relation-

---

61. Ibid., 62–63.

62. Ibid., 64.

63. Stanley Grenz and Denise Muir Kjesbo, *Women in the Church: A Biblical Theology of Women in Ministry* (Downers Grove, IL: InterVarsity Press, 1995), 114.

ship to the Father was the temporary submission of one divine person to another in the economy of salvation. We can readily understand how such a functional submission of one person to another reveals no ontological subordination."[64]

Now, however, Grenz's argument takes a decidedly different turn from that of most equivalentists, to the mutual dependence of the Son and the Father upon one another.

> Finally, the argument from Christ's example often overlooks the deeper dynamic of mutual dependence within the Trinity. Jesus willingly submitted himself to the One he called "Abba." Thereby he reveals that the Son is subordinate to the Father within the eternal Trinity. At the same time the Father is dependent on the Son for his deity. In sending his Son into the world, the Father entrusted his own reign—indeed his own deity—to the Son (for example, Lk 10:22). Likewise, the Father is dependent on the Son for his title as the Father. As Irenaeus pointed out in the second century, without the Son the Father is not the Father of the Son. Hence the subordination of the Son to the Father must be balanced by the subordination of the Father to the Son.[65]

Grenz terms the traditional view a linear or asymmetrical view of the relationship between Father and Son, which has then been used to justify a similarly asymmetrical view of the relationship between man and woman. He comments, "The classical asymmetrical understanding of the trinitarian relations is increasingly coming under attack today, even by otherwise classically oriented theologians. Indeed, because the Father is also dependent on the Son, a more nuanced, somewhat symmetrical model offers a better picture of God."[66] While one wishes that the expression "somewhat symmetrical model" had

---

64. Ibid., 152. Grenz here agrees with the gradationists that the subordination is functional, not ontological, but he makes it a temporary functional subordination, not an eternal functional relationship.

65. Ibid., 153–54.

66. Ibid., 154.

been elaborated, it is apparent that this is much more an equivalence than a gradational view of the relationship between the persons of the Trinity.

Kevin Giles

Without doubt, the most extended treatment of the issue of subordination from the equivalence point of view is by Kevin Giles, an Australian pastor who holds a doctorate in New Testament. His exploration of the subject began with a brief journal article, written in response to an increasing "number of evangelicals who were speaking of the eternal subordination of the Son in the Trinity."[67]

Giles had thought that in dealing with the subject he could simply consult the growing number of books that had been written on the Trinity in the immediately preceding years, but he found that he was mistaken. The only mention the authors of these books made of subordination was in connection with the early debates culminating with Arianism. He further discovered that these writers dealt only a little or not at all with the three issues that were being highlighted by the recent evangelical discussions: the headship of the Father, the significance of the subordination of the Son to the Father in the Incarnation, and the differences of the three persons being grounded in their respective roles or functions.[68] Because the recent evangelicals claimed that their view was the historic view of the church, held by many or even all orthodox theologians from earlier periods, he realized that he would need to do much more work to determine what the orthodox view of the Trinity was.[69] His research led him to publish his first major book on the subject, *The Trinity & Subordinationism*.

Giles made a significant discovery early in this process: "that the debate about the Trinity was in essence a debate about theological method," which was at the forefront of contemporary evangelical

---

67. Kevin Giles, *The Trinity and Subordinationism: The Doctrine of God and the Contemporary Gender Debate* (Downers Grove, IL: InterVarsity Press, 2002), 1.

68. Ibid.

69. Ibid., 1–2.

thinking.[70] Two interrelated questions underlay the debate: "how does one settle a theological dispute when what is asked is not directly answered by the Bible, and how does one weigh differing arguments when both sides appeal to the Bible to substantiate their opposing conclusions?"[71]

He also saw a deep and extensive connection between this debate and that over the relationship between men and women, both in the home and in the church.[72] This led him to a more general insight about theological method: "Quoting biblical texts and giving one's interpretation of them cannot resolve complex theological disputes. In the fourth century, this approach to 'doing' theology had to be abandoned, and I believe this approach should also be abandoned today because it always leads to a 'text-jam.' . . . A better way to understand how the Bible contributes to theology and what is involved in 'doing' evangelical theology is obviously demanded."[73]

Giles soon realized that he was not the first theologian to grapple with this issue or to come up with this conclusion. In particular, Athanasius, the great fourth-century theologian whose view had prevailed over that of Arius, saw that Arius had compiled an impressive collection of biblical texts in support of his view, but he believed that Arius was in error. It was possible for any sufficiently clever theologian to find texts that could be interpreted to prove almost anything that he wished. A better method was needed. According to Giles, "Athanasius argued in reply that to 'do' theology, one needed a profound grasp of what he called the 'scope' of Scripture—the overall drift of the Bible, its primary focus, its theological center."[74] When applied to Christology, this yielded a twofold account: "on the one hand, that the Son is eternally one in being and action with the Father and, on the other hand, that

---

70. Ibid., 2.
71. Ibid.
72. Ibid.
73. Ibid., 3.
74. Ibid.

the Son gladly and willingly subordinated himself temporarily for us and our salvation."[75]

The large issue, of course, was how one could obtain this insight into the overall thrust of Scripture. Here, according to Giles, Athanasius believed that anyone who had the spiritual eyes to see could discover the "scope" of Scripture, but it "was made plain by the 'tradition.'"[76] The evidence that our faith is right, according to Athanasius, is that it "starts from the teaching of the apostles and the tradition of the fathers."[77] Giles says he also discovered that Augustine followed the same theological method. He did not simply quote isolated texts of Scripture to substantiate already held belief but rather followed a "canonical" reading of Scripture.[78]

According to Giles, Athanasius also saw another significant problem: How does one utilize the Bible to address questions that the original biblical writers did not deal with in their time and context, but which arose later in the church? Since those questions were not dealt with formally in Scripture, it is ineffective to attempt to deal with them simply by quoting Scripture. Athanasius's greatness was in anticipating the problem and offering a method for dealing with it: "To answer questions the Bible does not anticipate, the theologian must first determine what is primary and foundational in Scripture on the matter under consideration and then work out the implications of this in dialogue with those theologians of other opinions."[79]

Giles notes that evangelicals often have disregarded the role of tradition in doing theology, claiming that their doctrines are derived directly from the study of the Bible. More recently, however, as they have wrestled with the complex problems of hermeneutics, they have begun to accept tradition as an important, if secondary, source of

---

75. Ibid.

76. Ibid., 4.

77. Athanasius, *Epistula ad Adelphium* 6, in *Nicene and Post-Nicene Fathers* 4:577; quoted in Giles, *The Trinity and Subordinationism*, 4.

78. Giles, *The Trinity and Subordinationism*, 4.

79. Ibid.

theology. Yet, Giles contends, we must not simply follow tradition uncritically: "Tradition should always be taken seriously and should never be ignored, but sometimes it needs to be corrected or rejected."[80] In this, he claims to be following the pattern of the Reformers, who recognized that the Catholic Church had misread the Scriptures, especially on the matter of salvation by grace alone, and did not hesitate to reject this traditional Catholic way of reading the Bible.

Giles asserts that there is one critical hermeneutical issue faced by the church: "Do changed historical-cultural contexts demand and provide new interpretations of the Bible?" His thesis is clear:

> This book is predicated on the view that the Bible can often be read in more than one way, even on important matters. This comment is uncontroversial because it is undeniable. History gives innumerable examples of learned and devout theologians who have differed from others in their interpretation of the Bible on almost every doctrine or ethical question imaginable. In relation to the doctrine of the Trinity my argument is that the tradition should prescribe the correct reading. This is claimed because this tradition is the fruit of deep and prolonged reflection by the best and most respected theologians across the centuries on what the Bible teaches on the Trinity, and their conclusions are now codified in the creeds and Reformation confessions of faith.[81]

Whereas some conservative evangelicals have assumed that biblical interpretation is a strictly objective process of discovering the authorial intent for any given passage, Giles contends that "the historical-cultural context is part of the exegetical outcome."[82] On such matters as the idea that the earth was flat, the ancient interpreters merely reflected the customary understanding held by everyone of their time. No other possibility could occur to them. At some points the biblical writers reflect those viewpoints as well. "Yet," says Giles, "new scientific

---

80. Ibid., 5.
81. Ibid., 8–9.
82. Ibid., 9.

discoveries have demanded that the old interpretations, with their good textual support, be abandoned. Only in a different cultural context could theologians discover a different reading of Scripture that made sense of the changed understanding of the world, an understanding that God himself had brought to pass."[83]

Giles notes that while "many conservative evangelicals . . . have been lead [*sic*] to believe that there can only be one correct interpretation of any given text, only one correct reading of the Bible on any particular matter," modern discussions of hermeneutics have challenged this type of objectivism, and evangelicals, including Anthony Thiselton and Kevin Vanhoozer, have contributed to those discussions.[84]

Giles's contention is that all interpreters bring to the task of interpretation their own presuppositions, which serve as spectacles through which they read the text. He adds, "From this observation the following hermeneutical rule may be deduced: *Context contributes to meaning.* Once this is recognized, one can no longer think of the Bible as a set of timeless, transcultural rulings or as propositions that speak in every age with one voice. The Bible is rather seen as a book written in history by human authors, inspired and directed by the Holy Spirit, through which and in which the Holy Spirit speaks afresh time and time again."[85]

This statement could itself be read in at least two different ways. First, it could be seen as reflecting a neo-orthodox view of revelation, in which revelation does not consist of a body of information fixed by God but of God speaking again and again through the words of the biblical authors.

Second, it could be understood as a more orthodox view, that there is a definite and objective meaning of the scriptural writing, which the Spirit illuminates and applies in different ways at different times. That the latter is what Giles is saying seems to emerge from his illustration of a person viewing a town from different elevations on a mountain: "His

83. Ibid.
84. Ibid., 10.
85. Ibid., 11.

changing context changes his perception of the town. The town does not change, but how he sees it changes."[86]

Giles's basic position then emerges quite clearly. The orthodox understanding of the relationship of the three persons within the Trinity has been that they are equal in their eternal authority. For a period of time and for a specific purpose within the redemptive economy of God, the Son and then the Spirit voluntarily assumed a position of functional subordination to the Father, and in the case of the Spirit, to the Son as well. At the completion of these respective redemptive tasks, however, the equal authority possessed in eternity past is reassumed and will continue to be possessed and exercised through all eternity future.

The problem, as Giles sees it, is that these conservative evangelicals in the late twentieth and then early twenty-first centuries have allowed their view of the respective roles of men and women to be affected by the cultural conceptions, without their realizing it. They have therefore interpreted the relevant biblical passages from a particular perspective and through particular historical-cultural spectacles. Then, in order to justify the permanent subordination of women, they have read the Bible in such a way as to find it teaching the eternal subordination of the Son (and the Spirit) to the Father. He says, "This innovative form of subordinationism arises entirely in connection with attempts to preserve what to them is a fundamental truth: namely, male 'headship.' In their concern to more securely ground their teaching on the male-female relationship, they have embraced an old error that undermines the most fundamental truth of all—the Christian doctrine of God."[87] In this, he contends, they are going against the stream of historic orthodox biblical interpretation and doctrinal formulation.

Giles argues for this position in several ways. One, pursued especially in his first book on the subject but then also expanded in a second book, is the use of historical argumentation.[88] This is within the

---

86. Ibid.
87. Ibid., 109.
88. Ibid., 32–59. Kevin Giles, *Jesus and the Father: Modern Evangelicals Reinvent the Doctrine of the Trinity* (Grand Rapids: Zondervan, 2006), 70–92, 129–204.

perspective of the role of tradition that he has developed. He shows how these earlier theologians support his position with respect to such specific issues as the differentiation of the divine persons. Beyond that, however, he has more recently done extensive exegesis of a number of significant biblical passages. Several critics had dismissed his theology because of his statements about the Bible not necessarily having just a single meaning. Perhaps at least in part to counter this, he gave more attention to Scripture in his second book. He stood by the earlier statement that the Bible can be read in more than one way.[89] Utilizing the type of hermeneutic employed by the Fathers and the Reformers, he shows how Paul, John, and the writer to the Hebrews spoke of the relationship between Jesus and the Father as one of eternal equality.[90]

Although he is primarily a biblical scholar and a church historian, Giles also engages in some philosophical argumentation, although somewhat informally. This is seen especially in his contention that the combination of eternal functional subordination and equality of essence cannot be maintained. A typical statement is: "If one party is forever excluded from certain responsibilities—no matter what their competency may be—simply on the basis of who they are, then this indicates they lack something that only their superior possesses. In other words, they are inferior in some *essential* way."[91]

Summary and Analysis of the Equivalence View

As with the gradational view, certain features of the equivalence view stand out:

1. The Father, Son, and Holy Spirit are thought of as completely and equally God in their being. Each is eternally and fully divine.

---

89. Giles, *Jesus and the Father*, 70.
90. Ibid., 93–128.
91. Giles, *The Trinity and Subordinationism*, 17 (emphasis added).

2. The terms *Father* and *Son* do not indicate the authority of the former over the latter but rather the similarity of the two to one another.

3. The Father-Son relationship is not to be understood on the analogy of human father-son relationships.

4. There is a reluctance to take literally the idea of eternal generation or begetting of the Son by the Father. When discussed, these are usually thought of as referring to the time of the Son's earthly ministry. There is no idea that the Son and the Spirit derive their being or their personhood from the Father.

5. References to the Father's commanding and the Son's obeying the Father are also considered as referring to the earthly ministry of the Son. This is also true of the Spirit's submission to the Father and to the Son.

6. Except for these temporary missions of special service, the Son and the Holy Spirit are completely equal in authority with the Father.

7. Texts such as Philippians 2:4–11 and Hebrews 5:8 are believed to indicate that the Son's submission to the Father began with the Incarnation.

8. First Corinthians 11:3 is believed not to support the idea of male supremacy over females. This is both because the analogy is not complete in that text and because *kephalē* should be interpreted as meaning source of, rather than controlling authority over.

9. This view of the eternal equality of authority of the three persons has been the dominant view of church theologians of the past.

It can be seen from this chapter and the immediately preceding chapter that despite some variations, these two views very clearly contrast and conflict with each other. In the chapters to follow, we will attempt further analysis and evaluation of the two.

CHAPTER 3

The Criteria for Evaluating Alternatives

W e have traced the basic contours of the two alternative views. The further question to be asked, however, is which of these we shall believe and practice. Each has its supporting arguments, which taken alone sound quite impressive. As sometimes happens in a debate, however, as we listen to each side, we may be virtually convinced; but as each makes rebuttal and refutation, the other's position sounds less impressive.

But even with the arguments placed side by side, we may seem to have reached a stalemate. The two views, however, appear, at least on the surface, to be complete and consistent in themselves, so that no eclectic picking and choosing of components appears possible, and they are mutually exclusive, so they cannot both be held. Choice must be made between them, but on what basis shall such a choice be made? They also appear to be exhaustive of the class of theories of the relationships between the members of the Trinity, so no third alternative appears possible. And, because this issue has far-reaching consequences, both for other areas of theology and for our practical living, we cannot simply ignore the choice. To do so is in effect to choose one of the views by default.

In a postmodern world, choices of this kind may be made for various reasons or on various bases. Since completely objective and neutral truth is not attainable for an individual according to this type of thinking, a measure of objectivity is often found in the community, the collective judgment of a group. Just as a given culture decides through its elected representatives what its norms of traffic operation should be for that community, but not necessarily for every conceivable community, so each community is the arbiter of what is truth for it. We may, then, turn to our community for the answer to our choice.

Unfortunately, however, this does not solve the problem; it only shifts it. For in this case, each of these views is held by a group of persons who constitute its community of validation. The problem then is, which community shall be the one whose judgment of validation I accept?

There was a time when this question was obviated by the fact that one had little choice of his or her community. He or she was born into a given cultural situation and therefore inherited the standards and judgments of that community. There was little likelihood of changing that milieu. We are not now talking about one's political party or religious denomination. In theory one could change that affiliation quite easily, although in practice the influence that community had already exerted upon one as a member thereof went far toward influencing the individual's judgment about whether it or an alternative was more desirable. There was truth to the old Roman Catholic claim that if the church could have persons through their childhood years, it would have them for life. The point is that even the discussions between political parties and religious denominations, although the conclusions were different in the case of the different groups, assumed a common set of categories, a sort of field of discussion or some sort of common ground within which or upon which the discussion could take place. That broader environment was not one that the individual was likely to change. Radical geographical location changes were not common, and worldwide communication was not yet a possibility. Now, however, one has exposure to much broader options, through both greatly enhanced communication and transportation. Consequently, the issue becomes, "Of which community shall I be a part? What community shall set the standards within which true and right and good are defined?" So it is still the individual who must choose the source of the objectivity.

Basically, the choice of a theory is a question of seeking to determine which is the "true" theory and adopting it. There are widespread differences regarding how one determines truth, but in today's environment there is even considerable controversy regarding the meaning of the concept of truth.

The conventional wisdom among philosophers is that there are three theories of truth: correspondence, coherence, and pragmatism. On such a scheme, the correspondence theory holds that truth is agreement of ideas or propositions with the actual state of affairs; the coherence theory is that truth is the agreement or coherence of ideas or propositions with others within their set; the pragmatic theory is that truth is the utility of ideas or propositions, the fact that they work out to have desirable consequences.

Upon closer examination, however, this analysis appears to be less than fully adequate. It appears instead that these theories may be differing ideas about the appropriate tests for truth, and that there is considerable agreement about the actual nature of truth itself. I have argued at length elsewhere that virtually every sane and functioning human being proceeds on the basis of what I call a primitive or naïve correspondence theory: that truth is the agreement of a statement with what it ostensibly represents.[1] I would point out that even William James, the father of pragmatism, begins his discussion of the topic of truth with a common definition: "Truth, as any dictionary will tell you, is a property of certain of our ideas. It means their 'agreement,' as falsity means their disagreement, with 'reality.' Pragmatists and intellectualists both accept this definition as a matter of course. They begin to quarrel only after the question is raised as to what may precisely be meant by the term 'agreement,' and what by the term 'reality,' when reality is taken as something for our ideas to agree with."[2]

Not all philosophers recognize that James's definition of truth was not as radically different from the common one as was generally thought. In my first teaching position, an undergraduate institution where philosophy and Bible were combined in one department, I once pointed

---

1. Millard J. Erickson, *Truth or Consequences: The Promise and Perils of Postmodernism* (Downers Grove, IL: InterVarsity Press, 2001), 234.

2. William James, "Pragmatism's Conception of Truth," in *Pragmatism and Four Essays from* The Meaning of Truth (New York: Meridian, 1955), 132.

out this quotation to the director of philosophy. He responded, "That's right. James did initially give a correspondence definition, before giving his pragmatic view," despite the fact that this man, not I, was supposed to be the professional philosopher in the department. He failed to realize that this was part of James's pragmatic definition of truth.

Similarly, it appears that coherence is actually a test, rather than a definition, of truth. The article on "Coherence Theory of Truth" in the *Encyclopedia of Philosophy* gives this interpretation. The author, Alan White, says that "what the coherence theory really does is to give the criteria for the truth and falsity of a priori, or analytic, statements."[3] He then goes on to criticize the coherence theory:

> Second, it confuses the reasons, or criteria, for calling a statement true or false with the meaning of "truth" or "falsity." As far as the criteria of truth are concerned, we can say only of a priori, or analytic, statements that they are true because they cohere with each other, and only of empirical statements that they are true because of what the world is like; however, as far as the meaning of truth is concerned, we can say of any kind of statement that it is true if it corresponds to the facts. Thus, as well as saying that a true a priori statement coheres with other statements in the system, we can also say that it corresponds to the a priori facts.[4]

When we ask about the different views of testing the truth of a theory, there are basically three. Foundationalism is the view that there are basic or foundational beliefs, and other propositions within a theory are justified by the demonstration of their relationship to these foundations. Determining whether these superstructure propositions are implied by the foundational propositions is therefore an accurate test of their truth. Coherence is the test for truth in which the relationships among the various propositions in a scheme of thought are the focus of interest. The positive agreement and coherence among these is regarded as an indication of

---

3. Alan R. White, "Coherence Theory of Truth," *The Encyclopedia of Philosophy*, ed. Paul Edwards (New York: Macmillan, 1967), 2:132.

4. Ibid., 133.

the presence of truth. Finally, pragmatism is the test for truth that measures it by the effect of those propositions or ideas, and regards practical benefit as being a major criterion of the truth. While these are regarded as alternatives, they may actually be complementary in nature.

These tests for truth in turn relate to three different dimensions of meaning. The pragmatist philosopher Charles Morris,[5] drawing heavily on the thought of the earlier pragmatist Charles Saunders Peirce, developed a scheme that has been applied to religious language in a somewhat adapted form by the philosopher of religion Frederick Ferré.[6] This scheme deals with three factors in meaning: the object referred to by a sign, often called the designatum or notatum; the sign itself; and the knower or interpreter of the sign. The overall scheme is what Morris calls semiotic, or a general theory of signs.[7] The relationship of the several signs in a system of meaning to one another is termed the syntactical dimension, or syntactics. The relationship of signs to that which they represent is termed the semantical dimension, or semantics.[8] The relationship of the sign to the knower or interpreter is termed the pragmatic dimension, or pragmatics, by Morris. Ferré has substituted the term *interpretics* for Morris's word *pragmatics*, but I have chosen to retain Morris's original nomenclature in this discussion.[9] Each of these dimensions of meaning may be evaluated by certain criteria, and thus the quality of a particular theory or set of signs can be measured by their use.

While Ferré intends the set of criteria to be used for evaluating competing worldviews, they also can be employed in grading theories of more modest proportions, such as the competing theories we are

---

5. Charles W. Morris, "Foundations of the Theory of Signs," in *International Encyclopedia of Unified Science*, vol. 1, no. 2, *Foundations of the Unity of Science*, ed. Otto Neurath (Chicago: University of Chicago Press, 1938), 1–59.

6. Frederick Ferré, *Language, Logic and God* (New York: Harper & Row, 1961), 146–66.

7. Morris, "Foundations of the Theory of Signs," 8.

8. This term is often popularly applied rather loosely to the entire complex of meaning relationships, but it seems more precise and accurate to restrict it to this dimension of meaning.

9. Ferré, *Language, Logic and God*, 148.

examining about the relative authority of the members of the Trinity. The aim in this chapter will not be to do the actual evaluation but rather to propose criteria. The actual evaluation will follow in the subsequent chapters, as application of what we do here.

Internal or Logical Factors

The first area of our concern will be the relationships among the signs or concepts in a system or theory. Thus, we may term these internal criteria. They are also appropriately designated as logical criteria. We observe two of these.

Consistency

This in itself is a negative criterion. That is to say, the presence of consistency in itself does not guarantee truth, but its absence signifies the lack of truth. Whether recognized or not, this criterion is used by all persons. The reason is that one simply cannot psychologically function on an ongoing basis in the face of logical contradiction. Sometimes the sphere of the contradiction is quite small, as that A implies B and B implies not-A. Here it is not possible to believe A and B at the same time and in the same respect. This is the law of contradiction, or as some term it, the law of noncontradiction: "Something cannot be A and not-A at the same time and in the same respect."

All of life depends on the assumption of this principle. I have sometimes tested this with students by displaying a T-shirt from the American Philosophical Association. On the front of the shirt appear the words, "The sentence on the back of this shirt is true." On the back is printed, "The sentence on the front of this shirt is false." It simply is not psychologically possible to believe both the front and the back simultaneously. This is similar to when I tell a class, "I am now telling an untruth. Do you believe me?" Other forms may involve another person, such as my favorite response to postmoderns: "I agree with you completely, and you are totally wrong."

Generally, however, the circle within which contradiction appears is much larger, making this contradiction more difficult to detect. So, if

A implies B, and B implies C, C implies D, D implies E, and E implies F, but F implies not-A, there is a contradiction within the system. The series of propositions may be much larger and more complex than this, requiring diligence in ferreting out potential or actual contradictions. A theory whose truth implies its falsity is not tenable.

It is important, however, to note the difference between logical consistency and customary consistency. By customary consistency I mean that the fact that a particular proposition, D, is generally found together with instances of A, B, and C, does not mean that it is inconsistent to deny D in a system that contains A, B, and C, unless it is the case that D is logically implied or required by A, B, and C. The fact that it is *customary* for these to be combined, or to appear together, does not in itself *require* that they must always be present together. For example, the concept of limited atonement (or "particular redemption," as it is sometimes termed) is frequently found together with other points of Calvinism, such as total depravity and unconditional predestination. That does not mean that the person is inconsistent if he holds the other tenets, but denies this one, unless it can be established that these logically imply it.

As another instance, I once had a colleague who was a five-point Calvinist and an annihilationist. Although this was the first time I had encountered such a combination, it was merely unusual, not contradictory or inconsistent logically. The belief in the eternal suffering or punishment of the non-elect is almost invariably found in Calvinism but need not logically be present. Instead of the non-elect or the reprobate being reprobated to eternal suffering, on this variation they were chosen in advance to be annihilated. Similarly, I remember being surprised to find that I had in one of my classes a Calvinistic Pentecostal. Every Pentecostal I had met previously had been an Arminian, but that is not logically required. The inconsistency was not logical, but rather customary. Another way of putting it is that this is an accidental, not an essential, element of the system. In terms of the foundationalist justification, these propositions cannot be justified by the foundational elements, or they are not implied by them.

It is important to bear in mind that the issue is *self*-consistency, the degree to which a system of thought does not contradict itself. It is not necessary that it be free from contradiction with another system, unless it can be shown that the latter system, or at least certain tenets of it, is implied by the former.

What sometimes happens is that inconsistency appears to be found within a system, but the apparent inconsistency is between one statement and another, as the one or both is interpreted by someone other than the author or speaker of the statement, rather than in terms of the meaning intended by the originator of the statement. This phenomenon, which results from a failure of the interpreter to be self-critical about his/her own interpretational presuppositions, is not a problem for the system itself, unless, of course, it can be shown that for some reason the statement(s) must be interpreted in the sense given by the latter party. If not, it is simply the case that A and B differ, and the issue that must be established is which party is correct. Postmodernists have helped make us more aware of the biases and conditioning that we all bring to any interpretational situation, although of course this is not an insight unique or original to postmodernism. It is a caution that needs to be heeded, however, if we are to be successful in this evaluational task.

Coherence

As we noted, consistency is a negative, not a positive, test. Beyond that, therefore, what is needed is coherence, the actual intermeshing of the elements of a theory.

It is quite possible for a set of propositions to be consistent with (not contradict) one another simply because they are unrelated. That the high temperature today at the place of this writing will exceed 80 degrees Fahrenheit, that the price of crude oil is in excess of $140 per barrel, and that my dog is pursuing small rodents are all true statements and in no sense contradictory. They do not, however, in any way support or enhance one another. There is consistency but not coherence.

Coherence means that the truth of certain propositions is established by a logical connection with other propositions in the set. Another way of putting this is that one proposition implies or entails another. I am not using *implies* in the popular, weak sense of the term to suggest something of a psychological inclination to believe a proposition, but not a logical necessity thereof. I am using it in the sense that if A is true, B must consequently also be true.

This means that we must search diligently for the presence of non sequiturs within arguments. These may take several different forms. One is when a formal logical fallacy is committed. Consider the following:

If it has rained, the grass will be wet.
The grass is wet.
Therefore, it has rained.

This is not a valid argument. It commits what is called the fallacy of affirming the consequent. The formal argument is A implies B; B; therefore, A.

Now consider this argument:

If it has rained, the grass will be wet.
It has rained.
Therefore, the grass is wet.

This is a valid argument, in which the antecedent is affirmed. The problem with the former argument is that there may be other reasons for the grass being wet than that it has rained. Perhaps there was an unusually heavy dew last night. Perhaps someone has taken a hose and sprayed water on the grass. This type of argument, although not valid, is more common than we would like to see.

The opposite problem also can occur. The following is the fallacy of denying the antecedent:

If it has rained, the grass will be wet.
It has not rained.
Therefore, the grass is not wet.

In reality, the grass may be wet without it having rained, for reasons such as those mentioned above. The absence of rain does not guarantee the absence of wetness of the grass. The valid form of argument would be,

> If it has rained, the grass will be wet.
> The grass is not wet.
> Therefore, it has not rained.

This form of argument is called denying the consequent. It is valid. If a sentence implies another proposition and the former sentence is true, then the second must be true as well. If the latter sentence is not true and is genuinely implied by the former, then the former must not be true either.

Another form often taken by non sequiturs is the fallacy of the suppressed premise. Here a conclusion is drawn on the basis of an assumption that is not made explicit and justified. Such an argument is also termed an enthymeme. The conclusion may be true or false, but that depends on the truth or falsity of the hidden premise. An example of an enthymeme with a true conclusion is,

> All trees are plants.
> Therefore, all maples are plants.

In this case, the suppressed premise, "All maples are trees," is true, so the argument is valid and yields a true conclusion. However, less felicitous results may follow from enthymemes such as the following:

> All trees are plants.
> Therefore, all rocks are plants.

Here the suppressed premise, "All rocks are trees," is plainly false. Although the conclusion could be true on other grounds, it does not follow from the offered premise, so one has no assurance of its truth.

Sometimes the omitted premise is treated as if it has been exposed and established. In some cases, the person making the assertion fills the gap with statements that seem to indicate such argumentation. For example, one may say, "clearly" or "obviously," where insufficient argumentation has been advanced to justify such a statement. Other expressions that betray such logical lacunae are, "it is commonly accepted that . . . ," "it stands to reason that . . . ," or the negative form, "no one believes that," and the like.

Other logical gaps come from a failure to deal with what has traditionally been termed the Aristotelian "square of opposition." In this, a universal affirmative statement, "All A is B," and a particular negative statement, "Some A is not B," are contradictories, as are universal negative statements, "No A is B," and particular affirmative statements, "Some A is B." Universal positive and negative statements ("All A is B" and "No A is B") are contraries, in other words, absolute contradictories. Particular affirmative and negative statements, called subcontraries ("Some A is B" and "Some A is not B," respectively), do not contradict each other at all, so both may be true.

Argumentation may overlook this. From the statement, "Some A is not B," it does not follow that "No A is B," nor from the assertion that "Some A is B" does it follow that "All A is B," or in other words, that "Some A is not B" is not true. Further, it is possible to have several contradictories to a universal statement. "Some A is not B," "A few A's are not B," "Most A's are not B," are all contradictories of "All A is B." By establishing that there is one case of A that is not B, it does not follow that a view that holds that a majority of A's are not B's is true. One case does not establish that 20 percent, 50 percent, or 80 percent are true. If, however, 80 percent has been demonstrated to be true, it does follow that any lesser percentage is also the case, but not the exclusive case.

One other factor that detracts from coherence or indicates a non sequitur is what is often referred to as "begging the question." This is a situation in which the conclusion is already present implicitly within one of the premises. This usually takes a form that is not easily recognized, including by the person making the assertion, but it is an illegitimate argument. A humorous version of this is the person who claimed to be the world's smartest human, but without offering any independent testimony regarding the matter. When challenged as to whether that claim was true, he replied, "Would the world's smartest human be wrong about something like this?" This is a form of circular reasoning. As with contradiction, if the chain of propositions is sufficiently large, it may be difficult to recognize circularity, but its inadequacy is genuine nonetheless.

Another positive sign of coherence is the filling in of gaps in a theory. There are always unanswered questions in any theory, but the ability of the theory to relate to other areas of concern is a plus. A theory that leaves too many gaps unexplained or unanswered, or simply cannot relate to what should be related issues, is weaker, all other things being equal, than a competitive view that gives a rationale for those issues. This is especially important when those are issues crucial to the larger system of which this theory's set of issues is a smaller part.

External Factors

The criteria we have been examining could be completely and perfectly fulfilled by a system or a theory and yet the theory still not be true if it failed to correspond to some reality external to itself. Indeed, there are numerous such cases as this. This is why libraries, publishers, and bookstores distinguish between fiction and nonfiction. A work of fiction might be perfectly consistent and even coherent, but unless the symbols that make it up relate to an existing, objective world, it is just that: a well-developed piece of fiction. It is the dimension of relationship of symbols to that which they purport to represent that constitutes the external measurement of truth. There are two aspects of this.

Applicability

Ferré's term *applicability* is an appropriate one. It is the issue of how well the symbols fit, or how accurately they describe, that which they represent. Two different symbols or symbol sets may be advanced, representing a given referent or set thereof. The question to be asked, by way of evaluation, is which one of these more accurately represents that referent, and with less distortion or artificiality. This is the question of whether this description "rings true," or has the "ring of authenticity" about it. It is the measure by which we often detect or attempt to detect prevarication, which is an intentional misrepresentation of a purported situation as factual when it is not.

I have suggested that in the context in which this debate is occurring, we might refer to the shape of the argument as "biblical foundationalism." That is to say, the basic substantive authority for both parties in the debate is the Bible. A proposition is ultimately justified by being shown to be taught by the Bible, or implied by a direct statement in the Bible. In terms of the issue of applicability, the question becomes how well the theory relates to the elements in the Bible that it claims to represent. In some cases, one interpretation of a given biblical text seems much more natural and accurate in its portrayal of the meaning of the text, while another strikes one as a bit forced or strained. The former, therefore, will be graded higher on the criterion of applicability. This is not to say that the interpretation that fits more easily with the apparent meaning of the text is preferable. Upon closer examination, the text may turn out to be saying something quite different from the seeming or surface meaning of it. Only thorough exegesis, taking account of nuances of grammar, syntax, and lexicography, will enable us to determine the more suitable or applicable interpretation.

Often in debates, formal or informal, the struggle is over how to characterize a situation, or what term to apply to it, or how to classify it. Alternatively, the term may be fixed, but the debate is over what it is to mean or to what state of affairs to apply it. We will judge as less satisfactory a theory that attempts to usurp the process of debate over either terms or meanings. This attempt is not uncommon among postmoderns, especially Stanley Fish, who contended, "Getting hold of the concept of merit and stamping it with your own brand is a good strategy."[10] Here we will have to ask whether an attempt has been made to affix one's own term to an idea utilized by both parties and thereby short-circuit the debate process. Similarly, the definition given to a term

---

10. Stanley Fish, *There's No Such Thing as Free Speech, and It's a Good Thing, Too* (New York: Oxford University Press, 1994), 6.

that both want to use may need close scrutiny. This is termed stipulative definition. Definitions should be argued, not decreed. Doing the latter may be a means of giving applicability that is more apparent than real.

The same is done with identifying the issue(s) to be discussed. In some circles, particularly in politics, this is called "framing." One of the better-known cases of this was the 1992 presidential election in the United States, when Bill Clinton succeeded in promoting the slogan, "It's the economy, stupid!" Sometimes a debater succeeds in convincing hearers that there is a difference between his view and that of his opponent, when there is none. At other times, the reverse is true. One party contends that the two parties have the same view on a given subject, when in reality they differ. This generally involves a popular position, where a "me-too" attitude is adopted.

The choice of label for a given view can produce very widely differing reactions. For example, in one survey, when voters were asked whether they would favor an estate tax, they were strongly favorable. However, when the same proposal was advanced to a comparable group of voters but labeled a "death tax," the voters were opposed by an equally strong percentage.

One can look at debates and tell by the language predominantly used which group has been successful in the labeling process. The lowering of a tax rate so that a smaller amount is taken from a taxpayer is sometimes labeled by those opposed to it as a "tax giveaway," even though the money in question belonged to the taxpayers, not the government that passed the law. This is an attempt by one group to attach its label to the process. Sometimes both parties are able to use their own labels for their own views. An example is the abortion debate, where the standard terminology is "pro-life" and "pro-choice." Labeling something as a right rather than a privilege is an attempt to win the debate over which it is, without the necessity of having the debate.

In the process of obtaining one's chosen label for one's view, there is also frequently an attempt to characterize one's opponent's view in an unfavorable light. This is sometimes an instance of the old maxim that a lie, if told often enough, will come to be accepted as the truth. This usually involves caricaturing the opposing view as an extreme position, while identifying one's own view with moderation. This is why there is a point to an observation I frequently make: If you ask each of two parties in a debate what his/her view is, they are often quite close together. If, on the other hand, you ask each to describe the opponent's view, the two views are frequently a vast distance apart.

It is especially important to be alert to the attempt to build evaluation into a term by the connotations given. For example, the same situation may be described as "rich diversity" or as a "confused hodgepodge." There is the familiar conjugation of an irregular verb: "I have firm convictions; you are stubborn; he is a pigheaded fool." Similarly, in politics one may characterize one's own approach as flexible and open-minded, while one's opponent, whose behavior in this respect is the same, is termed a "flip-flopper." Such use of slanted definitions to gain an advantage is disappointing and to an objective and analytical observer is a sign of weakness, like the proverbial comment in the margin of the preacher's sermon notes: "Weak point. Shout loudly."

I once received a letter from a former college professor of mine, in which he used expressions like "goose-stepping fundamentalists." What was especially disappointing was that this was the man from whom I had taken my introductory logic course. The use of objective, accurate, descriptive terminology is a positive, while the use of subjective, expressive, and tacitly evaluative language is a negative.

One source of distortion in the attempt at understanding is a lack of self-understanding, so that one's own biases are read into the text. All of us have such biases, of course, stemming from racial, social, gender, and other factors that have made us who we are. The postmodernists have made much of this, although they were by no means original in this observation. This means that we may see things in the text that are not there, because we import them into the text unconsciously, much as the color we perceive in an object is affected by tinted lenses through which we view it. Strikingly, this conditioning or bias is often presented as if it were something to which one's opponent is susceptible but to which we ourselves are immune.

Presuppositions, I often tell my students, are not something other people have; they are something everyone, myself included, has. The question of biases is not the end of the matter. The further and more important question is what shall be done about them. I advocate that scholars write their own intellectual autobiography, trying to identify their biases so that they may make a self-conscious attempt to compensate for, or neutralize, them. I can recall a class on critical thinking, in which it never occurred to the students in the class, most of whom were native Texans, that the cultural milieu in which they had grown up and were still functioning, with its strong individualism, might be affecting the way they read biblical passages dealing with the priesthood of the believer and soul competency. Even when using dictionaries and lexicons, I try to learn as much as I can about the author of the article, as, for example, in the *Theological Dictionary of the New Testament*, in order to detect when the meaning found for a word or passage may at least in part come from the interpreter rather than residing wholly in the text.

Is this really an accurate rendering of that which it purports to represent? That is a vital question that needs to be asked again and again. In a day when a given phenomenon may be approached and interpreted from the perspective of many different disciplines, it is especially important.

One factor useful for deciding between competing theories is the precision with which the symbols fit that which they assertedly represent. A view where the language is vague or ambiguous in its descriptive function is inferior to one where the language describes more thoroughly and precisely its referent.

Adequacy

If applicability is the ability of a theory to portray suitably and accurately what it purports to represent, then adequacy measures the extent of the relevant data that a theory can depict. Here the criterion is that a theory that can explain a larger percentage of the data is superior to one that can deal only with a smaller segment.

This means that we must constantly be inquiring about the boundaries of the data. Has the theory been formulated by ignoring or overlooking relevant data? This is referred to in some circles as "data mining," where some data is ignored, because it does not fit one's theory, or, worse yet, contradicts one's theory, while seeking for and carefully extracting data that would tend to substantiate one's own view. This may be done in such a way as to take the data out of its context, thus also violating the applicability principle we have discussed.

One sees this often in theological discussions where certain biblical texts are appealed to while others that also bear on the subject are bypassed. The difficulty comes because there are often numerous relevant texts, at least some of which tend to support opposing positions. Similarly, in scientific research, some data and some studies support differing conclusions than do others. Picking and choosing in such a way as to support the conclusion to which one is already committed betrays a weak theory. It is tempting to do this when dealing with figures from history, some of whom were not models of consistency, saying one thing at one point in their lives or in one situation and something else at another time or place. Good theories are built upon taking account of all the data, not just that which is favorable. In practice, sometimes one gets committed to a viewpoint and then is unable to admit an error or a change of mind and continues seeking for support. One research assistant reported that his supervising professor sent him to the library with the instruction, "Find supporting material for my position."

It is not uncommon for a theory to be built upon a carefully delimited set of data. Sometimes this limitation is based on the support of the presuppositions with which the inquiry begins. Candor requires that such arbitrary limitations be acknowledged. I recall as an undergraduate student, another student asking the behaviorist instructor of a psychology class what he did with the data emerging from the studies on extrasensory perception at Duke University at the time. The instructor was forthright: "They don't fit our frame of reference, so we ignore them." Sometimes a limit is drawn, perhaps by arbitrarily limiting the data to that from a given time period, often with the rationale that limitations of time and space required some circumscribing of the inquiry.

Every theory can appeal to some supporting evidence, or it would never gain any sort of hearing. Often one can learn more about a view by observing how it deals with the evidence that contradicts it than how it handles the supporting evidence. Searching for all the data and asking which view more adequately explains a larger swath of it is a good evaluative technique. It should be borne in mind, however, that this is not a strictly quantitative measure. Some data, in our case, some biblical passages, are more central and crucial than others, which may be more peripheral or incidental in nature. The ability of a theory to adequately handle the crucial passages must be weighted more heavily than its citing of numerous minor passages. At the same time, careful exegesis may reveal that a seemingly tangential passage actually is more relevant to the issue than was initially thought.

While the more common shortcoming is overlooking or disregarding contradictory material, there also may be a problem with introducing apparently relevant supporting material, when in reality it is not that. This is what I call, the fallacy of the irrelevant truth. So, for example, one book reviewer criticized an author because, in dealing with the view of another author, he quoted from the first edition of a book rather than the second edition. What the reviewer failed to mention was that on this particular point there was no difference between the two editions. In actuality, this was an omission of an important fact about the material mentioned. It is important to ask, of any given view, how broad a sweep of the relevant evidence it deals with, as contrasted with the opposing view.

One factor in determining the relevance of a passage or other type of datum is to determine accurately the question being addressed. Sometimes a passage seems on the surface to bear definitely on the issue at hand when the author was really answering a rather different question. We may recall the beer company advertisements on television featuring a series of noted professional football coaches at press conferences. By taking their answers out of the context in which they were originally given and placing them instead in a context of questions about beer, they seem to be giving answers to those questions. So it is possible to take the statement of a biblical or historical author and treat it as an answer to a contemporary question, when actually this is not what they were addressing at all. Giving the best treatment of the most statements, accurately understood, is the mark of superiority we are seeking.

In recent years, this approach of relying upon basic propositions as the basis for justification has come under severe criticism. Whether postfoundational, nonfoundational, or antifoundational, numerous critics have contended that the older approach is no longer tenable. For the most part, these criticisms have been directed toward classical foundationalism. This is the variety of foundationalism found in thinkers like Descartes and Locke, in which the basic or foundational premises are regarded as indubitable, incorrigible, or in some other way, absolutely certain. In the case of biblical foundationalism, this criticism has taken the form of rejection of, or at least suspicion of, the idea of biblical inerrancy. It is important to note, however, that this absolute certainty is not a necessary quality of foundationalism. Timm Triplett has characterized foundationalism simply:

EF1: There are basic propositions.
EF2: Any justified empirical proposition is either basic or derives its justification, at least in part, from the fact that it stands in an appropriate relation to propositions that are basic.[11]

This definition does not say anything about the quality of the basic propositions. This means that many recent criticisms of foundationalism apply only to one specific form of foundationalism, not to foundationalism in general. In fact, Triplett says, "It is not clear that the standard arguments against foundationalism will work against these newer, more modest theories. Indeed, these theories were by and large designed with the purpose of overcoming standard objections."[12]

---

11. Timm Triplett, "Recent Work on Foundationalism," *American Philosophical Quarterly* 27, no. 2 (April 1990): 96.

12. Ibid., 93.

It is noteworthy that the most vocal critics of foundationalism, such as Nancey Murphy,[13] Stanley Grenz and John Franke,[14] Wentzel van Huysteen,[15] and LeRon Shults,[16] make no mention in their writings of the work of William Alston, Robert Audi, or the article by Triplett, with the exception of brief references to Alston by Murphy and van Huysteen. Thus, it appears that their statements, unless supplemented, are seriously out of date by several decades. As such, their criticisms of foundationalism are actually caricatures of foundationalism as currently expounded. Audi puts it this way: "It requires epistemic unmoved movers, but not unmovable movers. Solid ground is enough, even if bedrock is better. There are also different kinds of bedrock, and not all of them have the invulnerability apparently belonging to beliefs of luminously self-evident truths of logic."[17] There are many types of foundationalism, some of which go by the name of "fallibilistic foundationalism," and with such the burden of proof is much less than that which contemporary critics would attempt to require of any foundationalist approach to justification.

In the discussions, the approach of foundationalism and of coherence are often contrasted. This is not necessarily the case, however, for both can work together well. For example, it may not be initially possible to relate a statement to the foundational elements. By tracing out the implications, however, one may find propositions that can be related to the foundation. A given assumption or presupposition may not be initially justifiable, but given some additional reflection and extrapolation, one may be able to achieve that goal.

---

13. Nancey Murphy, *Beyond Liberalism and Fundamentalism: How Modern and Postmodern Philosophy Set the Theological Agenda* (Valley Forge, PA: Trinity Press International, 1996).

14. Stanley J. Grenz and John R. Franke, *Beyond Foundationalism: Shaping Theology in a Postmodern Context* (Louisville: Westminster John Knox, 2001).

15. Wentzel van Huysteen, *Essays in Postfoundationalist Theology* (Grand Rapids: Eerdmans, 1997).

16. F. LeRon Shults, *The Postfoundationalist Task of Theology: Wolfhart Pannenberg and the New Theological Rationality* (Grand Rapids: Eerdmans, 1999).

17. Robert Audi, *The Structure of Justification* (Cambridge: Cambridge University Press, 1993), 134.

To a large extent, we are dealing here with inductive logic, which, as is well known, results in probable conclusions. The larger the sample of cases we draw from, and the larger the percentage of possible instances included in our sampling, the firmer will be the conclusions drawn from the endeavor.

Personal or Pragmatic

Finally, competing theories may be assessed in terms of how the signs constituting them relate to the knower of the theory or interpreter of the facts. Morris's original terminology of this relationship as pragmatics is helpful, so long as the term *pragmatics* is not construed too narrowly.

I have placed this criterion third, because without the other criteria being satisfied, the theory may be merely fictional or imaginary. Nonetheless, in terms of the sequence in which people come to adopt a given viewpoint, this element often has priority. An idea or theory or system is adopted because it meets a particular need or gives meaning to life. It is satisfying on a subjective, personal basis. Then, one moves outward from there, as questions arise as to whether there is actual objective reality to what has proved subjectively meaningful. Epistemologically, however, rather than biographically, it must take a subsidiary place to the other considerations.

This area of assessment focuses on the effect the theory has on those who espouse it. How does it affect their values, and what does it do to their motivations and actions? Does it enrich them? Does it contribute to the strengths of society? And, from the standpoint of Christian considerations, what does it produce in terms of the person's relationship to God? The pragmatic value should not be considered merely individually, but extend to the effects for society.

Because of the somewhat limited scope of the theory, the issues under consideration in this book may not seem to have a great deal of practical import. When examined, however, this initial assessment may not be fully accurate. For when the implications of the ideas are traced out in terms of what sort of affective or functional results there should be, there may be more than expected. It may be that while the theory cannot be initially strongly related to declarative statements about the nature of the triune God, they will be seen to imply certain actions as apparently commands of this same God. This will enable us to compare whether the imperatives and prohibitions entailed by one theory or another accord closely with those delivered to us in Scripture by this God. For example, if the nature of God as understood by a theory means that one shall consequently pray in a certain way, but the biblical revelation includes commands to pray in a rather different way, then we have a found a point in the practical realm where there is a weakness, as measured by that which we find elsewhere in Scripture.

The Status of the Conclusion

When we conclude our evaluation, we should not expect that the conclusion will be categorical. That is to say, it is unlikely that we will conclude that all the evidence is on one side and none on the other. We will not be able to say with absolute certainty that one theory is true and the other false.

In all disputed issues, the dispute is generally present because the evidence is distributed on more than one side or the evidence is ambiguous. What we can hope for is to "grade" the two theories relatively. Often, a party in a debate acts as if showing the difficulties with the opposing view establishes his or her own view. I often have quoted a statement from John Baillie's *Invitation to Pilgrimage*. As a student, Baillie had written a criticism of a particular theory. The professor, however, wrote on the paper, "Every theory has its difficulties, but you have not considered whether any other theory has less difficulties than the one you have criticised."[18] That is advice well taken. We may sometimes have to say something like, "Sixty-five percent of the evidence supports view A, and only 35 percent supports view B. I must therefore accept view A." Having said that, however, we must continue to hold our commitment to view A in tension with the evidence for view B and

---

18. John Baillie, *Invitation to Pilgrimage* (New York: Charles Scribner's Sons, 1942), 15.

be prepared, if in our judgment the balance of evidence shifts to the latter view, to alter our acceptance. In practice what sometimes happens is that once we arrive at a conclusion our minds snap shut, and no amount of evidence can open them.

Such a comparative-evidence approach frees us from the ludicrous practice of trying to rebut every argument against our view or trying to show that every smidgeon of evidence supports it. Such an approach frequently leads to a type of interpretation that distorts the evidence, or indicates tendentiousness in dealing with it that undermines our credibility. While weighing all the evidence and drawing conclusions about the relative strength of the competing theories may seem threatening if we require absolute security for our beliefs—in other words, the sort of certainty that classical foundationalism sought—it will, in the long run, prove more beneficial.

A Path Not to Be Traveled

One consideration that often arises within this discussion is the motivation of the parties to the discussion. On the one hand, the equivalentists contend that the gradationists adopt the position they do on the Trinity in order to justify a particular view on the relative roles of men and women within the family and within the church. Therefore, their scholarly treatment of the doctrinal issue of subordination in the Trinity is affected by their position on a practical issue of human relationships.

Conversely, some gradationists object that the equivalentists have taken the view they have of the relative authority of the divine persons because of their view of gender roles. Ignoring for the moment the appropriateness of the terms *complementarian* and *egalitarian* with respect to gender roles, the application of those same terms to relationships between the divine persons lends support, at least psychological, to the conception of the interconnection of the two issues.

What is done, whether overtly or tacitly, is to suggest that this motivation accounts for the doctrinal conclusion taken with respect to the Trinity. To the extent that this is being done, we are dealing here with instances of the "genetic fallacy": the idea that the truth or falsity of a belief can be determined by the issue of how it came to be held. Whether the debaters are aware of it or not, this also is a parallel to a type of postmodern approach to debate. While the earlier approach was to disprove the view, this postmodern way of arguing relies instead on discrediting the one who holds it. As such, it is a species of ad hominem argument.

Such sociopsychological analyses may be interesting and informative in terms of enabling us to understand the etiology of the belief. They should not, however, be regarded as bearing on the truth or falsity of the belief. I have worked with a formula as follows:

> Motivation is to argumentation
> as understanding is to evaluation.

Consequently, this type of argument will be disregarded in seeking to evaluate the two alternative positions. While one of these contentions may be correct and may become the occasion for us to urge caution on those who hold it, such a judgment will not be treated as relevant to the issue of the truthfulness of the view held. In the case of the president, my response was, "But disregarding why the special counsel may be bringing these charges, the question is, are they true? Did the president do it?" Similarly here, the question is not, "Why do they believe it?" Rather, the question should be, "But is the theory true?"

In closing, we should note that there are legitimate and illegitimate ways to apply these criteria. It is fair to assess a system of thought by the extent to which it fulfills the standards it sets for itself. It is not necessarily fair to fault it for not fulfilling objectives it does not espouse. That is the principle of self-consistency, of which we spoke earlier. There are, however, certain universal criteria in any area of endeavor that may legitimately be applied to any example within that field. So, for example, in the game of checkers, one player may be very skilled at preventing his opponent from capturing his pieces. This is good defensive checkers. Another may be more skilled at the offensive aspect of the game, jumping the other player's pieces, and crowning his pieces. It is universally agreed, however, that, by whatever means attained, there is one objective both styles of play seek to achieve: to win the game by coming to the point where one's opponent cannot make a move. So in judging a theory, this must be done either by the use of criteria it sets for itself or by criteria all theories must fulfill.

CHAPTER 4

The Biblical Evidence

Because both parties to this discussion are evangelicals, for whom the Bible is their primary authority, or source of knowledge about God, it is of paramount importance that we examine what the Bible has to say on the subject of the relative authority of the persons of the Trinity, and especially of the Father and the Son to one another. We begin by examining the texts each side cites in support of its view.

There are a large number of texts that both parties agree teach that the Son was subject to the Father's will during the period of his earthly, incarnate ministry. There is no point in citing these. In addition, both parties agree that those texts that seem to indicate a superior status for the Father over the Son during this time are referring only to a functional subordination, or a subordination of role (what Jesus did), rather than of essence or being (what Jesus was). They are agreed in rejecting Arian views that Jesus was in some sense less fully divine than the Father was.

Texts Supporting the Gradational Position

These texts fall into several groups. There are no texts that say in direct fashion, "The Father eternally has superior authority over the Son," but several that bear upon the issue. The point that the gradationists are arguing for is that Jesus' submission was not merely a temporary functional submission but rather a reflection of an eternal relationship, extending from eternity past to eternity future.

The Relationship of the Father and Son in Eternity Past

The first argument to show that the Son's submission was not merely temporary comes from an examination of what was transpiring before the Incarnation and even the creation. Here we note that the Father is the one who is said to have planned and determined what took place within time. Ware points out especially Ephesians 1:9–11, which speaks of how God "made known to us the mystery of his will according to his good pleasure, which he purposed in Christ" (v. 9).[1] Verse 11 says that "in [Christ] we were also chosen, having been predestined according to the plan of him who works out everything in conformity with the purpose of his will." This theme echoes what is stated earlier in the chapter: "For he chose us in him before the creation of the world to be holy and blameless in his sight. In love he predestined us to be adopted as his sons through Jesus Christ, in accordance with his pleasure and will" (vv. 4–5).

Numerous other verses similarly attribute to God (the Father) the initiative in planning and deciding in eternity what was to happen. A clear example is Romans 8:29: "For those God foreknew he also predestined to be conformed to the likeness of his Son, that he might be the firstborn among many brothers." Grudem puts the point strongly:

> In some places the Bible speaks of different roles for Father and Son *before* Creation. It was the Father who "predestined us" to be conformed to the image of His Son (Romans 8:29; compare 1 Peter 1:2). But if He "predestined us" to be like His Son, then, in the counsels of eternity in which predestination occurred, there had to be a Father who was predestining and a Son whom He decided we would be like. Paul also says that God the Father "chose us" in the Son *before the foundation of the world* (Ephesians 1:4). This means that before there was any Creation, before anything existed except God Himself, the Father was the one who chose, who initiated and planned, and, before creation, it was already decided that the Son would be the one to come to earth in obedience to the Father and die for our sins.[2]

---

1. Bruce Ware, *Father, Son, and Holy Spirit: Relationships, Roles, and Relevance* (Wheaton, IL: Crossway, 2005), 52–53.

2. Wayne Grudem, *Evangelical Feminism and Biblical Truth: An Analysis of More Than One Hundred Disputed Questions* (Sisters, OR: Multnomah, 2004), 407.

God also is the one who sent the Son, who came in obedience to the Father's command. Grudem cites John 3:16 and Galatians 4:4;[3] Ware quotes John 8:29, in which Jesus speaks of the one who sent him.[4] In addition to these texts, there are numerous others in which Jesus speaks of the one who sent him (Matt. 15:24; Mark 9:37; Luke 4:18, 43; 9:48; 10:16; John 4:34; 5:23–24, 30, 36–38; 6:29, 38–39, 44, 57; 7:16, 18, 28–29, 33; 8:16, 18, 26, 29, 42; 10:36; 11:42; 12:44–45, 49; 13:20; 14:24; 15:21; 16:5; 17:3, 8, 18, 21, 23, 25; 20:21). This is strong evidence of Jesus' consciousness of coming because of the Father's initiative.

The Meaning of the Names Father and Son

Another argument is that the very use of the names Father and Son to refer to the first two members of the Trinity indicates a difference in authority. Grudem says, "The Father and the Son relate to one another as a father and son relate to one another in a human family: the father directs and has authority over the son, and the son obeys and is responsive to the directions of the father."[5] Again, he alludes to this when he says, "The role of commanding, directing, and sending is appropriate to the position of the Father, after whom all human fatherhood is patterned (Eph. 3:14–15)."[6] He argues that the roles of the Father and the Son could not have been reversed, so that the Son would have commanded, directed, and sent, because then "the Father would have ceased to be the Father and the Son would have ceased to be the Son."[7]

He also speaks of the continuing designation of the two beyond this life: "The very names 'Father' and 'Son' also attest to this [Jesus being subject to the authority of the Father], and those names have belonged to the Father and the Son forever."[8] To the eternal functional subordinationists, it is apparent that the name Father reveals a position

3. Wayne Grudem, *Systematic Theology: An Introduction to Biblical Doctrine* (Grand Rapids: Zondervan, 1994), 249.

4. Ware, *Father, Son, and Holy Spirit*, 74.

5. Grudem, *Systematic Theology*, 249.

6. Ibid., 250.

7. Ibid.

8. Grudem, *Evangelical Feminism*, 413.

of superiority and command, and the name Son reveals a subordination, an obedience.

The Role of Order, or Taxis

The concept of taxis as an organizing principle includes the idea of priority of authority, according to the gradationists. As such, they regard the indication of this order in Scripture as a support for the idea of eternal functional subordination. This is especially emphasized by Ware, who describes this taxis as "an ordering in the Godhead, a 'built-in' structure of authority and submission that marks a significant respect in which the Persons of the Godhead are distinguished from one another."[9]

These distinctions cannot be based on a difference in essence, since they all share the same identical essence. Thus he says, "Their distinction, rather, is constituted, in part, by *taxis*—the ordering of Father, Son, and Holy Spirit within the Godhead. The order is not random or arbitrary; it is not Spirit first, Son second, and Father third, nor is it any way other than the one way that the early church, reflecting Scripture itself (Matt. 28:19), insisted on: Father, Son, and Holy Spirit."[10] While Ware does not say so explicitly, his reference to Matthew 28:19 and giving the names in the same sequence as they appear there suggests that the church named them in this order only ("the *one* way") and that this sequence reflected its conviction regarding the relative authority in eternity of the three persons.

God as the Source of All Gifts

Numerous texts attest to the Father as the one who gives gifts and blessings. The most inclusive of these is James 1:17, "Every good and perfect gift is from above, coming down from the Father of the heavenly lights, who does not change like shifting shadows." Ware appeals to another universal passage, Romans 8:32: "He who did not spare his own Son, but gave him up for us all—how will he not also, along with him, graciously give us all things?"[11] Horrell relies especially heavily

---

9. Ware, *Father, Son, and Holy Spirit*, 72.
10. Ibid.
11. Ibid., 54.

upon these gift passages, which enumerate a variety of gifts that are said to come from the Father.[12] The assumption here is that giving is an indication of the authority of the giver.

Future Submission of the Son

If these considerations establish that the Father's superiority of authority over the Son preceded the Incarnation, then the other consideration to be argued is that the difference in authority extends into the future as well. Grudem especially makes much of the pictures of the future that show the Son sitting at the right hand of the Father. Such a picture is found in Jesus' own words about the future state: "But I say to all of you: In the future you will see the Son of Man sitting at the right hand of the Mighty One and coming on the clouds of heaven" (Matt. 26:64). Biblical writers also present this picture in the narrative descriptions of the future state. It was part of the kerygma at Pentecost, when Peter declared, "God has raised this Jesus to life, and we are all witnesses of the fact. Exalted to the right hand of God, he has received from the Father the promised Holy Spirit and has poured out what you now see and hear" (Acts 2:32–33). Stephen glimpsed heaven and saw this: "But Stephen, full of the Holy Spirit, looked up to heaven and saw the glory of God, and Jesus standing at the right hand of God. 'Look,' he said, 'I see heaven open and the Son of Man standing at the right hand of God'" (Acts 7:55–56). Paul wrote of this as well: "Who is he that condemns? Christ Jesus, who died—more than that, who was raised to life—is at the right hand of God and is also interceding for us" (Rom. 8:34). Many other Scriptures contain the same imagery: Mark 14:62; Luke 22:69; Acts 5:31; Ephesians 1:20; Colossians 3:1; Hebrews 1:3, 13; 8:1; 10:12–13; 12:2; 1 Peter 3:22.

This position, according to Grudem, indicates the continuing subjection of the Son to the Father's authority. He says, "Nowhere is this pattern reversed. Nowhere is it said that the Father sits at the Son's right

---

12. J. Scott Horrell, "Toward a Biblical Model of the Social Trinity: Avoiding Equivocation of Nature and Order," *Journal of the Evangelical Theological Society* 47, no. 3 (2004): 410–11.

hand. Nowhere does the Son give the Father the authority to sit with Him on His throne. The supreme authority always belongs to the Father."[13]

There are, however, some texts that seem to contradict this uniform picture, by showing the Son sharing the Father's throne. Gilbert Bilezikian[14] pointed out a number of these: "To him who overcomes, I will give the right to sit with me on my throne, just as I overcame and sat down with my Father on his throne" (Rev. 3:21). "For the Lamb at the center of the throne will be their shepherd" (Rev. 7:17a.). "She gave birth to a son, a male child, who will rule all the nations with an iron scepter. And her child was snatched up to God and to his throne" (Rev. 12:5). "No longer will there be any curse. The throne of God and of the Lamb will be in the city, and his servants will serve him" (Rev. 22:3).

Grudem, however, dismisses these: "But these verses do not contradict the other verses that show Jesus at the right hand of God. Revelation 3:21 gives the answer: Just as we will sit *with* Christ on His throne, but He will still have the supreme authority, so Christ sits with the Father on His throne, but the Father still has supreme authority. . . . Both facts are true: Jesus sits with the Father on His throne, and Jesus is still at the right hand of the Father and the throne can still be called 'His [that is, the Father's] throne.'"[15]

Although there is an apparent contradiction between these two concepts, Grudem makes no effort to resolve it. Instead, he points out the passages (Rom. 8:34 and Heb. 7:25) that speak of Jesus interceding for us as indications of the Father's superior authority during that period between the ascension and the second coming.

Probably the most powerful argument for the continuing and even eternal future subordination of the Son to the Father is the great consummation passage in 1 Corinthians 15:24–28.

Then the end will come, when he hands over the kingdom to God the Father after he has destroyed all dominion, authority and

---

13. Grudem, *Evangelical Feminism*, 412.

14. Gilbert Bilezikian, "Hermeneutical Bungee-Jumping: Subordination in the Godhead," *Journal of the Evangelical Theological Society* 40, no. 1 (1997): 63–68.

15. Grudem, *Evangelical Feminism*, 413.

power. For he must reign until he has put all his enemies under his feet. The last enemy to be destroyed is death. For he "has put everything under his feet." Now when it says that "everything" has been put under him, it is clear that this does not include God himself, who put everything under Christ. When he has done this, then the Son himself will be made subject to him who put everything under him, so that God may be all in all.

This passage seems to be the strongest text of all in support of the gradational position. It could be argued that the command and the submission and obedience displayed in so many places speaks simply of the task of redemption that the Son carried out, under conditions necessarily requiring a dependence on the Father. This, however, speaks of "the end." Beyond this, there should be nothing further. Yet here the text indicates that having conquered all the enemies, the last of which is death, the Son hands over the kingdom to "God the Father," and then "the Son himself will be made subject to him who put everything under him, so that God may be all in all."

The plainest and most obvious interpretation is that which Grudem states: "Unless there is strong evidence in Scripture showing a later change in that situation [the Son being subject to the Father] (which there is not), the passage leads us to think that that situation will continue for eternity. . . . The relationship between Father and Son has always been that way, and it will be that way forever."[16] Ware is equally emphatic: "There is no question that this passage indicates the eternal future submission of the Son to the Father, in keeping with his submission to the Father both in the incarnation and in incarnation past."[17]

Passages Supporting Temporary Functional Subordination

The equivalentists have been quick to reply to these claims, both in terms of raising questions about the pertinence of the texts cited in support of the gradational view, and also in adducing texts that seem to

16. Ibid., 414.
17. Ware, *Father, Son, and Holy Spirit*, 84.

argue for an ultimate equality of the Father, Son, and Holy Spirit. The equivalentists' general argument is that those passages that speak of a functional subordination are referring to a temporary subordination for the purposes of fulfilling the unique functions of the Son and the Holy Spirit relative to the salvation of the fallen human race.

General Texts Troublesome for the Gradational View

The first of these pertains to the meaning of the term *Son*. An assumption seems to underlie the subordinationists' position, namely, that the term *Son* indicates a role subordinate to the Father. While this is often an implicit or unstated assumption, there are points at which it becomes a part of the argument, especially as we saw in Grudem's work, and the insistence that these names are the eternal names of the Father and the Son runs parallel to the argument that the authority structure is eternal. There is considerable biblical evidence, however, that the primary meaning of the biblical term *Son* as applied to Jesus is likeness, rather than subordinate authority. So, for example, the Jews saw Jesus' self-designation as the Son of God as a claim to deity or equality with God (e.g., John 5:18).

There is another problem with the term *Son*. While the argument of gradationists depends on this Son being the Son of the Father, or, in other words, the Son of God, that is not the only usage of the word *Son*. A close examination of the Gospels indicates that Jesus' preferred title for himself was "Son of Man" (78 times in the Gospels, including parallel passages), and others quite frequently addressed him as "Son of David" (16 times). By comparison, "Son of God" is used of Jesus 23 times in the Gospels. While these other expressions may well have the same import as Son of God, they do not as closely tie the term *Son* to that of *Father*.

A further consideration is the sequential order in which the names of the three persons are mentioned in Scripture. Contrary to what Ware seemed to be saying, there is no one uniform and invariable order in which they are named. Ware has cited the crucial baptismal formula, in which the order is indeed Father, Son, and Holy Spirit. However, he does not mention that in the Pauline benediction in 2 Corinthians

13:14 the order is Christ (Son), God (Father), Holy Spirit. He cites the verse, but does not comment on the sequence.[18] Grudem similarly invokes this verse as evidence of the Trinity but does not comment on the order of the names.[19] Giles, however, makes much of the variation, compiling the Pauline texts into a table, showing that the Son is mentioned first in sixteen lists, the Spirit first in nine, and the Father first in only six.[20] He comments, "This evidence suggests that Paul did not believe the three divine 'persons' are ordered hierarchically."[21] Gerald Bray[22] and Geoffrey Wainwright[23] have made similar observations. In addition to Paul, New Testament writers who list the three in a varied order are Peter, in 1 Peter 1:2, where the order is Father, Spirit, and Jesus Christ, and Jude 20–21, where the order is Holy Spirit, God, and Lord Jesus Christ. Almost a century ago, Warfield called attention to the same phenomenon and commented, "If in their conviction the very essence of the doctrine of the Trinity was embodied in this order, should we not anticipate that there should appear in their numerous allusions to the Trinity some suggestion of this conviction?"[24]

Yet another general consideration is the variations in the names used for the three persons. The terms *Father*, *Son*, and *Holy Spirit* are not the exclusive biblical designations of the three persons of the Godhead. While these are used almost invariably by Jesus and in John's writings, there is considerable variability in other biblical authors. This is especially true of Paul, who uses the names, God, Lord, and Spirit, even more frequently than the Father-Son terminology. As Warfield puts it, "It remains remarkable, nevertheless, if the very essence of the

---

18. Ibid., 40.

19. Grudem, *Systematic Theology*, 230.

20. Giles, *Jesus and the Father*, 109–10.

21. Ibid., 110.

22. Gerald Bray, *The Doctrine of God* (Downers Grove, IL: InterVarsity Press, 1993), 146.

23. Geoffrey Wainwright, *The Trinity in the New Testament* (London: SPCK, 1962), 109.

24. Benjamin B. Warfield, "Trinity," *The International Standard Bible Encyclopedia*, ed. James Orr (Grand Rapids: Eerdmans, 1952), 5:3020.

Trinity were thought of by him [Paul] as resident in the terms 'Father,' 'Son,' that in his numerous allusions to the Trinity in the Godhead, he never betrays any sense of this."[25]

One other interesting text is Isaiah 9:6, "For to us a child is born, to us a son is given, . . . And he shall be called . . . Everlasting Father, Prince of Peace." Since this is generally considered a messianic prophecy, it is unfortunate that the gradationists do not comment on this text, which from their perspective, is certainly at least paradoxical.

One other group of texts that are difficult to fit into a gradational scheme are those that seem to suggest that the Sonship had a point of temporal, rather than eternal, beginning. One of these is the indication of the fulfillment of Psalm 2:7, "You are my Son; today I have become your father," in connection with a reference to Jesus' resurrection (Acts 13:33). While many gradationists do not hold the generation concept in any very literal fashion, preferring to treat such references as pertaining to the birth or other aspects of the Incarnation, these types of texts call for more specific treatment. Exactly what does it mean for the Father to say, "Today I have *become* your Father," if he is *eternally* the Father of the Son?

Specific Passages Suggesting a Less Subordinate Position of the Son or the Holy Spirit

In the judgment passage in Matthew 25:31–46, verses 31 and 32 are especially instructive: "When the Son of Man comes in his glory, and all the angels with him, he will sit on his throne in heavenly glory. All the nations will be gathered before him, and he will separate the people one from another as a shepherd separates the sheep from the goats." Here is the Son, in the consummation of this world, exercising the supreme authority over that world, with such signs of authority as angels, a throne, and glory. The Father is nowhere present in this scene. Without detracting from the Father's authority, this certainly seems to indicate a position of ultimate authority in one of the most important events of all human history.

---

25. Ibid.

Further, we may look at a passage that seems to show the Holy Spirit exercising authority over the Son. In the temptation of Jesus, the leading by the Spirit is clear. Matthew 4:1 and Luke 4:1 speak of Jesus being led by the Spirit into the wilderness (Matthew uses *anēchthē* and Luke uses *ēgeto*). Mark's statement (1:12) is stronger, using the word *ekballei*, picturing the Spirit as virtually casting him out into the wilderness. In Luke 4:1, Jesus is said to be full of the Spirit when he is led into the wilderness. In verse 14 he returns in the power of the Spirit.

The logic of citing these passages is not to show some superiority of the Son over the Father or the Spirit over the Son. Rather, the force of these passages is to counter the claim that the texts that attribute to the Father alone certain acts of authority should be understood as signifying that his authority exceeds that of his partners in the Trinity. It also challenges the idea that the Son has inherent and permanent authority over the Spirit.

Less direct, but possibly also relevant, are the passages dealing with what is usually referred to as the blasphemy against the Holy Spirit, such as Matthew 12:31 and 32. Jesus says, "And so I tell you, every sin and blasphemy will be forgiven men, but the blasphemy against the Spirit will not be forgiven. Anyone who speaks a word against the Son of Man will be forgiven, but anyone who speaks against the Holy Spirit will not be forgiven, either in this age or in the age to come." Apparently it is more serious to speak against the Holy Spirit than against the Son. This hardly seems consistent with the idea that the Spirit has a lesser role than the Father and the Son.

Teachings Suggesting That the Father's Authority over the Son Was Especially Related to the Son's Redemptive Ministry

Certain passages suggest that the Son *became* a servant, or *became* obedient to the Father. Two in particular stand out.

Philippians 2:4–11

Here is a powerful passage describing the Incarnation. Several elements of the passage bear upon the issue under consideration. One is the statement, "Christ . . . did not consider equality with God something to be grasped." There has been considerable discussion regarding whether this should be understood in terms of his not seeking to take something he did not have or his giving up something he already possessed. Both parties to this debate, however, agree on the latter meaning, and it does seem to be the likelier rendition of the clause. This suggests that he had an equality with God that he gave up by coming, so that his status during the period of his earthly ministry was something less than it had been previously. While it would seem most natural to take this as being equal authority, Wayne Grudem contends that what Jesus gave up was simply equal glory and honor.[26] Does anything in the passage give us guidance?

The expression "taking the very nature of a servant" (Phil. 2:7) is a participial phrase, and seems to be an instrumental participle, so that it describes the means by which he "emptied himself." The fact that he took the nature of a servant, one who serves or does the will of another, suggests that he was not formerly a servant, or that he now subjected himself to someone else's will, which he had not done previously. This very expression suggests contextually that at least part of what he did not cling to was an equal authority with the Father.

"He humbled himself and became obedient to death" (Phil. 2:8) suggests that obedience also was something he acquired that was not present before. It is not death that he was obedient to, but someone else to whom he was obedient. "To death" marks the extent of that obedience.

On the basis of these considerations, I conclude that the interpretation that Jesus actually gave up equal authority with the Father and took on an obedience to him that was not previously present is superior to the view that he merely gave up equal honor and glory. This is underscored by the fact that nothing is said about honor and authority in this passage.[27]

---

26. Grudem, *Evangelical Feminism*, 409.

27. Robert L. Redmond, in a recent, rather confused chapter, refers to the classic interpretation as a "blunder" ("Classical Christology's Future in Systematic Theology," *Always Reforming: Explorations in Systematic Theology*, ed. A. T. B. McGowan

Hebrews 5:8

This is another significant passage: "Although he was a son, he learned obedience from what he suffered." This suggests that obedience was something that he learned. It does not, of course, follow that he had never previously learned obedience, for it certainly is theoretically possible to increase one's depth of obedience. So Grudem argues that this was not the first time he had learned obedience, although the passage says nothing about this. What is perhaps most significant for our purposes, however, is the adversative *kaiper*, "although," suggesting that obedience was perhaps something unusual or unexpected for a son. This passage, therefore, seems to support the temporary subordination view.

Texts Offering a Solution to the Dilemma

The result of our examination of the arguments advanced by the two sides has led to something of a stalemate. On the one hand, we have seen texts that seem to argue that the authority relationship of the Father over the Son was not restricted to the time of the Son's redemptive earthly ministry but is eternal in nature. On the other hand, we have seen texts that cannot easily be fitted into this scheme, and some that appear to argue more strongly for the idea that the command-obedience, or superiority-subordination relationship began with the coming of the second person of the Trinity in the Incarnation. Is there any direction we might go to attempt to resolve this dilemma in favor of one alternative or the other? Can we sharpen the issue more specifically?

One possible direction in which to turn our investigation was suggested by Warfield a century ago. Noting that the Son indeed came to earth to fulfill the decision that he should do so, Warfield raised

---

[Downers Grove, IL: InterVarsity Press, 2006], 67–124). His alternative, that "emptied himself" refers to his "pouring himself out of death," is based on questionable assumptions and falls far short exegetically of his confident statement that he has "demonstrated" it. See his *New Systematic Theology of the Christian Faith*, 2nd ed. (Nashville: Thomas Nelson, 1998), 253–65.

the question of the basis of that decision. The gradationists' answer is that this act of subordination was the extension of an eternal subordination, according to which the Father made such a decision and the Son carried it out. Warfield observed, however, that "these relations of subordination in mode of operation may just as well be due to a convention, an agreement, between the Persons of the Trinity—a 'Covenant' as it is technically called—by virtue of which a distinct function in the work of redemption is voluntarily assumed by each. It is eminently desirable, therefore, at the least, that some definite evidence of subordination in modes of subsistence should be discoverable before it is assumed."[28]

Warfield seems to be saying that there are two possible explanations of the decision that the second person should be the one to become incarnate and carry out the work of atonement and redemption: (1) that this was the sole decision of the Father; or (2) that this was an agreement the three persons of the Trinity made mutually, in which each voluntarily assumed a specific role. The two arguments could therefore be analyzed somewhat as follows:

1. Gradational-authority view
   - The person(s) making ultimate decisions and initiating actions possess(es) the supreme authority.
   - The Father makes ultimate decisions and initiates actions.
   - Therefore, the Father possesses supreme authority.

2. Equivalent-authority view
   - The person(s) making ultimate decisions and initiating actions possess(es) the supreme authority.
   - The Father, Son, and Holy Spirit jointly make ultimate decisions and initiate actions.
   - Therefore, the Father, Son, and Holy Spirit jointly possess supreme authority.

---

28. Warfield, "Trinity," 3021. It should be noted that Warfield defines "modes of subsistence" as "the necessary relation of the Persons of the Trinity to one another" (ibid.).

If this analysis is correct, then the difference between the two views is the assumption each makes regarding the second premise. Given each assumption, the conclusion follows validly.

The crucial question then becomes whether there is any way we can test these two assumptions, to justify one rather than the other. There may be. Hermeneutically, the task is to examine decisions and actions attributed to one or another person of the Trinity, to see whether they are done individually or collectively. Three hermeneutical stances regarding these texts seem possible:

1. Those decisions and actions attributed in Scripture to one person of the Trinity should be understood as the sole decision or action of that one person. This would seem to be the predominant stance of the gradationists, especially with respect to foreordination, sending, giving, and so on.

2. Those decisions and actions attributed in Scripture to one person of the Trinity should be understood as the sole decision or action of that one person if they are not elsewhere attributed to another person or persons of the Trinity. There could be a harder and a softer version of this stance, depending on whether the "if" is understood as meaning "if and only if."

3. Those decisions and actions attributed in Scripture to one person of the Trinity should be understood as the joint decision or action of all three persons of the Trinity. This position would tend to be associated with the equivalence position, and option 2 would also tend in that direction, though less obviously so. If only the second position were justified on textual grounds, some other basis, theological or philosophical, would be required to make the transition from 2 to 3.

Texts Suggesting Similar Action by the Different Persons

This last consideration introduces us to a large and important class of texts: those that attribute to a certain member of the Trinity an action that elsewhere is attributed to a different member.

Choosing

A number of passages identify the Father as predestinating, or choosing, persons for salvation. Representative of these are Romans 8:29, "For those God foreknew he also predestined to be conformed to the likeness of his Son, that he might be the firstborn among many brothers," and 1 Peter 1:2, "who have been chosen according to the foreknowledge of God the Father, through the sanctifying work of the Spirit, for obedience to Jesus Christ and sprinkling by his blood." These seem to indicate that the authority and the initiative in persons becoming the elect belongs to the Father. It may be instructive, however, to note that Jesus seems to be the one who chooses persons for service, at least those who were to be his first disciples: "Then Jesus replied, 'Have I not chosen you, the Twelve? Yet one of you is a devil!'" (John 6:70); "I am not referring to all of you; I know those I have chosen" (John 13:18a); "As it is, you do not belong to the world, but I have chosen you out of the world" (John 15:19). See also Acts 1:2, 24; 9:15. In fact, some texts may even attribute the electing to salvation to Jesus. Jesus said, "For just as the Father raises the dead and gives them life, even so the Son gives life to whom he is pleased to give it" (John 5:21). In Matthew 11:27, Jesus said, "No one knows the Son except the Father, and no one knows the Father except the Son and those to whom the Son chooses to reveal him."

It appears that Jesus chooses those to whom he reveals the Father. On Calvinistic grounds, this would seem to be virtually tantamount to electing, for those to whom God is made known in this fashion respond; and both Grudem and Ware are traditional Calvinists. In John 10:27 and Matthew 7:23, Jesus speaks of knowing or not knowing persons. The allusion here may be to the Hebraic concept of knowledge of a person, which is much more than simply being acquainted but is actually a matter of intimate knowledge.

> My sheep listen to my voice; I know them, and they follow me. (John 10:27)

> Then I will tell them plainly, "I never knew you. Away from me, you evildoers!" (Matt. 7:23)

The Holy Spirit also exercises determination. He is identified as the one who gives gifts to believers. In 1 Corinthians 12:11, after enumerating various gifts, Paul writes, "All these are the work of one and the same Spirit, and he gives them to each one, just as he determines." Evidently, the Spirit exercises sovereignty in this important matter.

Hermeneutic 2 would interpret these texts as suggesting that there is a division of duties: the Father chooses who is to receive eternal life; the Son chooses who is to serve in what capacity in the kingdom; the Holy Spirit decides what gifts will be given to whom. Hermeneutic 3 would interpret this complex of Scriptures, however, as teaching that each of these acts of sovereignty is the work of the triune God, and that one of the three is especially associated with a given choice, but that this should not be understood as exclusive.

Sending of the Holy Spirit

Who was it that sent the Holy Spirit into the world and into the lives of believers? Jesus' teachings in John 14–16 are instructive. Note John 14:16, "And I will ask the Father, and he will give you another Counselor to be with you forever," and 14:26, "But the Counselor, the Holy Spirit, whom the Father will send in my name, will teach you all things and will remind you of everything I have said to you." Here Jesus seems to be saying quite clearly that the Father will send the Spirit. In contrast, note 15:26, "When the Counselor comes, whom I will send to you from the Father, the Spirit of truth who goes out from the Father, he will testify about me." Later in that discourse, he said, "But I tell you the truth: It is for your good that I am going away. Unless I go away, the Counselor will not come to you; but if I go, I will send him to you" (John 16:7). Here Jesus claims that he will send the Spirit.

Access to the Father

Regarding access to the Father, Jesus said in John 14:6, "I am the way and the truth and the life. No one comes to the Father except through me." In Ephesians 2, however, the picture is somewhat more complex: "For through him we both have access to the Father by one Spirit" (v. 18). In some sense, both the Son and the Spirit are involved in the access to the Father, because here (v. 16), it is clear that Jesus is referring to the reconciling of both Jew and Gentile to God, which presumably is the same sort of coming to the Father that Jesus is referring to in the former text.

Judging of the World

We noted earlier the description of Jesus sitting on his throne and judging all persons in the final judgment (Matt. 25:31–32). This appears to be the same event referred to in 2 Corinthians 5:10: "For we must all appear before the judgment seat of Christ, that each one may receive what is due him for the things done while in the body, whether good or bad." Compare this, however, with Romans 14:10: "You, then, why do you judge your brother? Or why do you look down on your brother? For we will all stand before God's judgment seat." The judgment seat seems to be both that of Christ and that of God.

Intercession

It is common for believers to think of the Son as interceding for them with the Father. Hebrews 7:25 says of Christ, "Therefore he is able to save completely those who come to God through him, because he always lives to intercede for them." A similar idea is expressed in Romans 8:34: "Who is he that condemns? Christ Jesus, who died—more than that, who was raised to life—is at the right hand of God and is also interceding for us." Yet in this very same chapter, Paul twice refers to the intercessory work of the Holy Spirit on behalf of believers: "In the same way, the Spirit helps us in our weakness. We do not know what we ought to pray for, but the Spirit himself intercedes for us with groans that words cannot express. And he who searches our hearts knows the mind of the Spirit, because the Spirit intercedes for the saints in accordance with God's will" (vv. 26–27).

Indwelling of the Believer

An important question is that of the divine indwelling in the believer. In numerous places, Jesus is spoken of as being in the believer. Note the following examples:

Examine yourselves to see whether you are in the faith; test yourselves. Do you not realize that Christ Jesus is in you—unless, of course, you fail the test? (2 Cor. 13:5)

To them God has chosen to make known among the Gentiles the glorious riches of this mystery, which is Christ in you, the hope of glory. (Col. 1:27)

I have been crucified with Christ and I no longer live, but Christ lives in me. The life I live in the body, I live by faith in the Son of God, who loved me and gave himself for me. (Gal. 2:20)

Remain in me, and I will remain in you. No branch can bear fruit by itself; it must remain in the vine. Neither can you bear fruit unless you remain in me. I am the vine; you are the branches. If a man remains in me and I in him, he will bear much fruit; apart from me you can do nothing. (John 15:5)

It is necessary to pair these references together with those in which the Holy Spirit is said to be in the believer:

Don't you know that you yourselves are God's temple and that God's Spirit lives in you? (1 Cor. 3:16)

Do you not know that your body is a temple of the Holy Spirit, who is in you, whom you have received from God? You are not your own. (1 Cor. 6:19)

Of special interest are those passages where in close juxtaposition both the Son and the Spirit are said to dwell within the believer.

And I will ask the Father, and he will give you another Counselor to be with you forever—the Spirit of truth. The world cannot accept him, because it neither sees him nor knows him. But you know him, for he lives with you and will be in you. I will not leave you as orphans; I will come to you. Before long, the world will not see me anymore, but you will see me. Because I live, you also will live. On that day you will realize that I am in my Father, and you are in me, and I am in you. (John 14:16–20)

You, however, are controlled not by the sinful nature but by the Spirit, if the Spirit of God lives in you. And if anyone does not have the Spirit of Christ, he does not belong to Christ. But if Christ is in you, your body is dead because of sin, yet your spirit is alive because of righteousness. And if the Spirit of him who raised Jesus from the dead is living in you, he who raised Christ from the dead will also give life to your mortal bodies through his Spirit, who lives in you. (Rom. 8:9–11)

It is even interesting to find that Jesus spoke of the Father's presence with them.

Jesus replied, "If anyone loves me, he will obey my teaching. My Father will love him, and we will come to him and make our home with him." (John 14:23)

We noted a moment ago the two passages about our bodies being temples. If we read 1 Corinthians 3:16 carefully, it appears to speak of both the Father and the Spirit dwelling within the believer, if God can be understood to dwell within his temple.

Don't you know that you yourselves are God's temple and that God's Spirit lives in you? (1 Cor. 3:16)

Giving

Who is the one who gives to humans? On the one hand, it appears quite clear that the Father is the giver.

If you, then, though you are evil, know how to give good gifts to your children, how much more will your Father in heaven give good gifts to those who ask him! (Matt. 7:11)

For the one whom God has sent speaks the words of God, for God gives the Spirit without limit. (John 3:34; cf. 1 Thess. 4:8; 1 Tim. 6:13)

Jesus said to them, "I tell you the truth, it is not Moses who has given you the bread from heaven, but it is my Father who gives you the true bread from heaven. For the bread of God is he who comes down from heaven and gives life to the world." (John 6:32–33)

As it is written: "I have made you a father of many nations." He is our father in the sight of God, in whom he believed—the God who gives life to the dead and calls things that are not as though they were. (Rom. 4:17; cf. 1 Tim. 6:13)

Other gifts that the Father is said to give are endurance, encouragement, and a spirit of unity (Rom. 15:5); a body (1 Cor. 15:38); victory (1 Cor. 15:57); wisdom (James 1:5); and grace (1 Peter 5:5).

In light of texts such as this, it is not surprising that James wrote,

Every good and perfect gift is from above, coming down from the Father of the heavenly lights, who does not change like shifting shadows. (James 1:17)

From such textual considerations one might conclude on hermeneutic 1 that the Father is the exclusive giver. Note, however, the following:

For just as the Father raises the dead and gives them life, even so the Son gives life to whom he is pleased to give it. (John 5:21)

For the bread of God is he who comes down from heaven and gives life to the world. (John 6:33)

Peace I leave with you; my peace I give you. I do not give to you as the world gives. Do not let your hearts be troubled and do not be afraid. (John 14:27)

The Spirit gives life; the flesh counts for nothing. The words I have spoken to you are spirit and they are life. (John 6:63)

All these are the work of one and the same Spirit, and he gives them to each one, just as he determines. (1 Cor. 12:11)

He has made us competent as ministers of a new covenant—not of the letter but of the Spirit; for the letter kills, but the Spirit gives life. (2 Cor. 3:6)

This is an interesting collection of texts. In particular, if one asks, "Who is it that gives life?" the answer, based on these texts, has to be, the Father, the Son, and the Holy Spirit all give life.

One passage is particularly instructive in this matter, namely, John 10:28–30:

I give them eternal life, and they shall never perish; no one can snatch them out of my hand. My Father, who has given them to me, is greater than all; no one can snatch them out of my Father's hand. I and the Father are one.

Note that the preserving action of the Son and of the Father are described in identical terms.

Love

On the hermeneutic used by the gradationists, one might argue that because John 3:16 says, "For God so loved the world that he gave his one and only Son, that whoever believes in him shall not perish but have eternal life," it was only the Father who loved the world. Note, however, what Jesus said to his disciples:

As the Father has loved me, so have I loved you. Now remain in my love. If you obey my commands, you will remain in my love, just as I have obeyed my Father's commands and remain in his love. I have told you this so that my joy may be in you and that your joy may be complete. My command is this: Love each other as I have loved you. (John 15:9–12)

In theory, it would be possible to interpret these passages as involving a division of labor, according to which the Father loves some (perhaps the whole world, prior to the Son's coming), and the Son loves others (perhaps those whom he chose to be his disciples). The other interpretation would be that their love is not exclusive, but rather that they are the same thing, that they love together and inseparably.

Romans 8 seems to support the latter interpretation:

> Who shall separate us from the love of Christ? Shall trouble or hardship or persecution or famine or nakedness or danger or sword? As it is written: "For your sake we face death all day long; we are considered as sheep to be slaughtered." No, in all these things we are more than conquerors through him who loved us. For I am convinced that neither death nor life, neither angels nor demons, neither the present nor the future, nor any powers, neither height nor depth, nor anything else in all creation, will be able to separate us from the love of God that is in Christ Jesus our Lord. (Rom. 8:35–39)

Since the theme of the passage is the possibility of anything separating us from divine love, and since that phrase is attached both to the love of Christ and the love of God, they appear to be the same. It is notable, also, that Paul concludes by speaking of the love of God that *is in* Christ.

Reception of Prayer

The matter of prayer is a special case, particularly since Bruce Ware has made prayer exclusively to the Father an implication of the differing roles of the three persons of the Trinity. In several places in the New Testament, however, believers direct prayer to the Son: Acts 7:59–60; 2 Corinthians 12:8–9; and Revelation 22:20. Observe the similarity of Stephen's prayer to Jesus in Acts 7 to Jesus' prayer to the Father from the cross:

> Lord Jesus, receive my spirit. (Acts 7:59)

> Father, into your hands I commit my spirit. (Luke 23:46)

> Lord, do not hold this sin against them. (Acts 7:60)

> Father, forgive them, for they do not know what they are doing. (Luke 23:34)

The similarity of these prayers, one directed to the Father and the other to the Son, suggest that at least on these occasions believers prayed to either the Father or the Son.

Texts Suggesting Unity of the Persons

Are there texts that go beyond hermeneutic 2 to support hermeneutic 3? In a number of places, Jesus seemed to speak of himself and the Father in such a way as to suggest that the two somehow are one. We noted above that having described how the believer is in Jesus' hand and in the Father's hand in identical terms, he then adds, "I and the Father are one" (John 10:30). Another possibility is the passage where he says, "We [the Father and I] will come to him" (John 14:23). A more extended passage, speaking of the Father and the Son as being in one another, is John 17:20–23:

> My prayer is not for them alone. I pray also for those who will believe in me through their message, that all of them may be one, Father, just as you are in me and I am in you. May they also be in us so that the world may believe that you have sent me. I have given them the glory that you gave me, that they may be one as we are one: I in them and you in me. May they be brought to complete unity to let the world know that you sent me and have loved them even as you have loved me.

In another extended passage, Jesus suggests that the Father is in him and is doing his work through him:

> "If you really knew me, you would know my Father as well. From now on, you do know him and have seen him." Philip said, "Lord, show us the Father and that will be enough for us." Jesus answered: "Don't you know me, Philip, even after I have been among you such a long time? Anyone who has seen me has seen the Father. How can you say, 'Show us the Father'? Don't you believe that I am in the Father, and that the Father is in me? The words I say to you are not just my own. Rather, it is the Father,

living in me, who is doing his work. Believe me when I say that I am in the Father and the Father is in me; or at least believe on the evidence of the miracles themselves." (John 14:7–11)

In John 5, Jesus discusses the miracles he is doing and then comments,

> "My Father is always at his work to this very day, and I, too, am working." For this reason the Jews tried all the harder to kill him; not only was he breaking the Sabbath, but he was even calling God his own Father, making himself equal with God. Jesus gave them this answer: "I tell you the truth, the Son can do nothing by himself; he can do only what he sees his Father doing, because whatever the Father does the Son also does." (John 5:17–19)

These words can be understood simply as saying that Jesus does works similar to those the Father does, or they can be interpreted as teaching that his works are the works of the Father in and through him. The latter interpretation fits well with the passages cited earlier to the effect that he and the Father are one and that they are in one another.

There are other passages that suggest joint action by the Father and the Son. Earlier we noted that Jesus said he and the Father would come to the believers, and they would make their home with them (John 14:23). In John 10:27–29, Jesus described in identical terms the fact that no one could snatch the believer out of Jesus' hand and no one could snatch them out of the Father's hand. His closing comment is especially instructive: "I and the Father are one" (v. 30). Paul also says in 2 Corinthians 5:19 that "God was reconciling the world to himself in Christ" (ὡς ὅτι θεὸς ἦν ἐν Χριστῷ κόσμον καταλλάσσων ἑαυτῷ).

Finally, we should note a case of possible joint activity by the second and third persons of the Trinity. Although Jesus said that he must go away so that the Holy Spirit might come (John 16:7), in Matthew 28:20 he also promised that he would be with his followers always, to the end of the age, and apparently he was referring to a time including the period prior to his second coming.

Interpreting These Passages

We have seen a complex of passages. How can we best interpret them as a set? Perhaps a cue can be derived from historical theology. In general, I am quite reserved about the citations of figures from historical theology by persons on both sides of the debate. In large part, this is because citations are sometimes taken out of context and treated as answers to questions the theologian was not addressing and perhaps did not even anticipate. This is not to say, however, that a theologian may not reveal belief in a principle that can be applied to another issue. In this case, however, I believe the theologians I will cite were consciously addressing the specific hermeneutical issue we are considering.

In a chapter of *On the Trinity* titled, "All Are Sometimes Understood in One Person," Augustine suggests that what is said of one member of the Trinity can also be understood of the others. So, for example, he considers Jesus' promise that he and the Father will come to them and make their home with them (John 14:23). Note, however, the promise of the coming of the Spirit, given just before this: "And I will ask the Father, and he will give you another Counselor to be with you forever—the Spirit of truth. The world cannot accept him, because it neither sees him nor knows him. But you know him, for he lives with you and will be in you" (John 14:16–17). Does the coming of the Father and the Son mean that the Spirit will therefore depart? No, says Augustine, for the promise was that the Spirit would be with them forever. His comment reveals a broader aspect of his view of the Trinity.

> He [the Spirit] will not therefore depart when the Father and the Son come, but will be in the same abode with them eternally; because neither will He come without them, nor they without Him. But in order to intimate the Trinity, some things are separately affirmed, the Persons being also each severally named; and yet are not to be understood as though the other Persons were excluded, on account of the unity of the same Trinity and the One substance and Godhead of the Father and of the Son and of the Holy Spirit.[29]

---

29. Augustine, *On the Trinity*, 1.9.19.

Interestingly, John Calvin appears to operate from a similar principle. In discussing the Incarnation, he says, "Therefore our most merciful God, when he willed that we be redeemed, made himself our Redeemer in the person of his only-begotten Son."[30]

Based upon the induction of a number of passages, the hypothesis that in my judgment fits the largest number (including those cited by the gradationists) with the least distortion is the following. The various works attributed to the different persons of the Trinity are in fact works of the triune God. One member of the Godhead may in fact do this work on behalf of the three and be mentioned as the one who does that work, but all participate in what is done. So, for example, it was the Son who died on the cross, but in a very real sense, the Father and the Spirit also suffered. This is not the ancient teaching of patripassianism. This is referring to the other persons' sympathetic suffering in the Son's actual suffering on the cross. Probably most parents have experienced this, in seeing the pain of their child and in a very real sense feeling that pain themselves.

The other acts we have described need to be understood similarly. The love of God and the love of Christ are not two different things. The love that Jesus felt and showed to his disciples was the love of the triune God, expressed especially by and through him. Similarly, the intercession is not simply that of the Son or the Spirit with the Father. In a very real sense, it is intercession with the entire Godhead, expressed primarily by one of their number who has special contact with the one being interceded for. An illustration of this could be found when a member of a legislative body pleads before the group the cause of some person or organization external to the group. He is not asking that "you" vote in a certain way but that "we" do so.

On this basis, the sending of the Son to earth was done by the Father but on behalf of the Trinity. In a very real sense, all of them sent the Son, and all had jointly decided that he would go.[31] In the Atonement, the Son

---

30. John Calvin, *Institutes of the Christian Religion*, Battles translation, 2.12.2. I recommend reading the entire chapter.

31. We will note in the next chapter that Augustine said this very thing.

offers his life as a sacrifice to the Godhead, and the Father accepts it on behalf of the Godhead.

This, then, also offers a solution to that puzzling passage, 1 Corinthians 15:24–28. We have noted that this is perhaps the strongest passage in support of the eternal subordinationist or gradational-authority view. At least on its surface, the verses appear to contend that in the eschaton, the Son will turn over all authority (back) to the Father and will then himself become subject to the Father.

It should be noted, however, that a number of different interpretations have been offered over the years and that the traditional Reformed interpretation is quite different from this. Calvin offered an interpretation that has become the seed for later Reformed treatments. He asked how this could be, in light of the texts that teach that the Son's kingdom will be eternal (e.g., Dan. 7:13, 27; Luke 1:33; 2 Peter 1:11). He then adds,

> But Christ will then restore the kingdom which he has received, that we may cleave wholly to God. Nor will he in this way resign the kingdom, but will transfer it in a manner from his humanity to his glorious divinity, because a way of approach will then be opened up, from which our infirmity now keeps us back. Thus then Christ will be *subjected to the Father*, because the vail being then removed, we shall openly behold God reigning in his majesty, and Christ's humanity will then no longer be interposed to keep us back from a closer view of God.[32]

Charles Hodge elaborates on this suggestion in his commentary on 1 Corinthians:

> The thing done, and the person who does it, are the same. The subjection here spoken of is not predicated of the eternal Logos, the second person of the Trinity, any more than the kingdom spoken of in v. 24 is the dominion which belongs essentially to Christ

---

32. John Calvin, *Commentary on the Epistles of Paul the Apostle to the Corinthians* (Grand Rapids: Eerdmans, 1948), 2:32–33.

as God. As there the word *Christ* designates the Theanthropos, so does the word *Son* here designate, not the Logos as such, but the Logos as incarnate. . . . It is not the subjection of the Son as Son, but of the Son as Theanthropos of which the apostle here speaks. . . . The subordination, however, here spoken of, is not that of the human nature of Christ separately considered, as when he is said to suffer, or to die, or to be ignorant; but it is the official subordination of the incarnate Son to God as God. The words αὐτὸς ὁ υἱὸς, the Son himself, here designate, as in so many other places, not the second person of the Trinity as such, but that person as clothed in our nature. And the subjection spoken of, is not of the former, but of the latter, i.e. not of the Son as Son, but of the Son as incarnate; and the subjection itself is official and therefore perfectly consistent with equality of nature.[33]

What is especially interesting here is that although Hodge holds to the eternal subordination of the Son to the Father,[34] he does not believe that it is taught in this passage. Rather, the Incarnate Son, not the second person of the Trinity per se, is here spoken of as subject to the Father. While this interpretation may not seem as obvious as the one offered by Grudem, it has the value of fitting more harmoniously with the principle of mutual action, derived from the other texts we have examined.

In this chapter we have noted that there are some texts, which taken at face value and in isolation, clearly favor the gradational view. However, we have also examined other texts that tend to negate that view and to offer support for the equivalence view. In addition, there are a large number of texts that attribute similar actions to more than one member of the Trinity. When taken together with those that declare the unity of the persons, an overall principle can be formulated. Although one person of the Trinity may occupy a more prominent part in a given

---

33. Charles Hodge, *An Exposition of the First Epistle to the Corinthians* (New York: Robert Carter & Brothers, 1857), 333–34.

34. Charles Hodge, *Systematic Theology* (Grand Rapids: Eerdmans, 1952), 1:445.

divine action, the action is actually that of the entire Godhead, and the one person is acting on behalf of the three. This means that those passages that speak of the Father predestining, sending, commanding, and so on should not be taken as applying to the Father alone but to all members of the Trinity. Thus they do not count as evidence in support of an eternal supremacy of the Father and an eternal subordination of the Son.

CHAPTER 5

The Historical Considerations

As the discussion of subordination within the Trinity has proceeded, there has been an increasing concern to examine historical theology to determine the extent to which this view has been held within the history of the church. Perhaps the major initial impetus to this inquiry was given by Gilbert Bilezikian's article, in which he suggested, but without documentation, "Except for occasional and predictable deviations, this [the temporary-subordination view] is the historical Biblical trinitarian doctrine that has been defined in the creeds and generally defended by the Church, at least the western Church, throughout the centuries."[1]

This gave rise to an article by Kovach and Schemm, in which they challenged Bilezikian's assertion by showing a number of instances of early church theologians who, on their interpretation, actually supported the eternal subordination view. Their statement was equally categorical to Bilezikian's: "It cannot be legitimately denied that the eternal subordination of the Son is an orthodox doctrine and believed from the history of the early church to the present day."[2]

Similarly sweeping is the statement by Wayne Grudem in response to Richard and Catherine Kroeger's inclusion of functional subordination in the heresy of subordination: "They are condemning all orthodox Christology from the Nicene Creed onward and thereby condemning

---

1. Gilbert Bilezikian, "Hermeneutical Bungee-Jumping: Subordination in the Godhead," *Journal of the Evangelical Theological Society* 40, no. 1 (March 1997): 60.

2. Stephen D. Kovach and Peter R. Schemm Jr., "A Defense of the Doctrine of the Eternal Subordination of the Son," *Journal of the Evangelical Theological Society* 42, no. 3 (September 1999): 464.

a teaching that Charles Hodge says has been a teaching of the 'Church universal.'"[3]

While Grudem and Bruce Ware also cited alleged instances of subordination teaching, it is Kevin Giles who has done the most extensive research into the subject. As an Anglican, he naturally has a strong interest in the church's tradition. Beyond that, however, as we observed in the chapter on biblical material, he contends that since the Bible can be read in such a way as to support either position, the way to determine the correct hermeneutic is to examine the history of the church in order to ascertain how the church has understood those biblical passages in the past.

It is important to note that the context of the writing is vitally important here also, just as in the interpretation of biblical passages. When a biblical passage is taken out of context, it may be treated as addressing a different question than that which the author was dealing with. The resultant answer will actually be a distortion of the original meaning.

Similarly, a church father's statement may not have had in mind at all a question posed by a present-day debate. While it may seem to offer an answer to that question, taking it as such will be a misunderstanding of the author's intended meaning. I recall in a course on Augustine that members of the class would frequently remark, "Augustine seems to be confusing the Protestant and the Roman Catholic positions on this issue." Apart from the anachronism involved, the point was that those questions, at least in that form, had not yet faced the church. Thus, Augustine was not consciously addressing the issue we had in mind. Had he been, he might have written something quite different than he did. We must therefore probe thoroughly the background of the writer, including, in particular, the view of the opponent to whom he may have been responding.

This is not to say that statements not directed to the question before us are of no significance to us. The statement actually may be

---

3. Wayne Grudem, *Systematic Theology: An Introduction to Biblical Doctrine* (Grand Rapids: Zondervan, 1994), 251n. 35.

based on a principle that can be legitimately applied to a different issue. This is important, for without such principles, the Bible would be of no help to us in handling many current ethical issues that were not directly addressed in biblical times, and indeed could not have been, since the technology giving rise to the problem was not present at that time. So, for example, the Bible does not directly treat the question of global warming, which is so strongly debated at the present time. It does, however, offer teachings about God's concern and commands regarding the care and welfare of the entire creation that are based on principles that certainly are applicable to this issue. Great care must be taken, therefore, to determine that this principle is indeed at stake in a biblical passage, or in the writing of the theologian whose thought we are considering.

There is, however, one major difference in this respect and endeavor with regard to the Scriptures as contrasted to a figure from the history of the church. The authors of Scripture wrote under the inspiration of the Holy Spirit, and since this Holy Spirit was, as it were, the coauthor with all of these individual writers, there should be a harmony among their writings. This principle, known as "Scripture interpreting Scripture," can give us guidance in determining which of several possible interpretations of a passage is to be followed. While the theologians whose thought we will examine were men of godly lives who sought the guidance of the Holy Spirit in their thinking and expression, they were not inspired by the Holy Spirit in the same fashion as the biblical authors. It is not correct to speak of their writings as in some sense the Word of God.

The First Period: To the Year 400

Origen

While Origen was not necessarily the first of the ante-Nicene fathers to hold the doctrine of eternal divine generation of the Son by the Father, he certainly gave that teaching its greatest impetus. The doctrine is found in a number of places in his writings. One of the clearest is in his *De Principiis*: "Wherefore we have always held that

God is the Father of His only-begotten Son, who was born indeed of Him, and derives from Him what He is, but without any beginning, not only such as may be measured by any divisions of time, but even that which the mind alone can contemplate within itself, or behold, so to speak, with the naked powers of the understanding. And therefore we must believe that Wisdom was generated before any beginning that can be either comprehended or expressed."[4]

Several observations are appropriate regarding this generation. It is the Son's derivation from the Father of what he is. It is eternal, being without beginning. Finally, there is no reference here to the Son being subordinate to the Father in authority, or in any other way. Origen also makes clear that this is in no sense a division of the substance of the Father, or an emanation, or as he terms it, a "prolation": "For we do not say, as the heretics suppose, that some part of the substance of God was converted into the Son, or that the Son was procreated by the Father out of things non-existent, i.e., beyond His own substance, so that there once was a time when He did not exist; but, putting away all corporeal conceptions, we say that the Word and Wisdom was begotten out of the invisible and incorporeal without any corporeal feeling, as if it were an act of the will proceeding from the understanding."[5]

This was an act of the Father's will, a decision eternally to beget the Son without any other compulsion or cause, a concept taught elsewhere by Origen: "For in the exercise of His will He employs no other way than that which is made known by the counsel of His will. And thus also the existence of the Son is generated by Him."[6] It should be noted that Origen also believed in an eternal creation of the universe, and that this idea of eternal generation therefore fits well with that conception.

Novatian

Another ante-Nicene father who addressed the issue of the relationship between the Father and the Son and the basis of that differentiation

---

4. Origen, *De Principiis*, 1.2.2.
5. Ibid., 1.1.28.
6. Ibid., 1.2.6.

was Novatian. Ware quotes a lengthy statement by Novation in support of the eternal submission view:

> He is therefore the Son, not the Father: for He would have confessed that He was the Father had He considered Himself to be the Father; and He declares that He was sanctified by His Father. In receiving, then, sanctification from the Father, He is inferior to the Father. Now, consequently, He who is inferior to the Father, is *not the Father*, but the Son; for had He been the Father, He would have given, and not received, sanctification. Now, however, by declaring that He has received sanctification from the Father, by the very fact of proving Himself to be less than the Father, by receiving from Him sanctification, He has shown that He is the Son, and not the Father. Besides, He says that He is sent: so that by that obedience wherewith the Lord Christ came, being sent, He might be proved to be not the Father, but the Son, who assuredly would have sent had He been the Father; but being sent, He was not the Father, lest the Father should be proved, in being sent, to be subjected to another God.[7]

Here is one of the clearest statements by an early church father of the idea of the Son's dependence on the Father. Novatian consequently does not hesitate to speak of the Son as "inferior" to the Father. Ware's comment is that "clearly Novatian means only here that the Son follows the Father's command and submits to the Father's will."[8] It does not seem so clear that this is all that Novatian means, for he appears to be saying that the Son is dependent on the Father for his sanctification. It should be noted, further, that the text is actually referring to an incident that took place during the Son's earthly theanthropic ministry,

---

7. Novatian, *Concerning the Trinity*, chap. 27. Bruce Ware's quotation is in "Equal in Essence, Distinct in Roles: Eternal Functional Authority and Submission Among the Essentially Equal Persons of the Godhead" (unpublished paper presented at the 58th Annual Meeting of the Evangelical Theological Society, Washington, D.C., November 16, 2006), 9–10.

8. Ware, "Equal in Essence, Distinct in Roles," 10.

which Ware generalizes to eternal dimensions. It is also interesting to find Ware accepting Novatian's use of the term "inferior" here, albeit while qualifying its meaning, whereas he, Grudem, and other gradationists have resisted the use of that term in any sense.

The Councils and Creeds

Out of the series of councils held in the fourth and fifth centuries to decide the status of Jesus and his relationship to the Father, a corresponding series of creeds emerged, and additional creeds appeared within the church. Each of these addressed issues significant to the questions before us.[9]

Nicene Creed

We believe in . . . one Lord Jesus Christ, the Son of God begotten of the Father, Only-begotten, that is of the substance of the Father; God of God; Light of Light; very God of very God; begotten, not made; of the same substance with the Father.

Niceno-Constantinopolitan Creed

We believe in . . . one Lord Jesus Christ, the only-begotten Son of God, begotten of his Father [before all worlds]; (God of God), Light of Light, very God of very God, begotten, not made, being of one substance with the Father.

Athanasian Creed

For there is one person of the Father, another of the Son, and another of the Holy Ghost. But the Godhead of the Father, of the Son, and of the Holy Ghost is all one: the glory equal, the majesty coeternal. Such as the Father is, such is the Son, and such is the Holy Ghost. The Father uncreate, the Son uncreate, and the Holy Ghost uncreate. The Father incomprehensible, the Son incomprehensible, and the Holy Ghost incomprehensible.

---

9. The text of these is taken, with slight adaptation, from *The Creeds of Christendom: With a History and Critical Notes*, ed. Philip Schaff, rev. David S. Schaff, vol. 2, The Greek and Latin Creeds (Grand Rapids: Baker, 1983), 45–71.

The Father eternal, the Son eternal, and the Holy Ghost eternal. And yet they are not three eternals, but one eternal. As also there are not three incomprehensibles, nor three uncreated, but one uncreated, and one incomprehensible. So likewise the Father is almighty, the Son almighty, and the Holy Ghost almighty. And yet there are not three almightys, but one almighty. So the Father is God, the Son is God, and the Holy Ghost is God. And yet there are not three Gods, but one God. . . . The Father is made of none, neither created nor begotten. The Son is of the Father alone; not made, nor created, but begotten. The Holy Ghost is of the Father and of the Son; neither made, nor created, nor begotten, but proceeding.

Apostles' Creed

I believe . . . in Jesus Christ his [God the Father Almighty's] only Son our Lord, who was conceived by the Holy Ghost; born of the Virgin Mary.

Chalcedonian Creed

We . . . teach men to confess one and the same Son, our Lord Jesus Christ, perfect in the divinity, perfect in the humanity, truly God and truly man, consisting of a reasonable soul and body; consubstantial with the Father according to the Godhead, and consubstantial with us according to the manhood; in all things like unto us, sin only excepted; who was begotten of the Father before all ages, according to the Godhead.

Note certain points of similarity and difference among these creeds. Each, with the exception of the Apostles' Creed, speaks of the Son as begotten of the Father, and in the Nicene, the Niceno-Constantinopolitan, and the Chalcedonian, in terms that require an eternal generation. The Athanasian Creed adds of each of the members of the Trinity the term "uncreated." Thus, it is safe to say that in general these express the eternal generation or begetting of the Son by the Father.

Note, however, that nothing is said about subordination or relative authority. There is an order in which the three are mentioned: Father, Son, and Holy Spirit, but this appears to be merely logical or sequential, not an order of authority. For some current advocates of the position of gradational authority, the eternal subordination or submission of the Son is taken as an inference drawn from eternal generation. It will remain in latter chapters to investigate whether this concept of eternal generation is required by biblical teaching, whether this is a coherent concept, and whether eternal subordination is implied by it.

Athanasius

The great defender of orthodoxy had much to say on the subject of the Incarnation, the Trinity, and the relationship between Father and Son. Much of what Athanasius wrote was directed to the Arians, so the specific questions about which we are concerned did not draw his attention.

There can be little doubt that Athanasius held to the doctrine of the eternal generation of the Son by the Father. As a member of the Alexandrian school, he had been taught this doctrine, which originated with Origen. He espouses this doctrine in numerous places. An example can be found in his *Discourses*: "For the Father and the Son were not generated from some pre-existing origin, that we may account Them brothers, but the Father is the Origin of the Son and begat Him; and the Father is Father, and not born the Son of any; and the Son is Son, and not brother. Further, if He is called the eternal offspring of the Father, He is rightly so called."[10] Numerous other examples could be given. His dispute with the Arians was not over whether the Father had generated the Son, but whether, as the Arians insisted, there was a time before he was generated.[11]

One basic principle of Athanasius's interpretation of the biblical teachings is found in his famous conception of the double account of Scripture: "Now the scope and character of Holy Scripture, as we have often said, is this,—it contains a double account of the Savior;

---

10. Athanasius, *Four Discourses Against the Arians*, 1.5.14.
11. Ibid., 1.2.14.

that He was ever God, and is the Son, being the Father's Word and Radiance and Wisdom; and that afterward for us He took flesh of a Virgin, Mary Bearer of God, and was made man. And this scope is to be found throughout inspired Scripture."[12] This means that for Athanasius, much of what has been interpreted by others as teaching the subordination of the Son to the Father must be seen as relating to his redemptive ministry while on earth.

Countering the concept of the eternal generation of the Son is the radical unity of the three members of the Trinity, so that all are involved in each of the divine works. Athanasius frequently speaks of the Father as accomplishing his works through the Son. He teaches this in many places. Note the following example:

> Such then being the Son, therefore when the Son works, the Father is the Worker, and the Son coming to the Saints, the Father is He who cometh in the Son, as He promised when He said, "I and My Father will come, and will make Our abode with him;" for in the Image is contemplated the Father, and in the Radiance is the Light. Therefore also, as we said just now, when the Father gives grace and peace, the Son also gives it, as Paul signifies in every Epistle, writing, "Grace to you and peace from God our Father and the Lord Jesus Christ."[13]

Having said this, however, we should note that there are a number of places, especially in *De Synodis*, where Athanasius refers to the subordination of the Son to the Father, but without the context making clear that this refers to the Incarnation and humiliation of the Son.

> But the Lord, not being made subordinate to any reason why He should be Word, save only that He is the Father's Offspring and Only-begotten Wisdom, when He becomes man, then assigns the reason why He is about to take flesh.[14]

---

12. Ibid., 3.26.29.
13. Ibid., 3.25.11.
14. Ibid., 2.20.54.

For we acknowledge, that though He be subordinate to His Father and God, yet, being before ages begotten of God, He is God perfect according to nature and true, and not first man and then God, but first God and then becoming man for us, and never having been deprived of being.[15]

Believing then in the All-perfect Triad, . . . and one exact harmony of dominion the Father alone being Head over the whole universe wholly, and over the Son Himself, and the Son subordinated to the Father.[16]

For we do not place the Son in the Father's Order, but as subordinate to the Father; for He did not descend upon Sodom without the Father's will, nor did He rain from Himself, but from the Lord, that is, the Father authorizing it.[17]

And no one is ignorant, that it is Catholic doctrine, that there are two Persons of Father and Son, and that the Father is greater, and the Son subordinated to the Father together with all things which the Father has subordinated to Him.[18]

It is significant that even with his doctrine of the eternal generation of the Son, Athanasius, like the creeds, does not dwell on the obedience or submission of the Son to the Father, and especially does not teach this as a matter of eternal subordination of Son to Father. It is likely the principle of the radical unity of the two in their working prevents that transition from being made. For Athanasius to be enlisted in support of the present-day doctrine of the eternal subordination of the Son requires: (1) the validity of the doctrine of eternal generation; and (2) the implication from this of the eternal subordination of the Son to the Father. While Athanasius taught the former, he evidently did not see it as leading to the latter.

---

15. Athananasius, *De Synodis, Councils of Arimium and Seleucia,* part 2, History of Arian Opinions, par. 26 (4).

16. Ibid., (7).

17. Ibid., par. 27 (18).

18. Ibid., par. 28.

It appears that elements of Athanasius's background appear in his thought, so that he speaks in unqualified fashion of the Son's subordination. At the same time, he clearly speaks of a double principle of interpretation. Whether he saw the full implications of his view and would have applied them to these statements is not completely clear, but the principle of the double account, if carried through thoroughly, might have resolved these apparently contradictory statements.

Hilary of Poitiers

One early theologian often cited by the eternal subordinationists is Hilary of Poitiers.[19] Kovach and Schemm quote several passages from him in support of eternal subordination:

> For God the Father is One, from Whom are all things; and our Lord Jesus Christ the Only-begotten, through Whom are all things, is One; and the Spirit, God's Gift to us, Who pervades all things, is also One. Thus all are ranged according to powers possessed and benefits conferred;—the One Power from Whom all, the One Offspring through Whom all, the One Gift Who gives us perfect hope.[20]

> Who, indeed, would deny that the Father is the greater; the Unbegotten greater than the Begotten, the Father than the Son, the Sender than the Sent, He that wills than He that obeys? He Himself shall be His own witness:—The Father is greater than I. It is a fact which we must recognize, but we must take heed lest with unskilled thinkers the majesty of the Father should obscure the glory of the Son.[21]

In support of their interpretation of Hilary as teaching that the Son, while of equal essence with the Father, is subordinated in function,

---

19. Hilary's exact dates are uncertain, but he appears to have been born about 300 and died in 367. Kovach and Schemm give his dates as 291–371, apparently confusing him with St. Hilarion of Palestine.

20. Hilary of Poitiers, *On the Trinity*, 2.1.

21. Ibid., 3.12.

Kovach and Schemm quote historian Philip Schaff, who comments on the latter passage: "This subordination is most plainly expressed by Hilary of Poictiers, the champion of the Nicene doctrine in the West."[22] And again, "In the same way Hilary derives all the attributes of the Son from the Father."[23]

When taken in their entirety, the writings of Hilary reveal a clear and consistent teaching. He makes much of the distinction between the unbegotten, and the only begotten. Of the Father he says, "It is the Father to Whom all existence owes its origin. In Christ and through Christ He is the source of all. In contrast to all else He is self-existent. He does not draw His being from without, but possesses it from Himself and in Himself."[24] Contrasted with this is his depiction of the only begotten Son:

> The Son draws His life from that Father Who truly has life; the Only begotten from the Unbegotten, Offspring from Parent, Living from Living. As the Father hath life in Himself, even so gave He to the Son also to have life in Himself. The Son is perfect from Him that is perfect, for He is whole from Him that is whole. This is no division or severance, for Each is in the Other, and the fullness of the Godhead is in the Son. Incomprehensible is begotten of Incomprehensible, for none else knows Them, but Each knows the Other; Invisible is begotten of Invisible, for the Son is the Image of the invisible God, and he that has seen the Son has seen the Father also. There is a distinction, for They are Father and Son; not that Their Divinity is different in kind, for Both are One, God of God, One God Only begotten of One God Unbegotten.[25]

---

22. Philip Schaff, *A History of the Christian Church,* vol. 3, *Nicene and Post-Nicene Christianity,* 5th ed., rev. (Grand Rapids: Eerdmans, 1910), 682; quoted in Kovach and Schemm, "A Defense of the Doctrine of the Eternal Subordination of the Son," 466.

23. Ibid., 466n. 1.

24. Hilary, *On the Trinity,* 2.6.

25. Ibid., 2.11.

It is clear that for Hilary the concept of divine generation or begetting plays an important role. He struggles to explain it: "It remains to say something more concerning the mysterious generation of the Son; or rather this something more is everything. I quiver, I linger, my powers fail, I know not where to begin. . . . Whom shall I entreat? Whom shall I call to my aid?"[26] As Kovach and Schemm pointed out, Hilary definitely sees a gradation or order between the Unbegotten and the Only begotten.

In his treatise, *On the Councils*, Hilary elaborates this incomprehensible concept of generation to include the idea of eternal subordination:

> For it is plain that only the Father knows how He begot the Son, and the Son how He was begotten of the Father. There is no question that the Father is greater. No one can doubt that the Father is greater than the Son in honor, dignity, splendor, majesty, and in the very name of Father, the Son Himself testifying, *He that sent Me is greater than I*. And no one is ignorant that it is Catholic doctrine that there are two Persons of Father and Son; and that the Father is greater, and that the Son is subordinated to the Father, together with all things which the Father has subordinated to Him, and that the Father has no beginning and is invisible, immortal and impassible, but that the Son has been begotten of the Father, God of God, Light of Light, and that the generation of this Son, as is aforesaid, no one knows but His Father.[27]

However, Hilary is definite that this subordination is not of essence. He says, "It is here insisted that the nature is indistinguishable and entirely similar. For since He is the Only-begotten Son of God and the image of the invisible God, it is necessary that He should be of an essence similar in species and nature."[28]

His entire doctrine is clearly and succinctly summed up in one statement:

---

26. Ibid., 2.12.
27. Hilary, *On the Councils, or the Faith of the Easterns*, 11.
28. Ibid., 2.15.

That the Son is not on a level with the Father and is not equal to Him is chiefly shewn in the fact that He was subjected to Him to render obedience, in that the Lord rained from the Lord and that the Father did not, as Photinus and Sabellius say, rain from Himself, as the Lord from the Lord; in that He then sat down at the right hand of God when it was told Him to seat Himself; in that He is sent, in that He receives, in that He submits in all things to the will of Him who sent Him. But the subordination of filial love is not a diminution of essence, nor does pious duty cause a degeneration of nature, since in spite of the fact that both the Unborn Father is God and the Only-begotten Son of God is God, God is nevertheless One, and the subjection and dignity of the Son are both taught in that by being called Son He is made subject to that name which because it implies that God is His Father is yet a name which denotes His nature. Having a name which belongs to Him whose Son He is, He is subject to the Father both in service and name; yet in such a way that the subordination of His name bears witness to the true character of His natural and exactly similar essence.[29]

We may summarize Hilary's view as follows:

1. The Father and the Son are of the very same essence.
2. The Father has begotten the Son. Although both have their life in themselves, the Father has given it to the Son to have this life in himself. This begetting or generation is, in the final analysis, incomprehensible.
3. The Father is superior to the Son, who acts in obedience to the Father's will. In that sense, they are not equal, and one could say that the Son is thus inferior to the Father. In many cases, the Scriptures Hilary cites are referring to the time of the Son's

29. Ibid., 17.51. Also quoted by Bruce Ware in "Equal in Essence, Distinct in Roles," 10. Ware incorrectly documents the quotation as "Hilary of Poitiers, *Treatise on the Trinity*, in Philip Schaff, *The Nicene and Post-Nicene Fathers Second Series Vol. IX.* Hilary of Poitiers, *John of Damascus*, 27 *St. John* v. 36, 37" (14n. 18).

ministry on earth. Hilary teaches, however, that the obedience was to the eternal commands of the Father.

4. The Son is subordinate to the Father, but this subordination is not one of essence. Although not using the term, Hilary in effect says that the Son's subordination is one of role.

Having stated this view, however, the question of its significance remains. Kovach and Schemm correctly cite Schaff in support of their view that Hilary holds to subordination. However, they omit two very important comments Schaff then goes on to make about this type of subordination:

> But these and similar passages [cited in support of this view of subordination] refer to the historical relation of the Father to the incarnate Logos in his estate of humiliation, or to the elevation of human nature to participation in the glory and power of the divine, not to the eternal metaphysical relation of the Father to the Son.
>
> In this point, as in the doctrine of the Holy Ghost, the Nicene system yet needed further development. The logical consistency of the doctrine of the consubstantiality of the Son, upon which the Nicene fathers laid chief stress, must in time overcome this decaying remnant of the ante-Nicene subordinationism.[30]

Schaff holds that Augustine extended the doctrine of the Trinity to correct this shortcoming.[31] It will remain to be seen if this assertion is valid.

The Second Period: From the Year 400 Through the Reformation

Augustine

Called the great theologian of the Trinity, Augustine has been claimed by both parties as supporting their view. Kevin Giles states that "Augustine gives no support whatsoever to the idea that Christ is

---

30. Schaff, *A History of the Christian Church*, 3:683.
31. Ibid., 684.

eternally set under the Father's authority."[32] He understands Augustine's writing in light of several principles: the equality of the Father and the Son and the fact that their work is one, the necessity of a "canonical" reading of Scripture, and the recognition that texts speaking of the subjection of the Son are referring to his temporal incarnation.[33] He also contends that Augustine is using analogical language in his discussion of terms like *Father* and *Son*, and that he did not believe they should be understood as carrying the same meaning as when used of humans.[34] Further, Augustine rejects the contention that the one sending is greater than the one sent, only that the one sent is "from" the sender.[35] While Giles acknowledges that this was written with respect to the assertions of the Arians, it appears that the principle on which it rests can be applied to others as well.

Others have drawn a different conclusion from Augustine's writings. Kovach and Schemm acknowledge that "there are differing views on whether the father of the Western Church, Augustine (354–430), reflects a belief in the eternal subordination of the Son."[36] They acknowledge Augustine's unity of the members of the Trinity but say, "Even though there is an emphasis on unity, that does not mean Augustine did not teach the eternal subordination of the Son."[37] They cite J. N. D. Kelly, William G. T. Shedd, Charles Hodge, and Philip Schaff in support of this contention but offer only two brief quotes from Augustine, both of which say that the Father is the origin of the Son or begat him.[38]

Ware criticizes Giles for omitting a part of a quotation Ware has taken from Augustine, in which Augustine says of the coming of the Son,

---

32. Kevin Giles, *Jesus and the Father: Modern Evangelicals Reinvent the Doctrine of the Trinity* (Grand Rapids: Zondervan, 2006), 190.

33. Ibid.

34. Ibid., 191.

35. Ibid., 190–91.

36. Kovach and Schemm, "A Defense of the Doctrine of the Eternal Subordination of the Son," 468.

37. Ibid.

38. Ibid., 469.

And according to this manner we can now understand that the
Son is not only said to have been sent because "the Word was
made flesh," but therefore sent that the Word might be made
flesh, and that He might perform through His bodily presence
those things which were written; that is, that not only is He
understood to have been sent as man, which the Word was
made but the Word, too, was sent that it might be made man;
because He was not sent in respect to any inequality of power, or
substance, or anything that in Him was not equal to the Father;
but in respect to this, that the Son is from the Father, not the
Father from the Son.[39]

Ware feels that this omitted passage gives crucial support to eternal
subordination. Although he does not make his argument explicit, it
appears that he believes that Augustine is saying that the Father-Son
distinction made it necessary for the Son to be the one sent, and that
indicates a superiority of authority of the Father over the Son. It is
interesting to note that Ware omits a few words from the end of the last
sentence: "for the Son is the Word of the Father." The significance of
these additional words will become clear later.

Augustine himself lays down a very important interpretive principle for dealing with the apparently contradictory elements regarding
the Son:

Wherefore, having mastered this rule for interpreting the
Scriptures concerning the Son of God, that we are to distinguish
in them what relates to the form of God, in which He is equal
to the Father, and what to the form of a servant which He took,
in which He is less than the Father; we shall not be disquieted
by apparently contrary and mutually repugnant sayings of the
sacred books. For both the Son and the Holy Spirit, according
to the form of God, are equal to the Father, because neither of
them is a creature, as we have already shown: but according to

39. Augustine, *On the Trinity*, 4.20.27.

the form of a servant He is less than the Father, because He Himself has said, "My Father is greater than I;" and He is less than Himself, because it is said of Him, "He emptied Himself;" and He is less than the Holy Spirit, because He Himself says, "Whosoever speaketh a word against the Son of man, it shall be forgiven him; but whosoever speaketh against the Holy Ghost, it shall not be forgiven him." . . . According to the form of God, all things were made by Him; according to the form of a servant, He was Himself made of a woman, made under the law. According to the form of God, He and the Father are one; according to the form of a servant, He came not to do His own will, but the will of Him that sent Him. According to the form of God, "As the Father hath life in Himself, so hath He given to the Son to have life in Himself;" according to the form of a servant, His "soul is sorrowful even unto death;" and, "O my Father," He says, "if it be possible, let this cup pass from me." According to the form of God, "He is the True God, and eternal life;" according to the form of a servant, "He became obedient unto death, even the death of the cross."

According to the form of God, all things that the Father hath are His, and "All mine," He says, "are Thine, and Thine are mine;" according to the form of a servant, the doctrine is not His own, but His that sent Him.[40]

Augustine also directly inquires in what sense the Son is equal to and in what sense less than the Father, and, interestingly, also less than himself. He warns against misunderstanding: "Men have erred through a want of careful examination or consideration of the whole tenor of the Scriptures, and have endeavored to transfer those things which are said of Jesus Christ according to the flesh, to that substance of His which was eternal before the incarnation, and is eternal."[41] This means that the same must be said of the Son's own relationship to himself.

---

40. Ibid., 1.11.22–23.
41. Ibid., 1.7.14.

But the truth shows that after the same sense the Son is less also than Himself; for how was He not made less also than Himself, who "emptied Himself, and took upon Him the form of a servant?" For He did not so take the form of a servant as that He should lose the form of God, in which He was equal to the Father. If, then, the form of a servant was so taken that the form of God was not lost, since both in the form of a servant and in the form of God He Himself is the same only-begotten Son of God the Father, in the form of God equal to the Father, in the form of a servant the mediator between God and men, the man Christ Jesus; is there any one who cannot perceive that He Himself in the form of God is also greater than Himself, but yet likewise in the form of a servant less than Himself? And not, therefore, without cause the Scripture says both the one and the other, both that the Son is equal to the Father, and that the Father is greater than the Son. For there is no confusion when the former is understood as on account of the form of God, and the latter as on account of the form of a servant.[42]

Augustine finds Paul enunciating this principle quite clearly in Philippians 2. He concludes: "The Son of God, then, is equal to God the Father in nature, but less in 'fashion.' For in the form of a servant which He took He is less than the Father; but in the form of God, in which also He was before He took the form of a servant, He is equal to the Father."[43]

The other important principle that Augustine uses in interpreting passages such as those that speak of the Father sending the Son is that the actions of the members of the Trinity are not those of individual members alone but of all of the members collectively. We have noted this principle in the chapter on biblical teaching. Thus, he points out that Paul says both that the Father delivered up the Son for humans and that the Son delivered himself as well.[44] He then goes on to elaborate:

---

42. Ibid.
43. Ibid.
44. Ibid., 2.5.9.

He will reply, I suppose, if he has a right sense in these things, Because the will of the Father and the Son is one, and their working indivisible. In like manner, then, let him understand the incarnation and nativity of the Virgin, wherein the Son is understood as sent, to have been wrought by one and the same operation of the Father and of the Son indivisibly; the Holy Spirit certainly not being thence excluded, of whom it is expressly said, "She was found with child by the Holy Ghost." For perhaps our meaning will be more plainly unfolded, if we ask in what manner God sent His Son. He commanded that He should come, and He, complying with the commandment, came. Did He then request, or did He only suggest? But whichever of these it was, certainly it was done by a word, and the Word of God is the Son of God Himself. Wherefore, since the Father sent Him by a word, His being sent was the work of both the Father and His Word; therefore the same Son was sent by the Father and the Son, because the Son Himself is the Word of the Father that wisdom must needs appear in the flesh.[45]

This form of interpretation appears to reject the type of argumentation made by Grudem that the statements about the Father sending the Son indicate a subordination of the Son to the Father. It also undercuts Ware's claim that the fact that the Son was sent was because he was Son indicates a superiority of the Father over the Son, so that the Son was obeying a command of the Father, which presumably was by the Father's sole prerogative.

We may therefore summarize Augustine's view as follows:

1. The Son is from the Father, an apparent reference to the idea of eternal generation of the Son by the Father.
2. All works attributed to any one member of the Trinity are to be interpreted as actually being the work of all of them.
3. Statements about the Son's obedience or submission to the

---

45. Ibid.

Father are to be understood as referring to the Son's incarnate state and are not to be read back into the eternity preceding His coming.

4. Consequently, while it is said that the Father sent the Son because they are referred to respectively as the Father and the Son, it can as well be said that the Son also sent himself.

5. There is therefore no evidence of an eternal functional subordination of the Son to the Father, whereby the Son must always do the Father's will.

Thomas Aquinas

Relatively little is made of Thomas's writing by either side. Kovach and Schemm make no mention of him, nor does Ware. Giles lists him among his "omissions," explaining that evangelicals do not usually consider him "an authoritative voice from the past."[46] This is unfortunate, both because of the status of Thomas within Catholic theology and because of the directness and succinctness with which he writes on this subject.

Thomas's most direct treatment of the topic is in his "Treatise on the Incarnation" in his *Summa Theologica*, question 20, "Of Christ's Subjection to the Father." Citing Augustine with approval, Thomas says, "Now the less is subject to the greater. Therefore in the form of a servant Christ is subject to the Father."[47] He adds,

> As we are not to understand that Christ is a creature simply, but only in His human nature, whether this qualification be added or not, as stated above (Q (16), A(8)), so also we are to understand that Christ is subject to the Father not simply but in His human nature, even if this qualification be not added; and yet it is better to add this qualification in order to avoid the error of Arius, who held the Son to be less than the Father.[48]

---

46. Giles, *Jesus and the Father*, 90.

47. Thomas Aquinas, *Summa Theologica*, Book V, Question 20, P(3)-Q(20)-A(1).

48. Ibid., P(3)-Q(20)-A(1)-RO(1).

This subjection of the human nature to the divine means that there is even a sense in which Christ can be said to be subject to himself. After a rather extensive discussion of person or hypostasis and nature, Thomas concludes,

> Secondly, it may be understood of the diversity of natures in the one person or hypostasis. And thus we may say that in one of them, in which He agrees with the Father, He presides and rules together with the Father; and in the other nature, in which He agrees with us, He is subject and serves, and in this sense Augustine says that "the Son is less than Himself."[49]

In light of this similarity to the thought of Augustine, Thomas Aquinas also cannot be claimed in support of eternal subordination.

Martin Luther

Luther never really discusses the doctrine of the Trinity in any extended or systematic fashion. What we know of his view on the Trinity must be distilled from comments found in his sermons and elsewhere. In these he emphasizes that the doctrine is a matter of faith, not fully understood by human reason. Luther's messages reflect the conception of the Son as begotten by the Father. In a sermon on the Sunday after Christmas, he apparently subscribes to the procession of the Spirit from the Son as well as from the Father and gives some meaning to that: "For not only does the Spirit dwell in Christ as he does in men, but he also is Christ's, deriving his divine substance from him just as he does from the Father."[50]

In a sermon on Trinity Sunday, from Romans 11:33–36, he said of the first and second persons, "Here there are, therefore, two distinct persons, one of whom becomes reconciled, and the other is sent to reconcile and becomes man. The former is called the Father, being first in that he did not have his origin in any other; the latter is called

---

49. Ibid., P(3)-Q(20)-A(2).
50. Martin Luther, *Sermons*, vol. 6, "Sunday After Christmas," par. 90.

the Son, being born of the Father from eternity."[51] He does speak of the Son's submission to the Father's will, but he is here speaking of the Son's incarnation: "Christ Jesus, who for this purpose became man, and became like unto us, in order that he might help us out of the mire into which we are fallen. He loved God with all his heart and his neighbor as himself, and submitted his will to the will of his Father, fulfilled the law in every respect; this I could not do and yet I was required to do it."[52] Similarly, he says, "They will be helped to steadfastness and submission in suffering by perceiving that for their sakes Christ has submitted to far greater suffering, and has taken upon himself the infinitely heavier burden of their sins in the effort to redeem them."[53]

While all things are the work of the entire Godhead, yet each person has his own distinctive work: "The Scriptures teach us that all creation is the work of one God, or the whole Godhead; and yet, inasmuch as they make a distinction between the three persons of the one Godhead, we may properly say that everything had its origin, everything exists and continues, in the Father as the first person; through the Son, who is of the Father; and in the Holy Spirit, who proceeds from both the Father and the Son; which three, nevertheless, are comprehended in the one undivided essence."[54]

This division of labor, as it were, can be seen with respect to the spiritual gifts in 1 Corinthians 12:1–11: "He assigns to each the particular operation whereby he manifests himself. One is God the Father, and from him as the origin and first person emanates all power. Another is the Lord, Christ the Son of God, who as the head of the Church appoints all offices. The third is the Spirit, who produces and dispenses all gifts in the Church."[55]

---

51. Ibid., vol. 8, "Trinity Sunday," par. 11.
52. Ibid., vol. 5, "Eighteenth Sunday After Trinity," par. 30.
53. Ibid., vol. 6, "Second Sunday in Advent," par. 38.
54. Ibid., vol. 8, "Trinity Sunday," par. 41. See also another sermon on the same text, "The Doctrine of the Trinity," par. 23.
55. Ibid., vol. 8. "Tenth Sunday After Pentecost: Spiritual Counsel for Church Officers," par. 30.

John Calvin

Again, most of the commentators, especially the gradationists, do little with Calvin's thought. In his discussion of the Trinity in his *Institutes*, it is apparent that he follows Augustine rather closely. He does speak of the distinctions between the three persons of the Trinity: "To the Father is attributed the beginning of activity, and the fountain and wellspring of all things; to the Son, wisdom, counsel, and the ordered disposition of all things; but to the Spirit is assigned the power and efficacy of that activity."[56] There is a mutual dependence of each person on each of the others: "God could never exist apart from his wisdom and power."[57] There is a type of order, but this is only a logical or psychological order, and he suggests no subordination in connection with it: "Nevertheless the observance of an order is not meaningless or superfluous, when the Father is thought of as first, then from him the Son, and finally from both the Spirit. For the mind of each human being is naturally inclined to contemplate God first, then the wisdom coming forth from him, and lastly the power whereby he executes the decrees of his plan. For this reason, the Son is said to come forth from the Father alone; the Spirit, from the Father and the Son at the same time."[58]

Although "to each belongs his own peculiar quality," this must be understood in light of the fact that "the Father is wholly in the Son, the Son wholly in the Father."[59] By following Augustine's lead, we are able to reconcile what sometimes seem to be conflicting views among the ancients: "Therefore, when we speak simply of the Son without regard to the Father, we well and properly declare him to be of himself; and for this reason we call him the sole beginning. But when we mark the relation that he has with the Father, we rightly make the Father the beginning of the Son."[60]

Calvin showed little interest in the doctrine of eternal generation and did not discuss it. The one comment he makes leads the reader to

---

56. Calvin, *Institutes of the Christian Religion*, 1.13.18.
57. Ibid.
58. Ibid.
59. Ibid., 1.13.19.
60. Ibid.

believe that he did not personally espouse the doctrine or consider it to make any sense: "I felt that I would be better advised not to touch upon many things that would profit but little, and would burden my readers with useless trouble. For what is the point in disputing whether the Father always begets? Indeed, it is foolish to imagine a continuous act of begetting, since it is clear that three persons have subsisted in God from eternity."[61]

Some of Calvin's statements are ambiguous in themselves. The content of what he is saying often can be found by consulting his commentaries, where the most revealing ideas appear. Note, for example, his comment on 1 Corinthians 11:3: "God, then, occupies the first place: Christ holds the second place. How so? Inasmuch as he has in our flesh made himself subject to the Father, for, apart from this, being of one essence with the Father, he is his equal. Let us, therefore, bear it in mind, that this is spoken of Christ as mediator. He is, I say, inferior to the Father, inasmuch as he assumed our nature, that he might be the first-born among many brethren."[62] While Calvin accepts the idea that "head" here means "authority over," it is evident that he regards the Father's headship over Christ as resulting from, and therefore restricted to, Christ's role as the God-man.

When Calvin treats the kenosis passage in Philippians 2, it is also evident that in his judgment the obedience the Son offered to the Father was not merely a continuation of a previously existing relationship but began as part of the Incarnation: "Even this was great humility—that from being Lord he became a servant; but he says that he went further than this, because, while he was not only immortal, but the Lord of life and death, he nevertheless became obedient to his Father, even so far as to endure death."[63]

Another significant passage is the Hebrews 5 passage. Here Calvin follows the most direct meaning of the text in treating the obedience

---

61. Ibid., 1.13.29.

62. John Calvin, *Commentary on the Epistles of Paul the Apostle to the Corinthians* (Grand Rapids: Eerdmans, 1948), 1:353.

63. John Calvin, *Commentary on the Epistles of Paul the Apostle to the Philippians, Colossians, and Thessalonians* (Grand Rapids: Eerdmans, 1948), 182.

reference of verse 8: "The proximate end of Christ's sufferings was thus to habituate himself to obedience; not that he was driven to this by force, or that he had need of being thus exercised, as the case is with oxen or horses when their ferocity is to be tamed, for he was abundantly willing to render to his Father the obedience which he owed. But this was done from a regard to our benefit, that he might exhibit to us an instance and an example of subjection even to death itself."[64]

One final textual comment is especially instructive. As we noted in the chapter on biblical material, one of the strongest passages in support of the gradationist view is 1 Corinthians 15:24–28. Calvin's handling of this passage virtually has become the standard Reformed interpretation. Of the delivering up of dominion, mentioned in verse 24, he declares, "When he says, God and the Father, this may be taken in two senses— either that God the Father is called the God and Father of Christ, or that the name of Father is added by way of explanation. The conjunction et (and) will in the latter case mean namely. As to the former signification, there is nothing either absurd, or unusual, in the saying, that Christ is inferior to God, in respect of his human nature."[65]

The crucial reference to Christ becoming subjected to the Father is handled by Calvin as follows:

> But the reason why the Scripture testifies, that Christ now holds dominion over the heaven and the earth in the room of the Father is—that we may not think that there is any other governor, lord, protector, or judge of the dead and living, but may fix our contemplation on him alone. We acknowledge, it is true, God as the ruler, but it is in the face of the man Christ. But Christ will then restore the kingdom which he has received, that we may cleave wholly to God. Nor will he in this way resign the kingdom, but will transfer it in a manner from his humanity to his glorious divinity, because a way of approach will then be opened up, from

---

64. John Calvin, *Commentary on the Epistle to the Hebrews* (Grand Rapids: Eerdmans, 1949), 123.

65. Calvin, *Commentary on the Epistles of Paul the Apostle to the Corinthians*, 2:26.

which our infirmity now keeps us back. Thus then Christ will be *subjected to the Father*, because the vail being then removed, we shall openly behold God reigning in his majesty, and Christ's humanity will then no longer be interposed to keep us back from a closer view of God.[66]

Calvin also discussed this passage in his *Institutes*, and dealt thereby with the question of the Father's headship relative to the Son: "Then he returns the lordship to his Father so that—far from diminishing his own majesty—it may shine all the more brightly. Then, also, God shall cease to be the Head of Christ, for Christ's own deity will shine of itself, although as yet it is covered by a veil."[67]

The close connection Calvin sees between the persons of the Trinity and the fact that all participate in each act means that this text is to be understood as teaching that Christ will transfer the kingdom from his humanity to his deity.

It appears from Calvin's comments on these several crucial passages that his view of the Son's obedience to the Father is to be understood as a function of, and limited to, the time of his earthly ministry as the Incarnate One.

Conclusions

From this brief historical survey, several observations seem justified:

1. In the earliest period, prior to the ecumenical councils, a variety of conceptions of the status of Christ existed. Under the influence especially of Origen, the conception of him as begotten or generated by the Father developed.

2. Some subsequent theologians took this generation in a more literal fashion, as having taken place at some point of the Son's origin. These tended toward the idea that the Son was in some sense metaphysically inferior to the Father.

---

66. Ibid., 32–33.
67. Calvin, *Institutes*, 2.14.3.

3. Others spoke of the begetting as eternal in nature, emphasizing that the Son was fully equal with the Father and of the very same metaphysical essence as the Father.

4. The creeds of the church, including those arising from the ecumenical councils, quite uniformly reflect the idea of the eternal begetting of the Son by the Father, taking *monogenēs* to mean "only begotten" and applying this not to the birth of Jesus of Nazareth but to an eternal process. Insofar as the concept of "order" or *taxis* is discussed, it is generally taken in a formal sense as referring to a logical or organizational principle with no implication of greater or lesser status.

5. There was a difference of emphasis between the Eastern church, where subordination was taught, and the Western church, which more closely identified the acts of members of the Trinity as the acts of all three members together. So Harnack says, speaking of the dispute over the procession of the Spirit, "The doctrine of the procession of the Holy Spirit from the Father alone thus clearly shows that in the East the mutual indwelling of the Hypostases was not thought of as complete, and that the Father was regarded as greater than the Son. The spiritual representation of the Trinity was of a different kind in the East and the West, respectively, especially from the time of Augustine onwards."[68]

6. With Augustine a transition takes place. His position tended to be the dominant one through the Middle Ages and even through the Reformation. Great emphasis is placed on the unity of the three persons, in the sense that every act of any of them is the mutual act of all three persons of the Trinity, although they may have differing parts in that action and one may be particularly prominent in a given act.

The concept of eternal generation is generally held but is not emphasized; and in the case of some, such as Calvin, it is

---

68. Adolf Harnack, *History of Dogma* (New York: Dover, 1961), 4:127.

minimized or even rejected. Harnack describes Augustine's development of this Western emphasis: "In the West, Augustine, following an ancient Western tendency, destroyed the last remains of subordinationism, though just because of this he advanced in the direction of Modalism. According to him in constructing the doctrine of God we should not start from the person of the Father. On the contrary the conception of the Godhead ought from the very first to be personal and Trinitarian, so that the Father is regarded as being conditioned in His existence by the Son in the same way as the Son is by the Father."[69]

7. Throughout the period surveyed, there is little or no emphasis on the obedience of the Son to the Father, except for the period of the Son's earthly ministry. Where eternal subordination of authority is held, it is generally combined with a metaphysical subordination, as in the case of Arians and Semi-Arians.

8. It is difficult to contend that throughout its history the church has taught the eternal functional subordination of the Son (and the Spirit) to the Father. In order to make this assertion, certain additional assumptions must be made and argued, namely, that the Father-Son relationship bears a rather literal parallel to human father-son relationships, that their relationship during the Incarnation is a reflection of an eternal relationship, that generation involves a superiority status of the one generating over the one generated, or that the order or *taxis* is to be taken as a gradation of status among the persons.

There are no hard conclusions to be drawn from this historical survey, for neither position finds unequivocal support for its position. However, if one believes that the church made progress in its ongoing reflection on this matter, then it would seem that the view of equal authority has an advantage over that of gradational authority. While

---

69. Ibid., 129.

one might say that it is a choice of whether one follows the Eastern or the Western tradition, it is worth noting that in recent years the differences between the two traditions have become less.[70]

---

70. See "Agreed Statement on the Holy Trinity," Orthodox-Reformed dialogue, Kappel-am-Albis, Switzerland, March 1992. http://warc.jalb.de/warcajsp/news_file/15.pdf.

CHAPTER 6

The Philosophical Issues

I n the process of examining and comparing the two views under consideration, we have noted certain issues that were not merely biblical issues, and thus could not be settled simply by additional biblical inquiry. Rather, these were primarily philosophical in nature. They either contained concepts of a philosophical type (e.g., essence/function or identity/distinction) or arguments involving issues of logic. While these, particularly the former, also may be termed theological, they are not peculiar to theological discussion but are of a type found in other intellectual discourse. They therefore are susceptible to scrutiny and assessment by more general methods.

Our objective in this chapter will be to attempt to identify, analyze, and evaluate these philosophical issues. While the classification is not completely mutually exhaustive of the issues, nor are the two classes completely exclusive of one another, we can roughly classify them as metaphysical issues and logical issues.

Metaphysical Issues

At the heart of the disagreements between the two positions are certain basic ideas pertaining to the nature of God, humanity, or even reality in general. If these can be satisfactorily resolved, it may take us a long way toward reaching a conclusion on the debate.

Essence and Function

On a number of points, both parties are in agreement with each other. Both agree that God the Father, the Son, and the Holy Spirit are equally God and that they are divine in the same sense. Both vigorously oppose any type of Arian or Semi-Arian view of the deity of Christ. Thus, metaphysically, or in terms of their essence or being, or what they are, the three persons are fully equal. None is superior or inferior to either of the others.

Further, despite this belief in the metaphysical equality of the persons, both parties agree that there is some sense in which the members of the Trinity are functionally different. Each of the persons has a role in the economy of the Godhead, in which he primarily performs a function that is not in quite the same sense attributed to the other persons. For example, each holds that the Son, rather than the Father or the Spirit, atoned by dying on the cross. Both parties also agree that at least for a time, the Son and the Spirit were subordinate to the Father, or, in other words, that they obeyed the Father's commands or fulfilled the Father's desires. They agree that this subordination of one person to another does not contradict their essential equality.

Beyond this, however, there is a considerable difference between the two. The equivalentists hold that the subordination involved is only temporary, being (in the case of the Son) for the purpose of the Son's redemptive ministry while incarnate as the God-man. It was something that resulted from the Son's voluntary decision to take this lesser status relative to the Father. It began at a definite time and has ended or will end at some point. The gradationists, on the other hand, insist that this subordination is eternal. The Father has always been the supreme person of the Trinity, having superior authority over the Son and the Spirit. While using some different terms (*being, essence,* or *nature*) for the equality of the three, these theologians would insist that although permanent, the superiority and subordination are functional and do not preclude this equality of being. It is therefore our purpose here to ask about the nature of such distinctions.

Let us first review the fact that the gradationists indeed insist that this functional subordination is permanent and even intrinsic to the Trinity. Ware, for example, says, "This hierarchical structure of authority exists in the eternal Godhead even though it is also eternally true that each Person is fully equal to each other in their commonly possessed essence."[1] He describes it as a structure that "marks the very nature" of God.[2] Similarly, Grudem says that commanding is "appropriate to the position of the Father, after whom all human fatherhood is patterned (Eph. 3:14–15)" and obeying is "appropriate to the role of the Son,"[3] and he adds that "for all eternity the Father has been the Father, the Son has been the Son, and the Holy Spirit has been the Holy Spirit. These relationships are eternal, not something that occurred only in time." He also says that "the different functions that we see the Father, Son, and Holy Spirit performing are simply outworkings of an eternal relationship between the three persons, one that has always existed and will exist for eternity."[4] Further, "These distinctions are essential to the very nature of God himself, and they could not be otherwise."[5] These statements seem to make clear that this structure of authority and obedience is inherent in or intrinsic to the Trinity.

One way of characterizing these two different views is to say that on the gradational view, the Son is necessarily subordinate to the Father. He could not be otherwise. Under any and all circumstances (or as it is sometimes put in philosophical discussions, "in all possible worlds"), the Father has authority over the Son and the Son is subordinate to the Father. On the equivalence view, on the other hand, the Son is only contingently subordinate. His subordination is contingent upon a certain state of affairs, such as his being incarnate, or being in the state of humiliation. If those conditions do not pertain, then he is not subordinate but is equal in authority with the Father.

Another way of referring to the different views is in terms of the status of the attributes, or qualities, or properties involved. On the equivalence model, the quality of being subordinate is an accidental quality. It does not change what the Son is. He would be the Son, and

---

1. Bruce A. Ware, *Father, Son, and Holy Spirit: Relationships, Roles, and Relevance* (Wheaton, IL: Crossway, 2005), 21.

2. Ibid.

3. Wayne Grudem, *Systematic Theology: An Introduction to Biblical Doctrine* (Grand Rapids: Zondervan, 1994), 250.

4. Ibid.

5. Ibid., 251.

the Father would be the Father, even if this attribute were not present. While it modifies the possessor of the property, it does not change the nature of the possessor in any essential way. On the other hand, to the gradationist, authority and subordination are essential properties. If they were not possessed, the Father would not be the Father and the Son would not be the Son, and this is exactly what Ware and Grudem (especially the latter) mean when they say that if this structure were not present, the Trinity would cease to exist, or would not be the Trinity.

The problem is this. If authority over the Son is an essential, not an accidental, attribute of the Father, and subordination to the Father is an essential, not an accidental, attribute of the Son, then something significant follows. Authority is part of the Father's essence, and subordination is part of the Son's essence, and each attribute is not part of the essence of the other person. That means that the essence of the Son is different from the essence of the Father. The Father's essence includes omnipresence, omniscience, love, etc., and authority over the Son. The Son's essence includes omnipresence, omniscience, love, etc., and submission to the Father. But that is equivalent to saying that they are not *homoousious* with one another. Here is surely a problem for the gradationists, for they want to affirm the *homoousious*, in order to reject Arianism. On face value, therefore, there seems to be an internal contradiction in this doctrine.

This is not a charge that the gradationists are Arians. However, the way the gradationists have stated their doctrine implies a view of the nature of God that seems to entail some sort of Arian or Semi-Arian position.

Part of the confusion results from the lack of specificity in the terminology being used by the gradationists. The terms they use, *being*, *essence*, and the like, are quite common. However, in the history of philosophy, they have been used with a variety of meanings. What these theologians seem to intend by this terminology is simply "what something is" versus "what something does." They appear to be using it in some sort of commonsense or probably basically Aristotelian fashion. Perhaps they have in mind some quite specific variety that avoids the problem we have described here. If so, they need to elaborate what they have in mind. In fact, even if this problem were not present, it would be good to have a more complete explication of the concept involved. Until that is given, however, this problem appears to be unresolved.

In a debate at Trinity Evangelical Divinity School, Ware sought to resolve the difficulty by distinguishing properties of the person from properties of the divine essence: "We affirm that some properties that are distinct to each Person are essential to their personal identities, and we also affirm, without conflict or contradiction, that all properties of the divine essence are possessed fully and eternally by each of the three divine Persons without exception and without qualification."[6] This, however, does not seem to avoid the problem, because if these are necessary properties of the persons, then the persons have different essences.

One possible refuge from the difficulty for the gradationists would be a functionalist philosophy.[7] This places limitations on metaphysical inquiry, suggesting that we can describe only what something does but not press the more ultimate question of what that something really is, or its real nature.[8] This would say that we cannot really ask metaphysical questions, such as what kind of being is possessed by a person who did

---

6. The debate on the topic, "Do relations of authority and submission exist eternally among the Persons of the Godhead?" took place at Trinity Evangelical Divinity School, October 9, 2008. Wayne Grudem and Bruce Ware argued the affirmative and Tom McCall of Trinity Evangelical Divinity School and Keith Yandell of the department of philosophy of the University of Wisconsin, Madison, argued the negative. This debate will hereafter be referred to simply as "the TEDS debate." The debate can be accessed at http://www.henrycenter.org/media.php?link=all.

7. I see in Ware's discussion of the image of God a possible indication of the influence of functional philosophy. He notes the three major views (the structural, the relational, and the functional) and opts for a view that seems to combine the relational and the functional: "The image of God has to do primarily with how we are to live our lives as God's representatives, carrying out his will and 'ruling' on his behalf" (*Father, Son, and Holy Spirit*, 132–33).

8. For a brief but helpful summary of the implications for pragmatism's functional approach to truth, especially as it relates to questions of metaphysics, see Walter G. Muelder and Laurence Sears, "Introduction: Pragmatism and Critical Empiricism," in *The Development of American Philosophy*, ed. Walter G. Muelder and Laurence Sears (Boston: Houghton Mifflin Co., 1940), 311–16.

the types of things Jesus did while on this earth. We can only observe what he does; the more ontological question cannot legitimately be asked, or at least, if asked, cannot be satisfactorily answered. It might be accompanied by the tactic employed by the functional Christologists of a generation ago, who said that the basic biblical mentality was the Hebraic, not the Greek, mind and that the Hebrew mentality did not ask those questions of ultimate ontological identity. In other words, the New Testament writers did not ask whether Jesus was *homoousios* with the Father; they simply described him doing the works of God. Questions of nature and the like arose in a later period, in which a much more speculatively oriented type of thinking had supplanted the pure biblical mentality.

However, there are problems with such an approach. For one thing, this dichotomy of Hebrew and Greek thinking has come under serious criticism since the heyday of the biblical theology movement, most notably by James Barr,[9] but also by others, including Brevard Childs,[10] Reginald Fuller,[11] and Martin Hengel.[12] It seems to have been an imposition of an extraneous philosophy on the biblical materials, no less than is alleged to have been done by the Greek metaphysics.

A more serious problem is the tenability of such a functional philosophy. Must we not pose the question of what such function presupposes? I have characterized the functional Christology as "Cheshire Cat Christology," likening it to Lewis Carroll's Cheshire cat in *Alice in Wonderland*. The Cheshire cat sat in a tree with a grin on its face. Gradually, the cat faded away, leaving only a grin without a face to bear it. Like Alice, I find the idea of a grin without a face to be "quite curious," and the same would be true of a being who performs the works of God and

9. James Barr, *The Semantics of Biblical Language* (London: Oxford University Press, 1961).

10. Brevard Childs, *Biblical Theology in Crisis* (Philadelphia: Westminster, 1970).

11. Reginald Fuller, *The Foundations of New Testament Christology* (New York: Scribner's, 1965).

12. Martin Hengel, *Judaism and Hellenism: Studies in Their Encounter in Palestine During the Early Hellenistic Period*, 2 vols. (Philadelphia: Fortress, 1974).

makes the claims that he did about his relationship with the Father, unless that person is of such a "nature" as to be the same as God. The problem here is that in reverse. If we are dealing with a person, the Son, who is eternally and necessarily subordinate to the Father, don't we have to ask whether the nature (or "essence," "being," or "substance") of the Son is not somehow different and lesser than that of the Father?

There is yet another problem for the gradationists if they seek refuge in a functionalist philosophy. They want to maintain an ontological understanding of the three persons of the Trinity. They want to insist that the Son is fully divine, possessing all the attributes of deity, just as the Father. In other words, their very ontology seems inconsistent with a functionalism. If they use it to avoid the implications of this denial of difference of natures, they may thereby also lose the logical right to claim an ontological Trinity at all.

But what of the equivalentists? Is their view any better off? Here we should note again that these theologians hold to the metaphysical equality of the Father, Son, and Holy Spirit. All are God in the same way, and all are equally God. There is no difference of substance, essence, or being. They also insist that the three persons are eternally equal in authority. They claim, however, that the Son and the Spirit each became voluntarily and temporarily functionally subordinate to the Father (and the Spirit to the Son, as well). This was done for the purpose of carrying out a particular task. When that task is completed, full equality of authority will be reassumed.

Here we should note that the subordination to the Father is not necessary but contingent. If the Son is in the state of humiliation, incarnate and carrying out the redemptive task, then he is subordinate in authority to the Father; but if the former is not the case, then the latter is not, either. In other words, subordination is contingent upon or dependent upon being in the state of humiliation. This might be depicted somewhat as follows:

If DS (deity simpliciter), then EA (equal in authoritiy)
If DH (deity and humanity), then SA (subordinate in authority)

Now it might be argued that since DH is different from DS and since the Father is only and always DS, then the Son and the Father are of a different nature or essence, and the *homoousios* is also denied. Note, however, that both the Father and the Son are necessarily D. They cannot be otherwise. The Incarnation, which involves adding H to D, is contingent, so that the Son is only accidentally, not essentially, DH. The difference between him in the incarnate state and the Father is an accidental difference, not an essential one, so they are not of a different essence or nature. The Son is necessarily D but only contingently DS. Whether the Father is both necessarily D and necessarily DS is an issue that could be debated but need not really concern us here.

We also should note that although we cannot argue from human experience to the nature of the relationships within the Trinity, there is nothing in the concept of relative ranking of persons that precludes someone voluntarily and temporarily becoming subject to another of equal or even lesser rank, and this is illustrated in human relations. Numerous examples could be found in business, of one person serving as the lead person among a group of equals, perhaps by the choice of all involved.

In my own experience, I recall such an event. As a young second-year, untenured assistant professor, my family and I attended a faculty-staff summer family camp of the educational institution where I taught. One evening the recreational program consisted of a treasure hunt. There were four competing teams, and I was designated as captain of one of them. On my team was the dean of the college, a humble and unpretentious man. He came to me and asked where he should go and search for the next clue. I directed him to go up to the stables. It was my one moment of power, in which I gave orders to my superior (several steps my superior, I might add), and he obeyed them. However, on Monday morning, when we returned to the campus, he returned to his spacious administrative office and the prerogatives that went with it, and I returned to my little cubbyhole of a faculty office, with no authority. So, similarly, the temporary assumption of a subordinate or even inferior role by the Son, in which he became subject to the Father's authority, need have no permanent effect on their relative authority.

Our conclusion here is that the gradational view, at least as stated to the present, contains a rather serious problem of apparent contradiction of the *homoousios*, while the equivalence view does not appear to entail a similarly serious difficulty. It may be that the gradational view can be explained, restated, or modified in such a way as to obviate the difficulty noted, but to date that has not been done.

The Basis of Identity

We have noted in chapter 1 that Wayne Grudem was concerned about how to distinguish the three persons of the Trinity from one another, as Father, Son, and Holy Spirit. It cannot, he says, be on the basis of a difference of being, since each fully possesses the entire being, and thus the being of each is identical with the other. Further, it cannot be on the basis of a difference of attributes, since each has all the attributes of deity. It must, then, be a unique relationship between each of them, which in turn results in each having different roles from the other two. The alternative creates a serious problem: "But if there are no differences among them eternally, *then how does one person differ from the other?* They would no longer be Father, Son, and Holy Spirit, but rather Person A, Person A, and Person A, each identical to the other not only in being but also in role and in the way they relate to one another."[13]

Grudem finds this situation very troubling. "This would mean that the Trinity has not eternally existed."[14] Again he makes this point even more emphatically: "If we did not have such differences in authority in the relationships among the members of the Trinity, then we would not know of any differences at all, and it would be unclear whether there *are* any differences among the persons of the Trinity."[15] Similarly, he

---

13. Wayne Grudem, *Evangelical Feminism and Biblical Truth: An Analysis of More Than One Hundred Disputed Questions* (Sisters, OR: Multnomah, 2004), 433.

14. Grudem, *Systematic Theology*, 251.

15. Grudem, *Evangelical Feminism and Biblical Truth*, 433.

says, "If the Father also submitted to the authority of the Son, it would destroy the Trinity, because there would be no Father, Son, and Holy Spirit, but only Person A, Person A, and Person A."[16]

The point Grudem is making in these two statements is not entirely clear. Certainly, if there are three persons who in some sense are one, is this not a Trinity, even if each is identical in every respect? What he seems to be saying is that there would be no Trinity at all *as he defines Trinity*, namely, three persons having differing roles eternally, and in which one has authority over another, who is eternally subordinate. That, however, is not necessarily inherent in the idea of Trinity. It seems to beg the question that should be argued and proved. Otherwise, this seems to be a case of stipulative definition.

If this is all that Grudem means, then we may rest the discussion at this point. He seems, however, to have something more in mind, for he indicates that this has significant consequences even for human identity: "Once we lose personal distinctions among the members of the Trinity, we sacrifice the very idea that personal differences are eternally and fundamentally good, and we no longer have in the being of God a guarantee that God will eternally preserve our individual, personal distinctiveness either."[17]

Apparently Grudem is extending this principle even further, to make it a matter of the basis of identity of individuals in general. He does not clarify just how it is that the loss of such personal distinctions within the Godhead leads to the loss of assurance of divine preservation of our individual personal distinctiveness. Is he seriously saying that unless there are eternal and unchanging relationships of authority and subordination within the Trinity, our individual personal distinctiveness is in jeopardy? All he seems to offer is that such personal distinctions are no longer eternally and fundamentally good and presumably therefore would not be valued in humans by God either. But the issue there seems to be that unless there are qualitative distinctions among individuals, there is a loss of any real difference of identity among them.

---

16. Ibid.
17. Ibid.

This is an interesting theory and one that certainly deserves elaboration, elucidation, and defense. As it stands, this would seem to deny that there really are any such things as identical twins, since they presumably would not have different relationships and roles, at least early in their lives. Surely, this is not what Grudem is asserting, but without further explication, it is difficult to know how to evaluate the argument and especially difficult to know why this is so serious a threat to the eternal existence of the Trinity.

Eternal Generation

One issue that played a rather large part in the discussions in the earlier centuries of the church is the doctrine of the generation of the Son. It has received relatively little support among the later discussants.

One who has given considerable attention and argumentation to this more traditional doctrine is John Dahms, in a 1989 article.[18] The traditional doctrine is that the Father is in some sense eternally the basis or the source of the life or at least the distinct personal subsistence of the Son. This, however, is not in any sense to be confused with the doctrine of creation by the Father, as the Arians held. The ancient monks used to chant, "begotten, not made," as the creed had expressed the thought. Dahms, unfortunately, never gives any extensive definition of what he means by generated. What he does is quote the texts that speak of the Son as the begotten Son, or the begotten of the Father, such as John 1:14, 18; 3:16, 18; and 1 John 4:9. He is especially impressed with the text in 1 John 5:18, that the Son of God "was born of God." He comments, "In this verse it is explicitly stated that the Son was generated by the Father."[19]

Dahms believes not only that this doctrine is taught in Scripture but also that it is "essential to theological orthodoxy."[20] The first two of his conclusions are the most significant for our purposes:

---

18. John V. Dahms, "The Generation of the Son," *Journal of the Evangelical Theological Society* 32, no. 4 (December 1989): 493–501.

19. Ibid., 496.

20. Ibid., 497.

1. The doctrine provides an ontological basis for the dissimi-
   larity of the Father and the Son that is necessary for fellowship
   and interaction between them. . . .
2. The generation doctrine provides an ontological basis for
   the subordination of the Son of the Father, which the NT
   emphasizes (e.g., John 5:19–30).[21]

In many ways, Dahms's article is disappointing because of its
lack of argumentation and the logical leaps that he makes in his presentation. It does not represent the position of most contemporary
gradationists.

Ware, for one, does not hold to the doctrine of generation. He
regards the ideas of generation of the Son and procession of the Spirit as
"highly speculative and not grounded in biblical teaching," suggesting
that the passages that speak of the Son as begotten actually refer to his
earthly birth in the Incarnation.[22]

In his *Systematic Theology*, Grudem indicates that the terms *paternity* or *generation*, *begottenness* or *filiation*, and *procession* or *spiration*
should be understood simply as meaning, respectively, "relating as a
Father," "relating as a Son," and "relating as Spirit." To avoid confusion,
he has not used these terms, but he does not reject them outright.[23] In
an appendix added to later printings of the original and only edition
of *Systematic Theology* to appear to the present, Grudem discusses the
concept of *monogenēs*, in terms of whether it should be translated "only
begotten" or "only," and concludes in favor of the latter, as meaning
"unique," or "the only one of a kind."[24] From more recent linguistic
studies, we now know that if it were to be the former, it should have
been *monogennētos*, rather than *monogenēs*.[25] He asserts that "it would
be more helpful if the language of 'eternal begetting of the Son' (also
called the 'eternal generation of the Son') were not retained in any

21. Ibid.
22. Ware, *Father, Son, and Holy Spirit*, 162n. 3.
23. Grudem, *Systematic Theology*, 254n. 38.
24. Ibid., 1223.
25. Ibid.

modern theological formulations."[26] Rather, "What is needed is simply that we insist on *eternal personal differences* in the eternal relationships between the Father, Son, and Holy Spirit, and that the Son eternally relates to the Father as a son does to his father."[27] He contends that the 1 John 5:18 text should be understood as a reference to the earthly, human birth of Jesus, rather than some eternal, timeless begetting.[28]

Although Grudem does not explicitly reject the generation doctrine, he seems to reject the usual support for it. He concludes: "So long as we do not assume that these personal distinctions had a beginning at some point in time, nothing in Scripture would seem to contradict this idea, but nothing in Scripture would indicate that we should affirm it, either. Perhaps there is no meaningful sense in which we should speak about any one of the persons being a 'source' of these personal distinctions, for they have always existed and are essential to the nature of God himself."[29]

Interestingly, Giles seems to have no problem accepting the idea of generation, or the language of begetting, but he insists that this does not mean that the Father has any sort of preeminence over the Son.[30] He acknowledges that the idea is not explicitly taught in Scripture but believes it can be inferred from it.[31] He affirms that "nevertheless the idea that the Son is eternally begotten, or as Augustine says, eternally generated, has proved to be a helpful way to speak of the divine Father-Son relationship."[32] After examining Grudem's treatment of the *monogenēs* references, Giles asserts, "I therefore cannot agree with Grudem when he argues that the Son's eternal begetting or generation be removed 'from modern theological formulations' of the Trinity. To reject a theological idea enshrined in the creeds and confessions

---

26. Ibid., 1234.

27. Ibid.

28. Ibid.

29. Ibid.

30. Kevin Giles, *Jesus and the Father: Modern Evangelicals Reinvent the Doctrine of the Trinity* (Grand Rapids: Zondervan, 2006), 78.

31. Ibid., 239.

32. Ibid., 239–40.

seeking to replace it with another idea—the eternal subordination of the Son in authority—as the primary basis for differentiation, with no historical support at all, or any theological merit, is doctrinally dangerous."[33]

It must be acknowledged that for many persons today, the doctrine does not seem to make much sense. Just what does it mean to say that the Father eternally generates the Son, yet that the Son is not therefore inferior to the Father? How can the Father be the basis of the Son's being but without this constituting some species of creation of the latter by the former? It may well be that the difficulty of making sense of this concept today is because in our time we are working within a different philosophical framework than that which these earlier theologians were utilizing. It does seem evident that the concept is in need of further analysis and explication.

Paul Helm is a very competent contemporary Christian philosopher who has probed this concept. He attacks directly the central problem of the issue: "However mysterious this begetting—for those who drew up the credal and conciliar formulae held that it is a timelessly eternal, completed act of the Father, not an act in time—if the word 'begotten' is to retain any meaning then it must carry the implication that the Father caused the Son to be."[34] He further suggests that this means "an asymmetry between the being and agency of the Father (who begets) and the being and agency of the Son (who is begotten) is implied, and in some undeniable sense the Son is subordinate to the Father."[35]

This, however, poses the difficult question of how the fully divine Son could be caused to be: "How could the Son be begotten and nevertheless be unqualifiedly divine?"[36] As a philosopher and a student of the history of philosophy, Helm offers a specific content to the

---

33. Ibid., 240.

34. Paul Helm, "Of God, and of the Holy Trinity: A Response to Dr. Beckwith," *The Churchman* 115, no. 4 (2001): 350.

35. Ibid.

36. Ibid.

suggestion raised above about the difference between the framework within which those theologians were working and our own: "There is no question but those who formulated the doctrine of the Trinity in terms of the begetting of the Son and the processing of the Spirit were influenced by Neoplatonism, particularly by the idea that from the One emanated Mind and Soul (corresponding to the begottenness and procession of the Son and the Spirit), with the important difference that in the Trinity, Son and Spirit are hypostases in their own right, forming (with the Father) a Tri-unity."[37]

Helm finds a tension in the fourth-century Trinitarian views, and although he does not say so explicitly, it appears that on his analysis, the tension may arise from the attempt to combine biblical teaching with Neoplatonic philosophy: "A closer look at the Nicene and Contantinopolitan formulations shows that there is, in fact, a tension within them between a hierarchical view of the Son's existence, being begotten from the Father, in which the Son is caused to be, and a more egalitarian view, in which the equality and consubstantiality of the persons is stressed."[38]

Helms formulates what he understands the traditional subordinationist view of eternal generation to be asserting: "There is no state of the Father that is not a begetting of the Son, and no state of the Son which is not a being begotten by the Father and necessarily there is no time when the Father had not begotten the Son, and no time when the Son had not been begotten by the Father. . . . There is no possibility of the Father existing and the Son not existing."[39] His comment on this situation is: "But do these claims not take us far from the New Testament, and give rise to unnecessary speculation?"[40] Thus, as a philosopher, he indicates his purpose, which he apparently believes would eliminate the concept of eternal generation from discussion: "Finally, it may seem ironic that both the original lecture

---

37. Ibid., 351.
38. Ibid.
39. Ibid.
40. Ibid.

which called forth Dr. Beckwith's response, and this response to him, is from a philosopher who is making a plea for the removal from our understanding of the doctrine of the Trinity of certain concepts which derive not from the New Testament but from pagan philosophy, from Neoplatonism. The plea is made in order that our understanding of the Trinity may be more faithful to Scripture, and less open to speculative distraction."[41]

The doctrine of eternal generation does not play a large part in the discussions of subordination today. Philosophically, it has been deemed by many to draw a distinction that does not make sense: to insist on some sort of eternal derivation of being from the Father, or the Father being eternally the source of the subsistence of the other two persons, yet in such a way that they are not at all created by him. It is interesting that Calvin did not believe this to be a doctrine worth defending.[42]

We should note the effect of the contemporary rejection, or at least neglect, of the idea of eternal generation by contemporary gradationists like Ware and Grudem. Many of the historical references that they cite as support for a historical belief in functional subordination actually rest upon this idea of eternal generation. If Ware and Grudem do not hold this view, they cannot cite these earlier sources in support of their own view. This does not mean that if eternal generation implies eternal functional subordination, and if one rejects the former doctrine, the latter falls. That would be the fallacy of denying the antecedent. What it does say, however, is that eternal generation was regarded as implying eternal functional subordination, or that the former being true meant that the latter is necessarily true. If the former is denied, the latter may still be true, but it is not *necessarily* true, an important distinction. To put it differently, some other basis for the truth of eternal functional subordination must instead be found.

---

41. Ibid., 357. In the TEDS debate, Yandell made a similar point, that it was Grudem and Ware, not McCall and he, who had introduced the philosophical considerations, but his contention was more general than that of Helm, maintaining only that it was Greek philosophy that they had introduced.

42. John Calvin, *Institutes of the Christian Religion*, 1.13.29.

Logical Issues

In addition to these metaphysical or ontological issues, there are also several matters that involve logical argumentation, or the validity of the arguments presented.

Difference and Subordination

We noted that Grudem insisted that there must be differences of role for distinctions among the persons to exist. Without such differences, the very Trinity itself would not exist. Thus, the relationship of authority and obedience or submission is necessary.

Even if we were to grant the validity of this argument for the necessity of different roles, a further problem exists. Does it follow from the necessity of differences of role that there must be superiority and subordination of role? This is certainly assumed in the argument, but no argument for it is given. The argument seems to be something as follows:

> Distinctions of persons require different roles.
> Therefore, distinctions of persons require differences of authority.

What is missing from the argument, however, is the intermediate premise: Differences of role require differences of authority. Without that, the conclusion does not follow. There is a suppressed premise, and the argument is therefore an enthymeme.

Grudem is not the only one who works with this sort of argument. Scott Horrell similarly asserts, "A social model of the Godhead that does not recognize eternal differentiation of the Father, Son, and Holy Spirit based firmly in divine revelation easily loses all significant distinction. An egalitarian model of the immanent Godhead collapses trinitarian distinctions."[43]

Might it not be the case, however, that the Father, Son, and Holy Spirit perform different roles within the economy of the Godhead, and perhaps even that these are necessarily the roles they perform, without

---

43. J. Scott Horrell, "Toward a Biblical Model of the Social Trinity: Avoiding Equivocation of Nature and Order," *Journal of the Evangelical Theological Society* 47, no. 3 (2004): 417.

one having to be superior to the others? While I am not prepared to grant the former assumption, even if this were done, the argument is incomplete. It is interesting that Grudem speaks of "the fundamental egalitarian claim that if there is equality there cannot be difference in role, and if there is difference in role there cannot be equality."[44]

What is striking is that although Grudem claims that this is a fundamental egalitarian claim, he does not offer even one instance of documentation from an egalitarian source. If this is really such a fundamental claim, finding instances should constitute no problem. It appears that the claim is not so much in egalitarian thinking, as it is in Grudem's thinking, equating differences of role with differences in rank. This can also be seen in Ware's use of the analogy of harmony versus unison.[45] In unison, all voices sing the same notes. In harmony, one and only one carries the melody, but the other singers sing complementary notes, which produce a harmony. He believes this to be a good illustration of the varying roles but unified working of the members of the Trinity, which it is. The question to be asked, however, is whether the same person always carries the melody, and whether the same person always chooses which song will be sung. This does not follow from the concept of harmony. Yet in Ware's thinking, as in that of Grudem, differing roles necessarily require a differing ranking of those fulfilling the roles, and that does not seem to follow, at least not in the gradationists' statement of the argument. Therefore, this must be considered a fallacious argument as it stands, either a formal or an informal fallacy, whether a case of begging the question, circular argumentation, suppressed premise, or stipulative definition. Once again, more analysis and argumentation is necessary for the gradationist position to be tenable.

The Basis of the Eternal Decrees

To a large extent, the gradationist view rests on actions of the Father that seem to place him in a position of superiority over the Son.

---

44. Grudem, *Evangelical Feminism and Biblical Truth*, 428.
45. Ware, *Father, Son, and Holy Spirit*, 42.

This is particularly the case with the passages that speak of his sending the Son. Certainly, the argument seems to say, the one who sends does so because he has decided that the other should go. If one does the will of the other, it means that the one whose will is to be done has a position of superior authority over the one who carries out that will.

Here the argument seems to be something like this:

> The Father has sent the Son, who comes out of obedience to the Father's will.
>
> Therefore the Father is superior to the Son.

Here the suppressed premise seems to be, "The one who sends is superior to the one sent." That in turn assumes the premise, "The one who sends does so by virtue of a unilateral decision."

Warfield, however, has pointed out that it may be just as likely that the sending is the result of a covenant among the persons of the Trinity, established by the collective decision of the three persons; thus the decision that the Son should come, and the will that the Father therefore exercised in sending him, may have been as much the Son's decision as it was the Father's.

It should be noted, of course, that no biblical support is adduced for the existence of such a covenant. However, the point is that to rest any argument on an unproven assumption, when there are equally plausible alternatives, is an uncertain and shaky matter.

Usurpation of "Complementarian"

We noted in the earlier discussion the tendency to assume that difference necessarily involves ranking. This can be seen to be a more general assumption, revealed in Grudem's reference to egalitarians with respect to male-female relationships: ". . . the fundamental egalitarian claim that if there is equality there cannot be difference in role, and if there is difference in role there cannot be equality."[46] Actually, I do not know of any egalitarians who would make this claim or who assume it in their discussions. Of the egalitarian couples I know, most do not insist

---

46. Grudem, *Evangelical Feminism and Biblical Truth*, 428.

on each performing exactly half of all roles, so that their functions are identical. Where they disagree with "complementarians" is whether one member of the pair always has the final word, or the ultimate authority. Thus, it appears that the fundamental claim that Grudem finds actually has been read into or projected from the perspective that he himself takes.

Grudem has attempted to argue at some length for the justification of the use of the term *complementarian* to designate the hierarchical position with respect to men and women, and thus also with respect to the persons of the Trinity. He attempts to argue from the "established usage," that this term should be reserved for use by those who hold the position he does. He maintains that it has been in use as a designator of that specific position for a long enough period of time to have become the established meaning. In particular, reacting to William Webb, he says, "In addition, complementarians will consider Webb's terminology offensive and confusing. As a cofounder of the Council on Biblical Manhood and Womanhood in 1987, and as coauthor of the complementarian book *Recovering Biblical Manhood and Womanhood*, I wish to lodge a protest against Webb's use of two terms."[47] He claims that Webb applies the term *complementary egalitarianism* to what Grudem calls "a thoroughgoing egalitarian position." This, says Grudem, "simply confuses the issues by using *complementary* for a position totally antithetical to what complementarians hold."[48]

Grudem seeks to establish his group's exclusive right to the term by citing what he and John Piper had written in 1991 in the preface to the aforementioned volume: "If one word must be used to describe our position, we prefer the term *complementarian*, since it suggests both equality and beneficial differences between men and women. We are uncomfortable with the term 'traditionalist' because it implies an unwillingness to let Scripture challenge traditional patterns of behavior, and we certainly reject the term 'hierarchicalist' because it overem-

---

47. Ibid., 639.
48. Ibid.

phasizes structured authority while giving no suggestion of equality or the beauty of mutual interdependence."[49]

Grudem adds, "Since that time, *complementarian* has been the term we have consistently used to describe our position, and it has been widely (and courteously) used by others to describe our position as well. For Webb to apply it to an egalitarian position is to needlessly confuse the issue."[50] He goes on to argue that by analogy, Presbyterians could claim the right to call themselves Baptists, since they also baptize, and Democrats could call themselves Republicans, since they believe in a republic. The non sequiturs here are rampant. A long history of Baptists being called that (a name they did not necessarily choose for themselves) has gone on with no objection being raised by Presbyterians, and Democrats and Republicans would not dispute that members of both parties are both republicans and democrats. Webb is not the first one to dispute the exclusive right of one group to use the term.

By way of contrast, there is nothing in the usual definition of the term that carries the restrictions that Grudem's use of it entails. Strangely, this seems like a parallel to a common postmodern technique, which Stanley Fish spoke of this way: "Getting hold of the concept of merit and stamping it with your own brand is a good strategy."[51] Whether getting a concept and affixing one's term to it, or taking over a term and attaching it to one's meaning, the endeavor is similar.

This means that in my judgment these persons have engaged in stipulative definition and have usurped a term that probably should be shared. I find a better distinction to be between egalitarian complementarians and hierarchical complementarians. The question is not whether the roles are different. It is whether the difference necessarily involves

---

49. John Piper and Wayne Grudem, eds., *Recovering Biblical Manhood and Womanhood: A Response to Biblical Feminism* (Wheaton, IL: Crossway, 1991), xiv; quoted in Grudem, *Evangelical Feminism and Biblical Truth*, 640.

50. Grudem, *Evangelical Feminism and Biblical Truth*, 640. Peter R. Schemm Jr. makes the same point in "Kevin Giles's *The Trinity and Subordinationism*: A Review Article," *Journal of Biblical Manhood and Womanhood* 7, no. 2 (Fall 2002): 73–74.

51. Stanley Fish, *There's No Such Thing as Free Speech, and It's a Good Thing, Too* (New York: Oxford University Press, 1994), 6.

one person having the final authority in decision making. I believe this is actually an assumption present within the gradationists' thinking that has led them to confusion in their treatment of the structure of the Trinity. That assumption is that if there is difference in role, there also must be difference in relative authority. The failure to recognize their own assumptions leads them to find an assumption or a fundamental position in their opponents' thought that is not there. Until this is faced and made more than an assumption, no progress will be made in this matter. Arguments cannot be decided by stipulative definition.

The Terminology of "Subordination" and "Subordinationism"

Peter Schemm also contends that these two terms have definite meanings and they should not be interchanged or confused. He says,

> The second set of terms, "subordination and subordinationism," are used frequently in the context of trinitarian discussion, and have a clearly defined usage. Theologians of the past have spoken in some sense of the subordination of the Son and the Spirit within the boundaries of orthodoxy. Subordination*ism*, however, describes a heretical formulation of the doctrine of God, usually referred to as ontological subordinationism. Ontological subordinationism is recognized as heresy because it says the Son and Spirit do not share directly in the very being or essence of God the Father. The term subordinationism, then, is not used functionally (eternal or temporal) but rather ontologically (regarding being and essence only).[52]

Schemm believes that by using the two terms indiscriminately, Giles has misrepresented those who believe in the functional, but not ontological, subordination of the Son to the Father eternally. The term *subordination*, however, refers to a particular condition, while the addition of the ending -*ism* refers to a belief in or a system of thought based upon subordination. The established usage he refers to, however, is not so clear

---

52. Schemm, "Kevin Giles's *The Trinity and Subordinationism*," 73. Grudem and Ware made the same point in the TEDS debate.

as he would maintain. Note, for example, the comments of the church historian Philip Schaff: "This subordination is most plainly expressed by Hilary of Poictiers, the champion of the Nicene doctrine in the West,"[53] and, "In the same way Hilary derives all the attributes of the Son from the Father."[54] Schemm seems to be asserting that subordination always means functional difference and subordinationism always implies ontological difference. It would seem to be less confusing if instead of using this sort of stipulative definition, reference were made to ontological and functional subordination and subordinationism, and in the case of the functional variety, attaching the adjectives "eternal" or "temporary."

Rhetoric Substituted for Evidence

Ware frequently makes statements to the effect that something is "clear" or "obvious" when upon closer examination that proves not to be the case. It may be clear to Ware, but the clarity of the conclusion may be because of definitions and assumptions he makes that are in need of some definite argumentation and substantiation. While the use of such expressions may create the illusion of solid conclusions, it would be much better if the argument were made more explicit and the evidence clearly laid out, so that its adequacy could be assessed.

Ware is not the only one who engages in such a practice. In the Kovach and Schemm article, the authors make the sweeping statement, "It cannot be legitimately denied that the eternal subordination of the Son is an orthodox doctrine and believed from the history of the early church to the present day."[55] Here, by such a categorical statement, they have set the bar of disproof very low, and to the extent that the burden of proof rests on the affirmative, the bar of proof of their view exceedingly high. In the TEDS debate, Grudem used similar absolutistic language, answering the question, "Do relations of authority and

---

53. Philip Schaff, *A History of the Christian Church,* vol. 3, *Nicene and Post-Nicene Christianity,* 5th ed., rev. (Grand Rapids: Eerdmans, 1910), 682.

54. Ibid.

55. Stephen D. Kovach and Peter R. Schemm Jr., "A Defense of the Doctrine of the Eternal Subordination of the Son," *Journal of the Evangelical Theological Society* 42, no. 3 (September 1999): 464.

submission exist eternally among the Persons of the Godhead?" by saying, "Absolutely, undeniably, gloriously, yes."

In the case of Grudem, the practice takes a different form: of sometimes questioning the integrity of those who differ on a particular issue. So he says of Catherine Kroeger's work on *kephalē*, "In fact, in several sections its disregard of facts is so egregious that it fails even to meet fundamental requirements of truthfulness."[56] He also says of the view of eternal subordination, "This then has been the historic doctrine of the church. Egalitarians may differ with this doctrine today if they wish, and they may attempt to persuade us that they are right if they wish, but they must do so on the basis of arguments from Scripture, and they should also have the honesty and courtesy to explain to readers why they now feel it necessary to differ with the historic doctrine of the church as expressed in its major creeds."[57] Rather than suggesting that his opponents here have been mistaken, such statements seem to reflect a conviction that the case he has presented is so conclusive that those who differ have done so deliberately, in contradiction of the facts.

Substituting Interpretation for Statement

While we have focused especially on the logical and rhetorical problems attached to the gradational view, such problems also can be found in the presentation of the equivalence view. Giles especially will quote from a historical source and then give a paraphrase, often introduced by "in other words." What follows, however, is often one possible interpretation of the words quoted, but without argumentation that this is the correct, or at least preferred, interpretation. This can sometimes be detected by Giles's use of documentation for a quote but then going on to add a sentence or two, as if they were the words of the theologian cited, but without documentation. For example, he quotes from Athanasius, "It [Scripture] contains a double account of the Savior; that He was ever God, and is the Son, being the Father's Word and Radiance and Wisdom; and that afterward for us He took flesh of a

---

56. Grudem, *Evangelical Feminism and Biblical Truth,* 597.
57. Ibid., 422.

Virgin, Mary Bearer of God, and was made man. And this scope is to be found throughout inspired Scripture."[58]

It is true that Athanasius, in this context and elsewhere in his discussion of Philippians 2, does speak of Jesus humbling himself and becoming obedient. Giles gives a summary of Athanasius's teaching, as follows: "These texts, Athanasius maintains, give the interpretive key to the reading of the whole of Scripture. They indicate that texts found anywhere in the Bible speaking of the subordination of the Son refer to him as the incarnate Son."[59] This, however, is not Athanasius's statement in the contexts that Giles cites. Indeed, Athanasius does not use the word *subordination*, which may support Giles's case. This, rather, is Giles's interpretation of the collection of statements.

Actually, as we noted in the historical chapter, Giles's statement about Athanasius's view is not strictly correct, for there seems to be some ambiguity in Athanasius's statements. It may well be that Giles's appeal to the double principle is the solution to the puzzle, but it needs to be argued more thoroughly. It is at the point of what Athanasius meant that the dispute occurs, and Giles needs to distinguish more clearly between what Athanasius says and what Giles says Athanasius says, just as do the gradationists in some of their interpretations that Giles disputes.[60]

In this chapter we have examined a number of philosophical issues, both metaphysical and logical in nature, involved in the discussion as it has proceeded in recent years. While we have observed problems for both the gradational and the equivalence positions, it appears that considerably more unresolved difficulties exist for the gradationists.

---

58. Athanasius, "Four Discourses Against the Arians," 2.26.29; quoted in Giles, *Jesus and the Father*, 98.

59. Giles, *Jesus and the Father*, 99.

60. Similarly, Giles says that Athanasius "gladly accepts that there are many passages in Scripture that speak of the Son's subordination and obedience to the Father. These, he holds, emphasize the reality of the incarnation" (*Jesus and the Father*, 135). This may simply be failure to provide documentation for indirect discourse, but its absence, especially in light of using terminology not employed by Athanasius, creates a problem.

CHAPTER 7

The Theological Dimensions

In the chapter on evaluating alternatives, we noted that the factor of coherence involves how well one element of a theory relates to other elements of it. Christian theology is an organic whole, meaning that there is an aesthetic quality to the way the several doctrines interact and imply one another. We argued that greater coherence is a strength in the evaluation process.

There is another benefit, namely, that if an element of a theory is something we cannot check exhaustively against our sources (the Bible), coherence may nonetheless enable us to make such a check. The position on one doctrine may imply a particular position on another doctrine, and the second doctrine is one we can check against the data. Thus, an indirect proof or disproof may be possible. Agreement in the latter area does not establish the truth of the interpretation of the former doctrine, for to claim that would be an instance of the fallacy of affirming the consequent. Disagreement of the latter doctrine with the primary source, however, would count against the truth of the former doctrine, if indeed it implies the latter. That would be a case of denial of the consequent, a valid argument in which the antecedent is thereby disproved. A number of such doctrinal connections deserve our attention.

The Nature of Biblical Authority

A certain amount of controversy has focused on Kevin Giles's discussion of the use of the Bible. He stated in *The Trinity and Subordinationism* that the issues under debate could not be settled merely by quoting

Bible passages: "In seeking to make a response to my fellow evangelicals who subordinate the Son to the Father, I do not appeal directly to particular scriptural passages to establish who is right and who is wrong. I concede immediately that the New Testament *can* be read to teach that the Son is *eternally* subordinated to the Father; I seek rather to prove that orthodoxy rejects this way of reading the Scriptures."[1]

Giles regards the tradition as "an important, yet secondary, authority."[2] Athanasius realized that simply quoting Bible verses was insufficient in itself, because the Arians were able to compile a list of Scriptures that supported their view. Rather, the Bible must be read theologically; that is, it must be read in light of the "'scope' of Scripture—the overall drift of the Bible, its primary focus, its theological center."[3] This scope can be seen in the Bible but is made clear by the tradition.[4] According to Giles, the way that one decides how to read the Scriptures is by consulting the tradition.

While one can read the Bible to say that the Son is eternally subordinated to the Father, Giles says, "I seek rather to prove that orthodoxy rejects this way of reading the Scriptures."[5] The point of examining the tradition is to show that orthodoxy has indeed rejected this incorrect way of reading the Scriptures: "The quest for the orthodox doctrine of the Trinity is in part the story of how the best theologians across the centuries came to a common mind as to how the Scriptures should be read to inform and determine this doctrine."[6] He believes that his claim that the Bible can be read in more than one way is undeniable and therefore uncontroversial. An examination of the history of Christianity will show that learned and devout theologians have often had quite different interpretations of the same passages.[7]

---

1. Kevin Giles, *The Trinity and Subordinationism: The Doctrine of God and the Contemporary Gender Debate* (Downers Grove, IL: InterVarsity Press, 2002), 25.
2. Ibid., 5.
3. Ibid., 3.
4. Ibid., 4.
5. Ibid., 25.
6. Ibid.
7. Ibid., 9.

This does not mean that in every case the tradition should simply be accepted at face value. On the contrary, at times the tradition is wrong and should be flatly rejected. These are situations in which the interpretation merely reflects the way everyone thought on that subject in the world in which the interpretation was being given. Examples would be slavery, or the idea that the earth was flat. Exposure to later culture has revealed this: "Only in a different cultural context could theologians discover a different reading of Scripture that made sense of the changed understanding of the world, an understanding that God himself had brought to pass."[8]

Giles insists that texts in themselves are not self-interpreting: "They are only symbols on a page until a human agent gives them meaning. The interpreting agent, as has been noted, always reads through the 'spectacles' given by the presuppositions she or he holds or takes for granted." There is always this contribution of the interpreter to the meaning of the text, and "*context contributes to meaning*."[9] This leads Giles to a very important principle:

> Once this is recognized, one can no longer think of the Bible as a set of timeless, transcultural rulings or as propositions that speak in every age with one voice. The Bible is to be seen rather as a book written in history by human authors, inspired and directed by the Holy Spirit, through which and in which the Holy Spirit speaks afresh again and again. The Westminster Confession of Faith clearly reflects this pneumatic understanding of Scripture, which growing numbers of evangelicals have come to embrace in recent times. It declares, "The supreme judge by which all controversies of religion are determined . . . can be no other but the Holy Spirit speaking in the scriptures."[10]

As one might expect, the gradationists have criticized this hermeneutical stance vigorously. Grudem, for example, says, "Giles's fundamental approach should disturb evangelicals, for it means that appeals to

---

8. Ibid.

9. Ibid., 10–11.

10. Ibid., 11. The quotation is from the Westminster Confession of Faith, 1.10.

Scripture can have no effect in his system. He can just reply, 'Yes, the Bible can be read that way, but other readings are possible.' And thus the voice of God's Word is effectively silenced."[11] Grudem acknowledges that Giles uses church tradition to determine which is the correct interpretation but asserts that "unfortunately, Giles's understanding of the historic view of the church on the Trinity is deeply flawed."[12]

In an extended review of Giles's book, Peter Schemm has criticized his method on several grounds:

1. Giles has built his thesis on the wrong grounds: "the relationship between tradition (as a theological source) and the concept of subordination rather than on the more important question one must ask regarding the concept of subordination—that is, what does the Bible teach about the concept of subordination? He intentionally neglects this question because of his hermeneutical commitments."[13]

2. "Tradition as a source or contributor in theology has been invested with far too much hermeneutical value."[14]

3. "The cultural context of the interpreter has been invested with far too much hermeneutical value." While conceding the importance of the two horizons in biblical interpretation, Schemm feels that "this does not justify a variety of textual messages or valid interpretations." Instead of exalting the role of the cultural context of the interpreter as Giles had done, Schemm instead proposes "to refine the [interpretative] process through something similar to what Grant Osborne calls the 'hermeneutical spiral,' which continually revisits the biblical text to determine the author's intended meaning."[15]

---

11. Wayne Grudem, *Evangelical Feminism and Biblical Truth: An Analysis of More Than One Hundred Disputed Questions* (Sisters, OR: Multnomah, 2004), 426.

12. Ibid.

13. Peter R. Schemm Jr., "Kevin Giles's *The Trinity and Subordinationism:* A Review Article," *Journal of Biblical Manhood and Womanhood* 7, no. 2 (Fall 2002): 71.

14. Ibid., 72.

15. Ibid.

4. The most pressing question is: "Who decides which cultural context determines the meaning of the text?" Could not this method justify homosexuality, since there is now a much wider cultural acceptance of this? While conceding that Giles contends that the impact of culture is only to be considered, not made determinative, Schemm says this is not convincing, because, in effect, it is too little and too late, coming after "Giles has just argued for two-thirds of his book (parts two and three) that culture is determinative (cf. p. 203). He has clearly stated that there is not one correct interpretation of a biblical text. Ultimately then, the cultural experience of the interpreter is determinative in Giles's hermeneutical method."[16]

Here is a complex tangle of issues, but very important ones. The first observation I have is that Giles is to be commended for seeing the effect of cultural, historical, and other forms of conditioning on the interpreter, in ways that Grudem and Schemm do not seem to. They appear to display something of a naïve confidence that their understanding of the meaning of biblical passages is not an interpretation but is simply what the text says. This then leads them to overstate what Giles is saying, such as when Grudem remarks that thus "the voice of God's Word is effectively silenced." This appears to be a large leap from what Giles is saying. This may be an implication of Giles's position, but that needs to be argued. What Schemm recommends as an alternative to Giles's position is actually much closer to what Giles seems to be saying than Schemm's representation of Giles's. It is not apparent to me that Giles ever says that there are multiple possible meanings, all equally valid. He rather speaks of possible meanings and then offers a suggestion as to how one may find the correct, or at least a more adequate, meaning.

Giles makes an important point that we should be careful not to overlook. He is responding to those who allege that "the modern stress on the equality of the persons in the Trinity is a reading back of

---

16. Ibid.

contemporary egalitarian social ideals into the Godhead."[17] Rather, he says of this idea of the complete equality of the three persons, "It was consummately argued by Athanasius in the fourth century, Augustine in the fifth century and Calvin in the sixteenth century, when society was hierarchically ordered and patriarchy was the norm. The orthodox doctrine of the Trinity that excludes any subordination in being or act was developed counterculturally."[18] This he considers to be an evidence that God led these theologians to the correct formulation, since it was counter to what they would naturally have tended, on the basis of the prevailing culture, to believe. This would be a discriminating criterion. Of course, the gradationists could claim the same for their view, but the difference is that the present period was preceded by one in which the culture tended toward the hierarchical view, so their view is not counter to the immediately preceding culture, as was true for the earlier theologians mentioned. Thus, rather than the equivalentists reflecting twentieth-century culture, it may be the gradationists who reflect the influence of a nineteenth-century and earlier culture.

Having said that, there are a number of problems with Giles's view. For one thing, Schemm's last point is pertinent, namely, just how does one decide what is good tradition and bad tradition? Giles's only answer seems to be that later cultural changes show us that an earlier view was culturally controlled and was the only interpretation that would have occurred to someone at that time. The problem, however, is that future developments may supercede the current cultural understanding, perhaps even leading us to a reversal of the present understanding. Further, the problem of interpreting the biblical text also applies to interpreting the tradition or the culture. The same problems of conditioning also apply to this interpretive process. The disputes between these two parties over the writings of earlier theologians show this. Further, while it is commendable that Giles suggests using the tradition to reduce the cultural conditioning effect, other means of neutralizing this effect can and should be utilized. I have in mind such activities as

---

17. Giles, *The Trinity and Subordinationism*, 111.
18. Ibid.

interacting with those of different cultures and writing one's intellectual autobiography.[19]

Of greater potential concern is the question of what view of the nature of biblical revelation, inspiration, and authority underlies Giles's hermeneutical theory. As he describes the process of the Spirit's speaking afresh through Scripture, it could be interpreted in either of two ways. The traditional view is that the Bible is objectively God's revelation, preserved through inspiration, and that it conveys cognitive, objective, and informational truth. The work of the Holy Spirit then is that of illuminating, or bringing to understanding and conviction, the truth that is objectively present in the Scripture. That this is what Giles means by his statement is supported by his reference to the Bible's authors being inspired and his citation of the Westminster Confession.[20] However, his statement can also be interpreted in the neo-orthodox sense that the Bible is not a fixed, objective body of revealed information but that revelation is God himself in his full presence and that in that moment it becomes the Word of God. That this is what he means would be favored by his reference to the Holy Spirit speaking in the Scriptures and by his attribution of such a view to Donald Bloesch, whose view I have argued is much like that of Barth.[21] The problems with the neo-orthodox view are well known, and they contributed to the decline in popularity of that view. A major problem is that God may not "speak" the same message each time or to each person, which if Giles holds this view would make him vulnerable to the charge that there may be multiple valid meanings of Scripture.

---

19. I have sought to describe these processes in Millard J. Erickson, *Truth or Consequences: The Promise and Perils of Postmodernism* (Downers Grove, IL: InterVarsity Press, 2000), 237–51.

20. Some have sought to read the Westminster Confession as consonant with a neo-orthodox view, but those issues were scarcely in the minds of the authors of that confession, not having yet been raised. To read the confession in that fashion is an anachronism.

21. Millard J. Erickson, "Donald Bloesch's Doctrine of Scripture," *Evangelical Theology in Transition*, ed. Elmer Colyer (Downers Grove, IL: InterVarsity Press, 1999), 77–97.

One additional problem with Giles's use of the historical sources is that much has changed in the understanding of biblical exegesis since the time of the Fathers. In particular, certain aspects of biblical critical study were unknown to them. While it may be maintained that more radical criticism would be rejected by both parties to this dispute, nonetheless, certain conservative aspects of method, such as textual criticism and lexical studies, might well affect how both gradationists and equivalentists would understand some crucial passages.

It may be that Giles should make his view clearer in subsequent writings. It should be noted, however, that in *Jesus and the Father*, he devotes a considerably greater amount of space to citation and exegesis of biblical passages, showing what seems to be a greater confidence in the ability to determine the objective meaning of those passages than he had in his earlier volume.

The Relation of Authority and Power

In a recent article, Kevin Giles introduced a somewhat novel argument. He noted that the doctrinal basis of the Evangelical Theological Society (ETS) addresses only two issues: the inerrancy of the Bible in the original manuscripts and the Trinity. The latter statement, which was not in the original basis, but was added in 1990, includes the words, "one in essence, equal in power and glory." He contends that the position taken by the gradationist view of the Trinity contradicts this statement: "In this paper I argue that critical consideration should be given to what several leading theologians of the ETS are teaching on the Trinity because it would seem to implicitly contradict what the ETS statement of faith says on the Trinity. ETS members are bound to believe that the three divine persons are *one in essence and equal in power*. To argue that the Son is *eternally subordinate in authority* to the Father, denies that he is equal in power with the Father and the Spirit and by implication, that he is *one in essence/being* with the Father and the Spirit."[22]

---

22. Kevin Giles, "The Evangelical Theological Society and the doctrine of the Trinity," *Evangelical Quarterly* 80, no. 4 (October 2008): 323.

Giles acknowledges that a distinction is ordinarily drawn between power and authority: "The word 'authority,' technically defined, indicates that someone has the right to exercise leadership, whereas the word 'power' implies the ability to assert leadership or achieve an end."[23] Nonetheless, he says,

> However, the words may be used synonymously and often are in everyday speech. This is the case in the Bible (e.g. Lk 4:36; 9:1). It also seems this is the case with those with whom I am debating. When they speak of the differing *authority* of the Father and the Son they seem to mean much the same as if they had spoken of the differing *power* of the Father and the Son. In any case I cannot see how anyone could distinguish these terms when used of God. If the divine three are equal in power, as the ETS doctrinal statement says, then they must be equal in authority and vice versa.[24]

While recognizing that the two terms can be logically distinguished, he proceeds to press his argument: "Whether or not these two specific words can be distinguished when used of the triune God is in any case academic. The words 'power' and 'authority' in this discussion both designate divine attributes. Orthodoxy with one voice holds that all divine attributes are equally shared by all the divine persons. God is one in being and attributes. If the Father is all powerful, all loving, and all knowing, then so too are the Son and the Spirit."[25]

Giles therefore announces, "In what follows I will therefore assume that when the ETS doctrinal statement [*sic*] speaks of the triune God as 'one in essence' it means the same as if it had said *one in being*, the expression Knight, Grudem and most English speaking theologians today prefer. And when it speaks of the divine three as 'equal in power' it means the same as if it had said *equal in authority*, what Knight,

---

23. Ibid., 326.

24. Ibid., 326–27. Note that the ETS speaks of a doctrinal "basis," rather than a doctrinal "statement."

25. Ibid., 327.

Grudem and large numbers of contemporary conservative evangelicals deny."[26]

Giles then launches into a discussion of relevant biblical teachings, which discussion has been treated in chapter 4 of this book. For our purposes here, the theological implication is what is important to our consideration. The question is whether a declaration of difference of authority is tantamount to acknowledging a difference of power. While in the immediate context of Giles's presentation the importance of the question is whether certain members of the Evangelical Theological Society have taken positions that by implication place them outside the doctrinal boundaries of the society, we will not concern ourselves here with that specific political issue. Our concern will be the implications of a view of divine authority for the view of divine power.

Giles's acknowledged distinction between the two words is a common one in dictionary usage. Indeed, the common distinction between the right to exercise a power and the ability to do so is found within common society. Police, for example, may have the right to arrest members of an unruly crowd but be incapable of doing so. On the other hand, criminals, who have no right to take and possess certain property, may be able to do so by the use of force. Similarly, it seems appropriate to maintain that the three members of the Trinity have equal power, but without thereby committing oneself to the position that they have equal right to exercise it.

Nor does it appear that Giles has strong biblical support for his contention. In fact, the New Testament has two different words that serve to distinguish authority from power, namely *exousia* and *dunamis*. When Jesus healed the paralyzed man and in the process forgave sins (Matt. 9:6; Luke 5:24), it was the authority, not the ability, to do so that was at stake, although in a case such as that, the two were quite closely aligned. It would appear that the case must be made on other grounds.

In the TEDS debate, Tom McCall made a somewhat different point. He contended that if the Son was able to become incarnate but

---

26. Ibid.

the Father was not, then the Son had an attribute, omnipotence, that the Father did not. One could, of course, contend the reverse, that the Father was omnipotent because he was able not to become incarnate, but the Son was not. It appears to me that in this case the power to become or not become incarnate could be considered contingent upon the Father's will, rather than necessary, and therefore this is not a necessary attribute.

Giles has substituted "I will assume that" for "I have proven that" when he contends that "power" in the ETS statement means the same as authority. The fact that his contention has not met with any support by other members of the society, even those who agree with his position on relative eternal authority, is an indication that he must argue more convincingly, rather than making what appears to be an unwarranted, or at least an undemonstrated, assumption. His contention that both authority and power are essential attributes of God[27] seems to separate, not equate, the two, and itself needs further elaboration and argumentation. It may be that the eternal gradationists are vulnerable to this contention, but it appears to me that Giles has not sufficiently made his case beyond a reasonable doubt. Thus, at least for the time being, the gradationists should be judged not guilty of the charge.

The Basis for the Son Being the One to Become Incarnate

Bruce Ware has posed what he believes to be a serious problem for his opponents on the issue of eternal functional subordination. He contends that without eternal subordination, a major question is unanswerable: "Third, the egalitarian denial of any eternal submission of the Son to the Father makes it impossible to answer the question why it was the 'Son' and not the 'Father' or 'Spirit' who was sent to become incarnate."[28] He elaborates, showing what he believes are the serious consequences of such a denial:

---

27. Ibid.

28. Bruce Ware, *Father, Son, and Holy Spirit: Relationships, Roles, and Relevance* (Wheaton, IL: Crossway, 2005), 81–82.

Since, in their [the egalitarians'] understanding, nothing *in God* grounds the Son being the Son of the Father, and since every aspect of the Son's earthly submission to the Father is divorced altogether from any *eternal relation* that exists between the Father and the Son, there simply is no reason why the *Father* should send the *Son*. In Thompson's words, it appears that the egalitarian view would permit "any one of the three persons" to become incarnate. And yet we have clear and abundant scriptural revelation that the Son came down out of heaven to do the will of his Father. This sending is not *ad hoc*. In eternity, the Father commissioned the Son who then willingly laid aside the glory he had with the Father to come and purchase our pardon and renewal. Such glory is diminished if there is no eternal Father-Son relation on the basis of which the Father sends, the Son willingly comes, and the Spirit willingly empowers.[29]

Ware's statement appears to contain several contentions:

1. Apart from an eternal superiority-submission structure, there is no explanation for why the Son, rather than the Father or the Spirit, was the one who came to earth.
2. It is important to give such an explanation.
3. Without such, we could hold that any one of the three might have been the one to become incarnate.
4. We have evidence that the sending of the Son was not ad hoc. The Bible teaches that the Father commissioned the Son and the Son willingly obeyed the Father.
5. The glory the Son had with the Father is diminished if there is no eternal Father-Son relationship as the basis of the Son's coming.

Each of these needs to be examined and evaluated. Taking the second of these first, we ask why such an explanation is necessary. A number of theological questions can be posed to which we are currently

---

29. Ibid., 82.

unable to give answers. Why did the triune God choose to create at all? Why did he (they) decide to allow humans the ability to choose, resulting in the Fall? Why did he decide to provide atonement for sin? For each of these an answer of sorts can be given, such as, "to have objects of his love external to his nature," "so that their love might be a freely chosen love (and therefore presumably qualitatively superior), rather than a coerced allegiance," and "because his nature is love." But these are answers that are largely constructed by inference, rather than explicitly stated (with the exception of texts like John 3:16). The answers given are testimony to the psychological need of humans, Christians included, for answers to questions, but they scarcely seem to be answers without which our system of theology would collapse.

There are other questions to which we cannot currently give answers, such as "when will the Lord return?" and "how many will be saved?" and for such questions it appears that the answers are unattainable. Other questions appear in principle to be answerable, such as the relationship of predestination and free will, of the human and divine natures of Jesus, and of the three persons and one nature of the Trinity, but the answers are not readily forthcoming. To be sure, the ability to offer an answer to an important question is a strength of one view over another that cannot deal with it, but it is not necessarily an indispensable one, and the quality of the answer is highly important.

Second, however, strictly speaking it is not correct to say that the equivalentists have no answer to the question of why it was the Son who was sent. Although their answer is not the same as the gradationists', it is an answer nonetheless. Ware's assumption is that the only way to interpret the passages that speak of the Father sending the Son, or of the Son doing the Father's will, is that this means that the Father unilaterally made the decision that the Son should come and that the Son and the Spirit had no part in that. However, as we pointed out in both chapter 1 and chapter 4, B. B. Warfield held that that action might just as well be a matter of a covenant, in which the three persons of the Trinity jointly decided that the Son would come, and the Father did the sending on behalf of the other two. If Augustine and others are correct in saying that every action is an action of the triune God, in which one plays the most prominent role but all participate, then the decision that the Son would come would also be a joint decision. On that basis, the equivalentists' answer to the question, "Why did the Son, rather than the Father or the Spirit, come?" is "because they jointly decided that he would be the one to come." While it could be debated whether this is as adequate or as simple an answer as the gradational view, that is not what Ware specified. By saying that the equivalentists can give no answer to the question, he set the bar so low for them that this answer certainly suffices.

Third, while some equivalentists would contend that any one of the three might have come, this is not true of all. Some would say that there is an eternal distinction between the three, and that they have some unique characteristics. The terms *Father*, *Son*, and *Holy Spirit* may be eternal, and it may be that there is something about the Son that made him especially suitable, *in the judgment of the three*, to be the one to come.

Fourth, Ware assumes that if any one of the three could have become incarnate, that is a bad thing or it counts against the truth of the doctrine of the Trinity. That, however, seems to assume the very conception of the Trinity that he is arguing for.

Fifth, Ware asserts that there is clear biblical evidence that the Son's coming was not an ad hoc decision. Yet, the reality is that we do not know from Scripture what the basis for the decision was. Yes, Scripture says that the Son came to do the Father's will, but again, we do not know if that will was the will of the Father solely.

Sixth, much seems to be made of the fact that this is the way it happened. The Son became incarnate and did so in fulfillment of the Father's will. No one, however, is objecting to the idea that this is how it was in the actual instance of the Incarnation, as we have it recorded. What is at stake, rather, is the idea that it *must* have been that way, that it could not have been otherwise. It is the transition from the first of these two conceptions to the latter that must be argued for. Grudem contends,

> This relationship between Father and Son that is seen in so
> many passages is never reversed, not in predestination before the

foundation of the world, not in creation, not in sending the Son, not in directing what the Son would do, not in granting authority to the Son, not in the Son's work of redemption, not in the Son's return to sit at the Father's right hand, not in the Son's handing over the kingdom to God the Father, never. Never does Scripture say that the Son sends the Father into the world, or that the Holy Spirit sends the Father or the Son into the world, or that the Father obeys the commands of the Son or the Holy Spirit. Never does Scripture say that the Son predestines us to be conformed to the image of the Father. The role of planning, directing, sending, and commanding the Son belongs to the Father alone.[30]

Horrell makes a similar mistake when he says that in Scripture "there is never indication that in some future eon or in some deep blue past, the Son plays the role of the Father or the Holy Spirit plays the role of the Son, even though we say that each indwells the other."[31] Even D. A. Carson seems to allude to a similar idea: "Not once is there any hint that the Son commissions the Father, who obeys. Not once is there a hint that the Father submits to the Son or is dependent upon him for his own words and deeds. Historically, Christians avoiding the trap of Arianism have insisted that the Son is equal with God in substance or essence, but that there is an economic or functional subordination of the Son to the Father."[32]

No equivalentist that I know suggests that the Father or the Spirit ever became incarnate or that it will ever happen. What they reject is the idea that it could not have happened that way. From the fact that something happened, it cannot be deduced that it *necessarily* happened that way. That assumption, which seems to underlie the gradationist view at points, cannot be used unless it is justified.

---

30. Grudem, *Evangelical Feminism and Biblical Truth,* 414.

31. J. Scott Horrell, "Toward a Biblical Model of the Social Trinity: Avoiding Equivocation of Nature and Order," *Journal of the Evangelical Theological Society* 47, no. 3 (2004): 417.

32. D. A. Carson, *The Difficult Doctrine of the Love of God* (Wheaton, IL: Crossway, 2000), 40.

Seventh, it is not clear in what sense the glory of the Son is diminished if the equivalentist view is true. Without further specification of what is meant, it is difficult to evaluate this claim.

Inferiority of the Son

The gradationists have stressed the primacy of the Father within the Godhead. Ware even says, "The Father is, in his position and authority, supreme among the Persons of the Godhead."[33] Geoffrey Bromiley puts it similarly directly, relating the difference in status to the idea of eternal generation: "Between these persons there is a superiority and subordination of order. . . . Nor does this subordination imply inferiority."[34] It is apparent from the quotation that the subordination that Bromiley says does not imply inferiority is the same subordination that is the counterpart to superiority. It is interesting that Bromiley is reticent to use the term *inferiority* of the Son, even though it is the antonym to *superiority*. This appears to be a logical contradiction, in which A is superior to B, but B is not inferior to A.

I have pointed out this logical contradiction in commenting on Bromiley's article.[35] Grudem took exception to my comments in a revealing response: "But this paragraph by Erickson is just stating the historic position of the church (which Bromiley correctly summarizes) in apparently contradictory terms by leaving off the senses in which 'superiority' and 'inferiority' are intended. Bromiley specifies that it is a 'superiority and subordination of order,' similar to what I have here called 'relationship.' And yet there is no inferiority (or superiority) of being or essence: Father, Son, and Holy Spirit are each fully God and equal in all attributes."[36]

Bromiley does indeed specify that this superiority and subordination is that of order, which I have never denied. What is interesting,

---

33. Ware, *Father, Son, and Holy Spirit*, 46.

34. Geoffrey Bromiley, "Eternal Generation," in *Evangelical Dictionary of Theology*, ed. Walter Elwell (Grand Rapids: Baker, 1984), 368.

35. Millard Erickson, *God in Three Persons: A Contemporary Analysis of the Trinity* (Grand Rapids: Baker, 1995), 309.

36. Grudem, *Evangelical Feminism and Biblical Truth*, 428.

however, is that Bromiley's article does not specify the different senses of superiority and inferiority that Grudem claims. Indeed, Bromiley's use of the words "this subordination" seems to make clear that it is a superiority of order. Grudem apparently has read into Bromiley's article what is not explicitly there. To be sure, that may be what Bromiley had in mind, but there is nothing in his written statement that would indicate that. Nor have I suggested that inferiority must be of being. My point is simply that for A to be superior to B, but for B not to be inferior to A at the same time and in the same respect is a contradiction. Grudem has not only read into Bromiley's writing, but read into mine as well.

For our purposes here, what is interesting is Grudem's aversion to the word *inferiority*. Either he is unwilling to admit that the Father's superiority of order over the Son implies the Son's inferiority of order to the Father, or he holds that inferiority must always refer to being or essence, not order. Ware's similar hesitation can be seen in his constant use of the term *submission*, rather than *subordination*, and his avoidance of the words *inferior* or *inferiority*. It may be worth probing further these two alternative interpretations of Grudem's rejection of the term *inferiority*.

On the first alternative, Grudem simply does not want to speak of the Son as inferior in authority or order, even though the Father is superior in this respect. This may be a reflection of modern positive thinking, in which negative terms are steadfastly avoided. Children in school do good work but never poor work; rather, they "can do better." No one fails a course; he or she simply gets "no credit." For that matter, no one gets old or dies anymore, either. *Inferior* has a harsh quality about it, calling into question the worth of the person. This may be what lies behind Grudem's rejection of the term. Or, he may simply be guilty of the logical contradiction that seems to appear in Bromiley's article, which was first published in 1960, before positive psychology took the hold that it has in our society and in the educational system.

On the other hand, Grudem and the other gradationists may be working with a structure in which *inferior* always connotes being or essence, rather than rank, order, role, or relationship. That may be, but if so, two requirements seem incumbent upon them: that they state this connection overtly and that they offer some argumentation in support of it.

I suspect that what is at work here is an unconscious or intuitive sense of what they are denying explicitly: that in a situation in which one member of a pair is always the one exercising the superior authority and the other one always submitting or obeying—and this relationship is fixed and necessary, not simply arbitrary or temporary—there is indeed something of a difference of the essence of the two, that the inherent superiority of authority is also a superiority in essence, and that, therefore, the latter is of an inferior or lesser essence.

The Significance of the Incarnation

The gradationists have contended that the Son's glory is diminished if there is not an eternal Father-Son relationship on the basis of which the Father commands and the Son obeys.[37] But in light of the questions we have just raised, others arise. It is necessary to ask the impact of each of these two views on the extent and the wonder of the Incarnation. Both sides agree that the Son, by becoming incarnate, became subject to certain conditions of humanity such as the physical pain, discomfort, and deprivations connected with a physical nature and the temptation to which he was submitted. That he left the splendor, glory, and comfort that was his in heaven is not in dispute.

There is, however, one major point of difference between the two views. On the gradational view, the submission or subordination to the Father that was involved in subjecting himself to the Father's will and becoming obedient to him in the Incarnation was just a continuation of what had been true for all eternity. He did not add obedience or subordination to his situation, although he may have added some dimensions of this by virtue of now being a human. His status, relative to the Father, however, was not something different from what it had been.

---

37. Ware, *Father, Son, and Holy Spirit*, 82.

On the equivalence view, part of what becoming incarnate meant was taking on a subordinate role relative to the Father. Rather than having equal authority with the Father, as he did in heaven from eternity, he now became subject to the will of another and became obedient to the commands of the Father. He not only took on the physical circumstances of humanity and the humble dwelling of a servant but also became a servant of the Father, rather than his equal.

This means that on the equivalence view, the act of self-denial and "emptying" that Paul speaks of in Philippians 2 is of greater magnitude than on the gradational view. The equality that he gave up included a status of equal authority, which, as we noted in chapter 4, seems to be implied by expressions like his taking the form of a *servant*, and *becoming obedient*. There was an even greater disparity between his incarnate and his pre-incarnate states than the gradational view describes.

Of course, increasing the magnitude of the Incarnation does not establish that this is the true view. It is possible to make a statement stronger than Scripture teaches or than was actually the case, and that does not mean the theory is thereby correct. As Edward Carnell once pointed out in response to Søren Kierkegaard, it would be a greater paradox if, instead of the infinite divine being becoming incarnate in a finite human, he had become instead incarnate in an earthworm.[38] While this argument does not settle matters of truth and falsity, it does establish that the nature of the Incarnation is different on this basis.

The Future Glorification of the Son

A similar argument can be made regarding the glorification of the Son. On the gradational view, with respect to authority, the Son's status in the eternity future is not too different from that which he possessed during his earthy incarnate ministry. He has always been subordinate and obedient to the Father, the supreme member of the Trinity; he was that during his earthly ministry, and he will be that in the eternity to come. While that

---

38. Edward John Carnell, *A Philosophy of the Christian Religion* (Grand Rapids: Eerdmans, 452), 485–86.

obedience was perhaps exercised under somewhat different conditions while he was on earth, there is only a quantitative, not a qualitative, difference between the states. The Lamb will always be sitting on the right hand of the Father's throne, not equal with him. On the equivalence model, the authority of the Son in his glorified state will be greater than during his earthly redemptive ministry and will be equal to that of the Father.

The ascension of Christ is one of the weakest points of evangelical theology, for it is sometimes depicted as accomplishing little more than a change of geographical location. Similarly, the gradational view of glorification, which includes in part the ascension, sees the change as being largely one of circumstance, the resumption of the splendor and comfort possessed before the Incarnation. A view that sees the Son's authority as becoming fully equal to that of the Father enhances this aspect of the work of Christ. While humiliation is a greater humiliation on this view, glorification is similarly a greater glorification.

Divine Immutability

Grudem invokes the doctrine of immutability as one means of supporting the contention that the Father-Son relationship is eternal: "We may conclude this first from the unchangeableness of God . . . if God now exists as Father, Son, and Holy Spirit, then he has always existed as Father, Son, and Holy Spirit."[39] This becomes a means for arguing back from Christ's self-declared earthly relationship to the Father to an eternal subordination relationship. To put it differently, this becomes one basis for an equation of the economic Trinity with the immanent Trinity.

Usually, the doctrine of immutability has been used to speak of the nature of God and the fact that he cannot change in what he is. Here, as the gradationists have repeatedly pointed out, the question of the difference between the persons is not of being or essence but of role. Grudem seems to be saying that the role of any person of the Trinity in relationship to another cannot change. This, however, resembles the

---

39. Wayne Grudem, *Systematic Theology: An Introduction to Biblical Doctrine* (Grand Rapids: Zondervan, 1994), 250.

ancient Greek doctrine of virtual immobility, rather than the Christian doctrine of dynamic mobility. According to the latter, God is able to act and to act in different ways. Presumably, he can assume different roles at different times and in different situations. Grudem's argument seems to have fallen into the category of excessive proof: by attempting to guarantee the eternality of the relationship, he may have proved more than he intended. He may have proved that God cannot change the way he acts. In fact, given this model of immutability, he may have precluded the possibility of a member of the Trinity becoming incarnate. There is another problematic dimension of the argument. Grudem's claim for the continuing Incarnation on the basis of Hebrews 13:8 may have an unfortunate result, for it may thereby also have proved that Jesus was eternally incarnate, rather than becoming so at the point of his birth.

In recent years, there have been efforts by evangelical theologians to redefine the doctrine of immutability to separate it from the influence of Greek philosophy.[40] One of the leaders in this endeavor has been Bruce Ware.[41] It may be significant that Ware does not employ Grudem's argument at this point, for it seems to have more far-reaching consequences than those that Grudem states.

Divine Will(s) and Divine Unity

Kevin Giles has argued emphatically that the gradational view jeopardizes the unity of the three persons of the Trinity. In particular, he focuses his critique on the question of whether there is/are one will or three wills within the Trinity. He puts his assertion quite strongly:

> *The three divine "persons" have one will.* To be one in being, operations, and authority implies one will. The thesis that the Son must eternally obey the Father suggests that the Father and the Son each have their own will. The Son must submit his will to

---

40. John Feinberg, *No One Like Him* (Wheaton, IL: Crossway, 2001), 264–76.
41. Bruce Ware, "An Evangelical Reformulation of the Doctrine of the Immutability of God," *Journal of the Evangelical Theological Society* 29, no. 4 (December 1986): 431–46.

the will of the Father. If the divine three each have their own will, then divine unity is breached and tritheism follows.[42]

Giles does not really argue his point. He does say, correctly, that "if the Father and the Son (and the Spirit) have one will, the actions of one cannot be conceived as obedience to another."[43] The question, however, is whether they indeed do have one will.

What makes Giles's case more difficult is the clear biblical revelation that, at least during his earthly ministry, Jesus indicated a difference between his will and that of the Father. For example, in Luke 22:42 Jesus says, "Father, if you are willing, take this cup from me; yet not my will, but yours be done." This seems to indicate at least an interaction between his will and that of the Father. This should drive Giles to the only possible interpretation, given his presuppositions, that the will of Jesus, as separate from the will of the Father, is present only because of his having assumed human nature. That in turn indicates that prior to and apart from the Incarnation there was only one will, that of the triune God. Giles says, "In the New Testament Jesus Christ is obedient as incarnate God. It is the human will of Jesus that is obedient to the one divine will. In the immanent Trinity the Father and the Son live in perfect unity and perichoretic communion, having one mind and one will in all things."[44] The attempt to see the Son as eternally having a will of his own is seen as a case of projection: "To speak of the Father eternally commanding and the Son obeying, freely or otherwise, is to depict the Father-Son relationship in terms of fallen human relationships."[45]

In Giles's theology, the will is attached to the nature, not the person. So, Jesus, having two natures, had two wills, a theory traditionally denominated as diotheletism. In this case, however, the will of the divine nature is the common will of all three members of the Godhead.

---

42. Giles, *Jesus and the Father*, 310.

43. Ibid.

44. Ibid. This seems to imply that during the Incarnation Jesus had two wills, a human and a divine, the latter of which he shared with the Father and the Holy Spirit.

45. Ibid.

It may be that Giles is correct, but he has not really established his case by argument. He has stated it in a sufficiently extreme fashion that if there are three wills rather than one will, the situation is tritheism.[46] Of course, in any situation of this type, the dilemma is the danger of either falling into tritheism if the threeness is emphasized or, on the other hand, falling into modalism if the oneness is made the stronger point.

Historically, there has been an alternative offered to Giles's position, which also strives to preserve the unity of the Trinity. That is the doctrine of perichoresis, the view that the three persons exist in such close relationship that the common life of the Godhead flows through each of them and that they are so close in harmony that they act in a unitary fashion. In one version of this model, there are three wills, but the persons are in such close harmony that their willing is one of consensus. Not one will, but three acting in unity is the case. This alternative seems as plausible as the solution that Giles adopts. In his case, he seems to have engaged in stipulative definition of such a sort that if there is eternal subordination, the result is inevitably tritheism. That premise, however, must itself be argued more persuasively than Giles has.

Giles insists that "in relations between the Father, Son, and Spirit, perfect harmony prevails. They are one in mind and will. The idea that each divine person has his own will, and the Son in particular is called to submit his will to that of the Father's will implies tritheism."[47] It appears that there is an equivocation here on the concept of "being of the same will," or "having one will." One possibility, which Giles follows, is that there is literally just one will. That will, defined as the faculty or capacity of choosing, is one, and that one will is shared or jointly possessed by the three persons. The other possibility is that there are three different wills, in the sense that each person has the capacity of choosing, but that they are in such harmony with each other that each of the three chooses to do the same as each of the others. Each, with his will, wills the same as the others. Thus, what each will chooses

---

46. Ibid., 203.
47. Ibid.

is the same option, so there is one thing that is willed alike by the three wills. The tacit transition from one meaning of will ("what one chooses with") to the other meaning ("what one chooses") is what makes Giles's conclusion follow, namely, that this leads to tritheism.

Yet, even given this reservation about Giles's argument, the gradationists still have a problem of unity to deal with. The idea that there is one supreme will, that of the Father, and that the will of the Son and that of the Spirit are so separate from the will of the Father that they must eternally submit to that will does separate the persons considerably. Here the will of one person is definitive, rather than the three being so close in harmony and in exchange of life that differences of will are inconceivable. There is indeed a problem as to whether the gradational view can be preserved from falling into tritheism, but preserving that unity may be accomplished by three wills in perichoretic unity, without the necessity of only one will.

The Names of the Persons

One argument Grudem especially appeals to is the use of the names "Father" and "Son" to designate the first two persons of the Trinity. He says, "The Father and the Son relate to one another as a father and son relate to one another in a human family: the father directs and has authority over the son, and the son obeys and is responsive to the directions of the father. . . . The role of commanding, directing, and sending is appropriate to the position of the Father, after whom all human fatherhood is patterned (Eph. 3:14–15)."[48]

Often, in discussions of religious language, the language is classified in terms of how different usages of the same word compare. One common approach is to categorize the language as univocal, equivocal, or analogical. In language that is univocal, the same term means exactly the same thing in different contexts. If language is equivocal, there is no relationship between how these words are used in two different contexts. In analogical language the same quality is found in different

---

48. Grudem, *Systematic Theology*, 249–50.

usages, but in differing degrees. Thus, if both God and humans are powerful, then they both have the capability of doing certain things, but God's ability far exceeds that of humans. Humans have power to accomplish things, and some can accomplish quite amazing physical feats, such as lifting very large and heavy objects, for example. God, however, has this attribute to an unlimited degree. He is all-powerful. The problem with an analogical statement is to know to how great a degree these two differ. What is often done is to attach the qualifier "all" to the attribute when speaking of God—God is all-powerful, all-wise, all-knowing—to indicate the possession of the same quality as the human but to an infinite degree.

In this case, it appears that the gradationists have taken one aspect of the father-son relationship, namely, authority of the father over the son, and applied it to the divine Father-Son relationship univocally. Grudem's language is, "The Father and the Son relate to one another *as* a father and son relate to one another in a human family" (emphasis added). There is nothing in the statement to indicate a differentiation of the divine authority-submission relationship from the human authority-submission relationship. Thus the language is taken quite literally in the case of the divine relationship, assuming that the description of the human form of the relationship is a literal one. In the case of the equiv-alentists, the term (with respect to this dimension of authority) is taken more literally when speaking of the relationship of Jesus the God-man to the divine first person but less so when speaking of the eternal rela-tionship between the two. There, if the terms are to be applied, they mean something quite different from what they do in the former case. The language is being used metaphorically rather than literally.

Unfortunately, the gradationists do not spell out in detail a the-ory of religious language. Grudem's systematic theology text does not have a section on religious language, and only a couple of paragraphs discuss the anthropomorphic nature of language about God. Both Grudem and Ware have strongly opposed open theism, and Ware has written two books on the subject. One of their objections is that the open theists interpret some passages (such as those that speak of God changing his mind or discovering something) literally that should be taken metaphorically. Yet, as Giles has pointed out, they themselves have followed a hermeneutic with respect to these names that strongly resembles what they reject in the open theist treatment of the actions of God.[49] At least on the surface, this appears to be something of an inconsistency in their treatment of God-language. This is not to say that no justification for this exception can be made but simply that no such justification or explanation thus far has been forthcoming.

The gradationists insist that the names "Father" and "Son" are not just used of the persons during Jesus' earthly ministry but have always applied to the two persons. After arguing that the Son's submission to the Father must have been from all eternity and citing Augustine to the effect that the Son was sent because he was the Son and the Father did the sending because he was the Father, Ware says,

> Even more basic is the question why the eternal names for "Father" and "Son" would be exactly *these* names. One must come to terms with the fact that God specifically revealed himself to us with the names "Father" and "Son" for the first and second Persons of the Trinity. Certainly these names carry connotations of authority and submission, as is confirmed by the Son's uniform declaration that he, the Son, sought only to do the will of his Father. Unless one is prepared to say that these names apply only to the incarnational relationship of the first and second Persons of the Trinity, in which case we simply don't know who these first and second Persons are eternally, we must admit that God's self-revelation would indicate an identity of the Persons of Father and Son which also marks their respective roles. Authority and submission, then, seem clearly to be built into the eternal relationship of the Father and Son, by virtue of their being who they eternally are: God the Father and God the Son.[50]

---

49. Giles, *Jesus and the Father*, 65.
50. Ware, *Father, Son, and Holy Spirit*, 82–83.

Note that Ware speaks of these as the eternal names of the Father and the Son. Similarly, Grudem says that the names are applied to the persons in terms of relationships and actions that were present before the Incarnation. We noted earlier that he based this first on divine immutability. He then adds, "We may also conclude that the relationships are eternal from other verses in Scripture that speak of the relationships the members of the Trinity had to one another before the creation of the world. For instance, when Scripture speaks of God's work of election . . . before the creation of the world, it speaks of the Father choosing us 'in' the Son."[51]

If taken at face value, these statements seem to indicate that "Father" and "Son" have from all eternity been the names of these two persons. However, certain conceptual difficulties arise that Ware and Grudem do not discuss. Who used these names for the persons in eternity past? Did the angels refer to them this way? That, however, does not take us to eternity, since the angels are created beings. Are these names by which the two persons (as well as the Holy Spirit) addressed one another? If so, what was the nature of the "speaking" of these names to one another? These issues probably need to be clarified.

Note that the equivalentists can deal with this by the use of indexical references, temporally considered. That is to say, because the references to these eternal matters were written within time and since the coming of Jesus Christ, the references to the names may be those used at the time of the writing but may not indicate that the persons actually had those names at the time to which the writing refers. This type of reference can be seen even within temporal bounds, when a historical writing uses a place-name that was current at the time of writing but was not the name of the place at an earlier time, sometimes with an explanatory comment: "They advanced against the Canaanites living in Hebron (formerly called Kiriath Arba) and defeated Sheshai, Ahiman and Talmai. From there they advanced against the people living in Debir (formerly called Kiriath Sepher)" (Judg. 1:10–11).

---

51. Grudem, *Systematic Theology*, 250.

The Basis of the Trinity

By this title we have in mind a very specific topic, introduced especially by Grudem. As we saw in chapter 1, he asks on what basis the persons of the Trinity are distinguished from each other, and he replies that it cannot be on the basis of a difference in essence or being. Each person possesses the entire divine nature. It also cannot be in any difference in attributes possessed by different members of the Trinity. He concludes that the distinction among the persons must be in the unique relationship of each to the other, which in turn is revealed in the different roles they perform. So he says, "But if there are no differences among them eternally, *then how does one person differ from the other*? They would no longer be Father, Son, and Holy Spirit, but rather Person A, Person A, and Person A, each identical to the other not only in being but also in role and in the way they relate to one another."[52] If this is the case, however, then according to Grudem, "this would mean that the Trinity has not eternally existed."[53] What he means by this is made clear in another statement: "If we did not have such differences in authority in the relationships among the members of the Trinity, then we would not know of any differences at all, and it would be unclear whether there *are* any differences among the persons of the Trinity."[54]

We must now ask about the cogency of this argument. In the chapter on philosophical issues, we discussed the meaning and importance of this principle of identity and differentiation. Here our question is this: Is it really the case that three persons who are identical do not constitute what could be called a trinity, so that he can say that under such circumstances, the Trinity has not eternally existed? It most certainly would constitute a triad of persons. It seems that what Grudem is actually saying is that "the Trinity (defined as three persons with differing degrees of authority) has not eternally existed." That, however, is a case of stipulative definition. What he may have succeeded in doing is demonstrating that the Trinity, as he has defined it, has not eternally

---

52. Grudem, *Evangelical Feminism and Biblical Truth*, 433.

53. Grudem, *Systematic Theology*, 251.

54. Grudem, *Evangelical Feminism and Biblical Truth*, 433.

existed. That, however, is a two-edged sword, which may instead serve to refute his view.

The Son's Obedience

One additional question pertains to whether the Son's obedience is voluntary or necessary. In the larger sense of whether the Son voluntarily obeyed each specific command of the Father, this is difficult to determine. Could he have decided not to obey the Father? If not, was it genuine obedience; and if he could have, what would the consequences have been?

A more limited and yet more crucial question pertains to whether the Son's coming was voluntary on his part. Could he have declined to come, and if so, can we say that he was free in this action? For that matter, was the Father free in the act of sending? Here it appears that on the gradational view, these were not free actions in the fullest sense. Presumably, it was a free decision whether someone should come at all. But since on the gradational view the relationship of authority is necessary, then that decision, if made, had to be that the Son would be the one to come. It could not have been the Father, although conceivably the Father (and the Son?) could have decided that the third person of the Trinity would have been the one to come. In that respect, then, the decision was not a free one, and neither the Father nor the Son was free as to whether the Son was to be sent.

Status of the Holy Spirit

The Holy Spirit has received relatively little attention in these discussions, as indeed was true in the debates over the Trinity in the early centuries of the church. In general, each group has treated the Holy Spirit in much the same fashion as they have the Son. The equivalentists regard him as having equal eternal authority with the Father and the Son, but having become subordinate to both for the purpose of his ministry in the individual believer and the church. The gradationists regard him as eternally subordinate to the Father and to the Son as well.

Herein is a problem for the gradational view. If the relationship of the Son to the Father is like that of an earthly son to his father, then since the Holy Spirit is similarly subordinate not only to the Father but also to the Son, does not the Holy Spirit also bear a relationship to the Son similar to an earthly son to his father? And, if so, is the Spirit's relationship then one step further removed from the Father?

Athanasius attempted to argue that the Spirit must be divine because his relation to the Son was the same as that of the Son to the Father.[55] But, as Pelikan observes, "This provoked the not unwarranted taunt that the Holy Spirit would then have to be interpreted as the son of the Son and hence the grandson of the Father."[56] As Gregory of Nazianzus put it,

> Either He is altogether Unbegotten, or else He is Begotten. If He is Unbegotten, there are two Unoriginates. If He is Begotten, you must make a further subdivision. He is so either by the Father or by the Son. And if by the Father, there are two Sons, and they are Brothers. And you may make them twins if you like, or the one older and the other younger, since you are so very fond of the bodily conceptions. But if by the Son, then such a one will say, we get a glimpse of a Grandson God, than which nothing could be more absurd.[57]

As strange as these ideas may seem, it makes sense to ask such questions if one is to press the Father-Son, command-obedience structure along the lines of human relationships. It remains for the gradationists to spell out the fashion in which the Spirit relates to the Son, and thus to the Father, whether directly or indirectly.

The Morality of the Atonement

Those who advocate the substitutionary-penal view of the atonement sometimes encounter a point of strong resistance in presenting it.

---

55. Athanasius, *Epistles to Serapion*, 1.21.

56. Jaroslav Pelikan, *The Christian Tradition: A History of the Development of Doctrine*, vol. 1, *The Emergence of the Catholic Tradition (100–600)* (Chicago: University of Chicago Press, 1971), 213.

57. Gregory of Nazianzus, *Orations* 31.7.

The courtroom analogy often used seems to suggest a sort of unjust or immoral dimension. The accused is found guilty and sentenced, in this case, to eternal death. Instead of the defendant having to pay the penalty, however, a third party, Jesus Christ, takes the place of the condemned and suffers the punishment instead.

The apparent injustice occurs in the judge seemingly requiring a sentence be served by an innocent third party. To the extent that this is imposed by the judge upon the innocent party, it seems unfair. It should be noted that on the eternal functional subordinationist model, this charge has an element of validity, for it is the Father who decides that the Son shall die and commands him to go and give his life.

However, if the model that has been emerging from our biblical and historical investigation is followed, the situation is quite different. Now the judge and the one punished are not separate. Rather, because the actions of any member of the Trinity involve the participation of the others as well, the analogy is more like this: the judge pronounces judgment and orders that the third party be punished instead of the guilty person. Then he steps down from the bench, doffs his robes, and himself goes off to serve the imposed sentence. It is the case that the one who suffers in our place and the one who transfers the guilt of humans to Christ and the merit of Christ's death to us are the same. Rather than having to obey a command issued by another, Christ himself participated in the decision that he should do this.

We have examined a number of theological issues that arise out of the two positions on the relationship of the Son to the Father. While both the gradational and the equivalence views possess theological strengths and weaknesses, it appears that the number and severity of the theological problems arising from the gradational view are greater than those occasioned by tracing out the implications of the equivalence view.

CHAPTER 8

The Practical Implications

One further area of consideration is the practical differences that may emerge from the two differing theories. Does the choice of one or the other of these views of the eternal relative authority of the Father and the Son make any difference in the religious or ethical practice of the believer, and does this bear on the truth of the respective views? Are the practical implications of a view such that they can be tested against divine commands or instructions that have been revealed to us? There are certain issues of a practical nature that deserve to be addressed by the two parties.

Prayer

Probably the primary issue is the nature of prayer, and particularly, the matter of which members of the Trinity we should address in our prayers. Should prayer be addressed only to one member of the Trinity or to all the members?

Ware is very definite on this matter. He acknowledges that sometimes children are taught to preface their prayers by saying "Dear Jesus." He proposes instead something that he considers both "clear and radical": that we pray to the Father alone. There are two reasons for this: Jesus taught us to pray that way in the Lord's Prayer, and a correct understanding of the Trinity requires it. He says, "The Christian's life of *prayer* must rightly acknowledge the roles of Father, Son and Spirit as we pray to the Father, through the Son, in the power of the Spirit."[1] Since Jesus taught us to pray, "Our Father," this is how we are to pray.

---

1. Bruce A. Ware, *Father, Son, and Holy Spirit: Relationships, Roles, and Relevance* (Wheaton, IL: Crossway, 2005), 18.

Beyond that, the reason why we may pray and encourage children to pray incorrectly is because of a misunderstanding of the doctrine of the Trinity. Ware says, "Perhaps we do not think about prayer as we should because we do not understand the doctrine of the Trinity."[2] I take it Ware is saying that this practice is an implication of the doctrine of the Trinity, as he formulates it, since he says that this life of prayer *must* acknowledge the roles.

However, there is one rather major problem with this view. In several instances in the New Testament, prayer is addressed to the Son. One notable one is Stephen's prayer in Acts 7:59–60, where he definitely addresses his prayer to the "Lord Jesus." Similarly, in 2 Corinthians 12:8–9, Paul recounts praying for a pressing need, that the stake in the flesh might be removed, and receiving an answer. In verse 8 he says, "Three times I pleaded with the Lord to take it away from me." The answer comes in verse 9: "But he said to me, 'My grace is sufficient for you, for my power is made perfect in weakness.' Therefore I will boast all the more gladly about my weaknesses, so that Christ's power may rest on me." Since the Lord to whom he prayed spoke of "my power," and since Paul then described this as "Christ's power," it is evident that Jesus is the Lord who here received and replied to the prayer. Yet another instance is the "Come, Lord Jesus," prayer in Revelation 22:20, which became commonly known as the *maranatha* prayer of the early church. The practice in these three cases conflicts with the command that Jesus gave. There are four possible responses Ware could make to this apparent conflict:

1. He could contend that the restriction of prayer to the Father is not actually implied by this view of the Trinity. Yet the language in which he has advanced this teaching on prayer hardly admits such a claim, and indeed his whole argument seems to rest upon it. This option does not seem viable.

2. He could contend that these are not actually prayers. Yet the form of the utterances is that of requests presumably directed

---

2. Ibid.

to a divine being. This also does not seem to provide an adequate solution.

3. He could contend that those who prayed these prayers prayed wrongly. My understanding of the work of the Spirit in the life of the believer does not guarantee that the person never errs in what he does. In the instances at hand, however, the action seems to be approved and even responded to positively. This option does not appear to be a good solution, therefore.

4. Finally, he could decide that his subordinationist view of the Trinity is incorrect. The logical structure of his argument seems to be:

A implies B
A, therefore B

This is a common form of argument, termed affirming the antecedent, and it is a valid argument. Note, however, that the argument

A implies B
Not B, therefore not A

also is a valid argument, termed denying the consequent. On this basis, if the eternal subordinationist view of the Trinity implies the "Father-only" view of prayer, but the Father-only view is not true, then that implies that the eternal subordinationist view of the Trinity is false. By "implies" here we mean not merely the weak sense of the word, of suggesting or rendering psychologically appealing, but the strong sense of strict logical implication.

It would seem to me to be a better approach to regard Jesus' command to pray to the Father as the logical way to pray during Jesus' earthly ministry (although note that the numerous requests brought to Jesus were actually prayers to him uttered in his bodily presence). Now that he has ascended to his previous place, at least some prayers may and even should be addressed to him, although not necessarily exclusively so. Support for this can be seen in noting how similar was Stephen's prayer at his moment of death to Jesus' prayer in a similar situation. Compare, for example, Acts 7:59, "Lord Jesus, receive my spirit," with Luke 23:46, "Father, into your hands I commit my spirit," and Acts 7:60, "Lord, do not hold this sin against them," with Luke 23:34, "Father, forgive them, for they do not know what they are doing."

What of the other eternal subordinationists? Horrell seems to endorse in passing what has evidently been the formula in some conservative circles: to the Father, through the Son, in the Holy Spirit.[3] Grudem, however, says, "We may pray either to the Father or to the Son," and "it does not seem wrong to pray directly to the Holy Spirit at times."[4] Thus he does not seem to be vulnerable to the criticism above.

However, if we look more closely at the nature of the requests made in the prayers to Jesus that Grudem cites, one must ask whether, on his view of the roles of the respective members of the Trinity, those requests should really be directed to the Son. If indeed the Son acts in obedience to the Father's will, should we not pray for the Father to command the Son to do these things? Whether one holds that prayer actually affects what God wills and does, or that it is simply an affirmation to God of our concern that his will be done, the predominance of the Father's will over that of the Son and the Spirit would seem to require that prayer, to the extent that it is petitionary prayer, be addressed to the Father. For example, given Grudem's view of the Father sending the Son in the first coming, would it not be more appropriate to pray to the Father to send the Son a second time than to ask Jesus to return? Perhaps the Lord has not yet returned because we have been praying wrongly. Thus, Grudem's view of the respective roles of the three members may actually imply the view of prayer that he rejects on the basis of these biblical texts. So it appears that in the understanding of prayer, Ware has been more consistent than Grudem in drawing the implication of the view of

---

3. J. Scott Horrell, "Toward a Biblical Model of the Social Trinity: Avoiding Equivocation of Nature and Order," *Journal of the Evangelical Theological Society* 47, no. 3 (2004): 421.

4. Wayne Grudem, *Systematic Theology: An Introduction to Biblical Doctrine* (Grand Rapids: Zondervan, 1994), 381.

the eternal authority-subordination relationship. Unfortunately, as we have seen, that view of prayer is contradictory to the biblical practice and thus constitutes a refutation of the theory (eternal gradation of authority) that implies it.

It is interesting to note that this formula is not something new in the church. Origen argued for a similar position in his treatise on the Lord's Prayer. He says, "Now if we observe the proper nature of prayer we should not pray to any begotten being, not even to Christ himself, but only to God the Father of all, to whom even our Saviour himself prayed, as we have already recorded, and to whom he teaches us to pray."[5] Origen adds, "That prayer to the Son and not to the Father is absurd, and contrary to obvious evidence, would be universally agreed."[6]

However, if Origen restricts prayer to being directed only to the Father, not the Son, he also makes a further restriction: that the prayers are only to be through the Son.

> Therefore the saints, when they give thanks to God in their prayers, confess their thanks to him through Jesus Christ. Just as it is improper for somebody who is scrupulous in prayer to pray to one who himself prays but to the one whom our Lord Jesus taught to address as "Father" in our prayers, so no prayer should be offered to the Father except through him; as he himself made clear when he said: "Truly, truly I say to you, if you should ask anything of my Father, he will grant it you in my name. Until now you have asked nothing in my name; ask, and you shall receive, so that your joy may be completed" (Jn 16.23–24). For he did not say: "Ask me," or simply "Ask the Father," but "If you should ask anything of the Father he will grant it you in my name." For until Jesus taught this, nobody besought the Father in the name

---

5. Origen, *On Prayer* 15; taken from *Tertullian, Cyprian, Origen on the Lord's Prayer*, translated and introduced, with brief annotations, by Alistair Stewart-Sykes (Crestwood, NY: St. Vladimir's Seminary Press, 2004), 146–47.

6. Ibid.

of the Son, so Jesus' words, "until now you have asked nothing in my name" are true. And true also is the statement: "Ask, and you shall receive, so that your joy may be completed" (Jn 16.24).

Philip Schaff says that this is because Origen, with his belief in the eternal generation of the Son, regarded the Father as "the fountain and root of the divinity." He goes on to add, "Hence, he also taught, that the Son should not be directly addressed in prayer, but the Father through the Son in the Holy Spirit. This must be limited, no doubt, to absolute worship, for he elsewhere recognizes prayer to the Son and to the Holy Spirit. Yet this subordination of the Son formed a stepping-stone to Arianism, and some disciples of Origen, particularly Dionysius of Alexandria, decidedly approached that heresy."[7]

If Schaff's interpretation is correct, we have Ware, who rejects the idea of eternal generation, following a pattern that was commended by Origen, who had novel ideas on a number of subjects on the basis of his view of generation. The point, however, is that here, in the judgment of Schaff, the pattern of prayer is related to Origen's idea of eternal generation, an idea that Ware rejects. A number of questions remain, which may not be fully resolvable. Whether both hold to the same sort of functional subordination and whether that is the basis of this form of prayer might be debated. Whether that functional subordination assumes some sort of ontological subordination is also in question and has been addressed elsewhere in this volume. It does appear, however, that Ware may, in his recommended practice, be more consistent with his theological tenets than is Grudem. Thus, he has done us a favor by showing the practical conclusion to which that view leads.

Worship and Praise

Ware examines the Philippians 2 passage and notes especially the way it culminates. He notes that Paul says that every knee will bow and

---

7. Philip Schaff, *History of the Christian Church* (Grand Rapids: Eerdmans, 1948), 2:552. Schaff cites *De Orat.*, chap. 15, as the source for Origen's statement about prayer (ibid., n. 7).

every tongue confess that Jesus Christ is Lord. That amazing offering of praise is not the final word of the passage, however. In Ware's words,

> This glorious statement of the exaltation of Christ does not end with every knee bowing and every tongue confessing that Jesus Christ is Lord. Rather, this action is penultimate while the ultimate glory is extended to God the Father (v. 11b). God the Father receives the ultimate and supreme glory, for the Father sent the Son to accomplish redemption in his humiliation, and the Father exalted the Son over all creation; in all these things, the Father stands supreme over all—including supreme over his very Son. All praise of the Son ultimately and rightly redounds to the Father. It is the Father, then, who is supreme in the Godhead—in the triune relationships of Father, Son, and Holy Spirit—and supreme over all the very creation over which the Son rules as its Lord.[8]

Ware declares this fact to be "perhaps the single most important feature of this passage" for the present discussion.[9]

Ware wants us to realize that every gift comes from the Father. This is apparent from texts like James 1:17: "Every good and perfect gift is from above, coming down from the Father of the heavenly lights, who does not change like shifting shadows." It is not just for those gifts the Bible tells us come from the Father, or more generally, simply from God, that he is to be praised. Rather, Ware points out that Ephesians 1:3 specifically places God's gifts in a Trinitarian setting: "[Paul] writes, 'Blessed be the God and Father of our Lord Jesus Christ, who has blessed us in Christ with every spiritual blessing in the heavenly places.'" Then Ware goes on to comment, "The Father gets top billing, as it were. All the blessings that we receive come to us from the Father, through the Son, as mediated to us by the Spirit."[10]

---

8. Ware, *Father, Son, and Holy Spirit*, 50–51.

9. Ibid., 50.

10. Ibid., 51.

The pattern here is interestingly similar to the formula Ware has suggested with respect to prayer. While he does not tell us that we are to direct praise only to the Father, not the Son, we are to keep in mind that the ultimate glory is to go to the Father. It is as if what the Son does, he does because the Father has decided and commanded him to do it. The real source of the actions, and the blessings emanating from them, is the Father.

In some ways, although Ware does not state it, there is a parallel between the work of the Son and the work of the human as God's agent and steward of the creation, in fulfillment of the command in Genesis 2 to have dominion over the earth. The dominion that the human exercises is really God's authority delegated to him. Similarly, the believer is representing Christ in carrying out the Great Commission and apparently is exercising the delegated authority that Christ says has been given to him (Matt. 28:19–20). Christ is carrying out the Father's command, and we are carrying out the command Christ has given to us, which is thus the Father's will, mediated through the Son.

One interesting feature of Ware's position is that it seems to involve a perichoresis, but it is asymmetrical. Jesus did say, "Don't you believe that I am in the Father, and that the Father is in me? The words I say to you are not just my own. Rather, it is the Father, living in me, who is doing his work. Believe me when I say that I am in the Father and the Father is in me; or at least believe on the evidence of the miracles themselves" (John 14:10–11). Here there is a symmetry, in which Jesus is in the Father and the Father is in him. The works Jesus does are not just his own, but the Father is doing his work through Jesus. Ware would strongly agree and probably would see this text as supporting his position, although he does not specifically cite it. What is interesting, however, is that both the Father and Son are in each other, from which some have drawn the conclusion that not only is each work of the Son a work in which the Father participates, but also each work of the Father is one in which the Son (and the Spirit) participate. Ware does not draw that parallel.

Giles, on the other hand, does see the relationship as reciprocal. It is not that the Father does the Son's will but that the works done by the Father are not his alone. They are done by both, and actually by all three, including the Holy Spirit. Citing Marianne Thompson, he notes, "John never envisages a disjunction in will or work between the Father and the Son. He consistently teaches that the Son does the work of the Father (5:17, 19; 10:32, 37; 14:10–11). What Jesus does the Father does and *vice versa*. They work as one."[11]

I take it that the difference between worship based on Ware's theology at this point and that flowing from Giles's theology would be this. According to Ware, the Father should be praised and thanked for those works that are attributed to him. The works done by Jesus should be the occasion of our praising Jesus, but also always praising the Father, who is the source of the decision and therefore deserving of the ultimate praise. And, although Ware does not discuss the subject, I assume that he would say that the works of the Holy Spirit are works for which we should also praise the Son and, even more completely, the Father.

Grudem does not address the issue of differences of worship in relationship to the members of the Trinity. He does say that the equality with the Father that the Son gave up (Phil. 2:6) was an equality of glory and honor, not of authority, so one might infer that Grudem would make no differences in worshiping and praising the Father and the Son.[12] Giles, and presumably other equivalentists, however, while especially praising the member of the Trinity who plays the primary role in a given work, would praise the triune God, Father, Son, and Holy Spirit, for all the works and blessings of God and thank him (them) for all gifts.

Based on the texts that we examined in chapter 4, the equivalence view is more expressive of the biblical teaching. And the commonly sung doxology expresses more closely the equivalence view than it does the gradational view:

Praise God from whom all blessings flow,
Praise Him all creatures here below.

---

11. Giles, *Jesus and the Father*, 122.

12. Wayne Grudem, *Evangelical Feminism and Biblical Truth: An Analysis of More Than One Hundred Disputed Questions* (Sisters, OR: Multnomah, 2004), 409.

Praise Him above, ye heav'nly host.
Praise Father, Son, and Holy Ghost.

Order or Taxis

It appears that in the matters of both prayer and worship, the concept of order, or taxis, plays a large part in the thinking of the gradationists, especially of Ware. He says,

> A word often used by early church theologians for the evident authority structure of the Father-Son relationship in the Godhead is *taxis*, which means "ordering." There is an ordering in the Godhead, a "built-in" structure of authority and submission that marks a significant respect in which the Persons of the Godhead are distinguished from one another. Surely, they are not distinct in essence, for each shares fully the identically same divine nature. Their distinction, rather, is constituted, in part, by *taxis*—the ordering of Father, Son, and Holy Spirit within the Godhead.[13]

Ware does not offer lexicographical or historical arguments in support of this contention, so it is important that this concept be more closely examined. The word *taxis* can have several different meanings. Arndt and Gingrich, for example, give four different meanings:

1. Fixed succession or order
2. (Good) order, or in an orderly manner
3. Position or post
4. Nature, quality, manner, condition, appearance[14]

It appears that the gradationists take the word in the third sense, which derives from the sense of *tassō* as putting someone in a position in which the person is in charge or is over someone else.[15] On the other

---

13. Ware, *Father, Son, and Holy Spirit*, 72.

14. William F. Arndt and F. Wilbur Gingrich, *A Greek-English Lexicon of the New Testament and Other Early Christian Literature*, 2nd ed. (Chicago: University of Chicago Press, 1979), 803–4.

15. Ibid., 805–6.

hand, the equivalentists would say that order is simply an organizational matter. So Giles says,

> This is not to suggest, however, that Paul denied divine order
> as such. For Paul there is nothing arbitrary or random in how
> God the Father and God the Son work or function. He indicates
> that he believed they always work cooperatively in an orderly
> manner. There is a given divine disposition. . . . Such order does
> not imply the subordination of any party. Rather, it envisages
> harmonious and agreed ways of cooperatively and reciprocally
> working together. God the Father does nothing apart from God
> the Son and vice versa. They are distinct "persons," yet they work
> as one in an ordered, in the sense of orderly, manner.[16]

Note the key word in Giles's statement: "agreed." The order is not
something unilaterally imposed by the Father but mutually agreed on
for purposes of organization.

There are many situations in which first in order does not connote
a primacy of rank. Soldiers have their fixed places in formation, but
that is not entirely based on rank. Although Matthew is the first of the
four Gospels, probably no one seriously believes that this indicates that
the "first" gospel is also first in importance. Priority in time often does
not indicate superiority; indeed, the later often exceeds the earlier. In
fact, in some organizational structures, the most important comes last.
In academic processions, the president, as the highest-ranking officer,
is the last in and the first out.[17]

We might debate the extent to which the use of the term historically carried one or another of these meanings, but it does not necessarily follow from the concept of taxis that there must be gradations of
rank and thus differences in glory and praise. If this is implied by the
term, then the gradationist approach of ultimate praise being given to

---

16. Giles, *Jesus and the Father*, 110.

17. I did teach in two institutions, which had a rather close connection, historically and otherwise, in which the president was both the first in and the first out, but
this is an unusual exception, apparently reflecting local culture and customs.

the Father is appropriate. What is needed, however, is some additional argumentation for that point. It is our judgment that the gradationists have not sufficiently made their point here.

The Family

The gradationists make a particularly strong application of their view of the Trinity to the family. Time and time again in his book, Ware says things like this:

> It seems that 1 Corinthians 11:3 suggests this [that the invariable order is Father, Son, and Holy Spirit] and then applies this same *taxis* to God-designed human relationships. For all eternity, the order establishes that God is the head of Christ; within the created sphere, there is an ordering such that Christ is the head of man; and within human relationships, the order establishes that man is the head of woman. Intrinsic to God's own nature is a fundamental *taxis*, and he has so designed creation to reflect his own being, his own internal and eternal relationships, in part, through created and designed relationships of *taxis*.[18]

Grudem also argues for the parallel between God's headship over Christ and the husband's headship over his wife:

> Why was the Son eternally subject to the Father? Simply because He eternally existed as Son, and submission to the Father was inherent in that relationship. Why should a wife be subject to her husband? Simply because she is a wife and he is a husband, she is a woman and he is a man. "Wives, be subject to your own husbands as to the Lord" (Eph. 5:22). "But I want you to understand that the head of every man is Christ, the head of the wife is her husband, and the head of Christ is God" (1 Cor. 11:3). In the one case, submission is grounded in the Son's existence as Son. In the other case, submission is grounded in a wife's existence as a woman. This is a wonderful parallel between the

18. Ware, *Father, Son, and Holy Spirit*, 72.

submission (with equal dignity and value) of the Son of God to the Father and the submission (with equal dignity and value) of the wife to her husband.[19]

Similarly, Grudem writes, "Thus, in a marriage relationship . . . there is a reflection of the equality and difference between Father and Son in the Trinity, a beautiful reflection of the image of God. And so it is with differences in role but equality in value and gifting in the church."[20]

On the other hand, equivalentists for the most part have contended that the relationships among the members of the Trinity do not really bear on the structure of the relationships within the family. Their discussion of the former has been to show, not that their view of the family is correct, but that the gradationist case for their view of the latter cannot be derived from a supposed parallel. Gilbert Bilezikian's plea was that evangelicals stop trying to exploit the doctrine of the Trinity to justify a social or ethical matter. The same is true of Kevin Giles's arguments. In the case of equivalentists, the relevance of the relationships within the Trinity to those within the family and society is more general and related to the manner in which those relationships are exercised, rather than the structure of the latter.[21]

Ware clearly expresses the implications of this structure in several places. He suggests that those who are in positions of authority should exercise that authority as the Father does his authority over the Son: "Who is in a position of authority, with responsibility to pattern his manner of leadership after the Father? Clearly, every married man is in this category. Husbands have rightful authority in their homes with their wives, and if God has blessed them with children, their authority extends also to these precious gifts from the Lord. Husbands should exercise their authority

---

19. Wayne Grudem, *Evangelical Feminism and Biblical Truth*, 435–36.

20. Ibid., 453–54.

21. Despite this, Fred Sanders, in an unpublished paper read at the 2006 annual meeting of the Evangelical Theological Society, decried the use of the doctrine of the Trinity to justify a view of marital relationships but chose to attribute this to what I have here termed the equivalentists, rather than the gradationists.

with wisdom, goodness, carefulness, and thoroughness in order to seek the well-being of those under their charge. Husbands should seek to be like their heavenly Father in increasing measure."[22]

It is clear that the gradationists rest much of their case for the transition from the eternal subordination within the Trinity to the permanent and invariable subordination of wife to husband on the text of 1 Corinthians 11:3. In his book *Evangelical Feminism and Biblical Truth*, Grudem has one appendix of fifty-six pages, in which he argues on the basis of this text, patristic literature, and extrabiblical Greek literature, that the correct translation of the word *kephalē* here should be "head," in the sense of "authority over." In addition, he discusses the word in five other places in the book, and the Scripture index to the book contains twenty references to this verse, as well as seven references to the longer passage, verses 2–16. Giles points out that the book *Biblical Foundations for Manhood and Womanhood* contains eleven discussions of this verse, most of them more than a page in length.[23] It is apparent that Grudem feels strongly about this subject, saying of Catherine Kroeger's article on "head" in *Dictionary of Paul and His Letters*, that although the article gives an apparent wealth of documentation, only someone with extensive library resources available and willing to devote a large amount of time to the investigation would discover that "this is not careful scholarship." As we noted earlier, he goes on to say, "In fact, in several sections its disregard of facts is so egregious that it fails even to meet fundamental requirements of truthfulness."[24]

Grudem's claim for the evidence supporting his rendering of the meaning of the word is challenged by equivalentist scholars. Several years ago at an evening-long debate at the annual meeting of the Evangelical Theological Society, he and Gilbert Bilezikian examined thirty instances of the word *kephalē* in classical Greek writings. Each contended that all thirty instances supported his view! Philip Barton Payne contends, "There are fourteen primary reasons to interpret head

---

22. Ware, *Father, Son, and Holy Spirit,* 59–60.
23. Giles, *Jesus and the Father,* 111n. 73.
24. Grudem, *Evangelical Feminism and Biblical Truth,* 597.

as referring to 'source' rather than 'authority' in this passage [1 Cor. 11:2–16]."[25] Among the reasons he offers are that the Septuagint rarely used *kephalē* to translate the Hebrew word for "head" in those places where it seems to mean "superior rank," even though the Septuagint strongly tended to translate Hebrew words literally; that not a single example of head as implying authority is given by any of several significant Greek lexicons: Liddell Scott Jones, Renehan, Moulton and Milligan, Friedrich Preisigke, Pierre Chantraine, and S. C. Woodhouse; that Paul elsewhere repeatedly "referred to Christ as head in the sense of source of life or nourishment," in passages such as Colossians 1:18; 2:19; Ephesians 4:15–16; and 5:23. These and other considerations suggest that the case is not necessarily as conclusive as Grudem contends.

In addition to the requirement that the word *kephalē* means authority, the gradationist argument in this application requires that Paul is arguing in 1 Corinthians 11:3 that because God is the "head" of Christ, the man is similarly the "head" of the woman. Here, however, equivalentists offer several negative considerations. Payne claims that "the items listed in verse 3 are not listed in a descending or ascending order of authority, but they are listed chronologically: Christ, the creative source of man; the man, the source from which God took woman; God, the source of Christ in the incarnation."[26] Giles also challenges Grudem's interpretation of the logical structure of the passage:

> In 1 Cor. 11:3 Paul does not allude to a fourfold hierarchy, God-Christ-man-woman, but to three paired relationships in which in each case one party is the *kephale* of the other. They are not ordered hierarchically. Paul speaks first of Christ and man, then man and woman, and last of God and Christ. Rather than subordinating the persons in a descending "chain of command," or "hierarchy of headship," Paul is differentiating the persons paired to introduce the main point he wants to make in the whole passage, namely

---

25. Philip B. Payne, "Wild Hair and Gender Equality in 1 Corinthians 11:2–16," *Priscilla Papers* 20, no. 3 (Summer 2006): 10.

26. Ibid.

that men and women are differentiated by God. This sexual differentiation is to be demonstrated by what they have or do not have on their head when leading in public worship.[27]

On these two points, it appears to me that the case for the gradational application is not sufficiently established. Bear in mind that in a chain of propositions, the probabilities of the statements are not added to each other, but multiplied by each other. So, if each of two statements is 80 percent probable, the composite is 64 percent probable; if 70 percent, 49 percent; if 60 percent, 36 percent; if 50 percent, 25 percent. Because of the debatability of each assertion, the composite argument is unconvincing in this case.

Church Government

In his discussion of the pertinence of supremacy and subordination within the Trinity, Ware applies this not only to family relationships but also more broadly: "Others with this responsibility, such as elders in a local church, mothers (as well as fathers) with their children, or employers in the workplace, or in any arena of life where people are placed under another's authority—these are all spheres where we can look to the Father for the model on how to lead, or how to exercise rightful authority."[28]

It is not just those who possess the authority who should look for guidance to the patterns within the Trinity, however. Those placed under authority should do similarly: "*Those under authority* need to be more like the Son, who gratefully and obediently embraces the work given him by his Father, and gives highest honor to the Father for all that is accomplished."[29]

As with the treatment of family relationships, Ware is careful to specify that just as the Father possesses authority but exercises it gently and lovingly, here also those who are in places of authority are not to

---

27. Giles, *Jesus and the Father*, 112.
28. Ware, *Father, Son, and Holy Spirit*, 59–60.
29. Ibid., 67.

exercise it in a domineering fashion. They also are not to utilize it for their own pleasure, profit, or aggrandizement. They are to be careful to call attention to those placed under them and to give them credit for what they have done.[30] Conversely, just as the Son gives ultimate glory to the Father, those under authority are to reflect credit on those who prepared them for their specific ministry and granted them the privilege of carrying it out.

> While *those in authority* need to be more like the Father, who lavishes favor on others by calling them to participate in his work, often putting the spotlight on them for their labors of love, *those under authority* need to be more like the Son, who gratefully and obediently embraces the work given him by his Father, and gives highest honor to the Father for all that is accomplished. What a revolution would take place in our homes and churches if such reciprocal honoring of one another took place, all the while maintaining clearly the lines of authority that exist, by God's good purpose and wise design. What lessons we learn, then, from seeing more clearly the distinct role of the Father among the Persons of the triune Godhead.[31]

It is apparent, from Ware's wording, that he believes this mode of operation, where some have the authority and administer it lovingly and others submit obediently and humbly, is an implication of the authority pattern within the eternal Trinity. His position on this matter, unlike the familial relationships, does not depend on the particular rendering of 1 Corinthians 11:3. Rather, both parties seem to be following the interpretation that humans bear the image of God, not just individually but collectively, and that consequently the relations among them should mirror the relations among the members of the Trinity.

In terms of church government, the general principles of humility and unselfishness are harmonious with several types of organization,

---

30. Ibid., 59–71.
31. Ibid., 67.

but the pattern that tends to fit best with the gradational view of the Trinity is an episcopal or, to a lesser extent, a presbyterial type of government. There, authority is vested in an individual or ascending series of individuals or bishops, or in a select group of leaders, known as elders, and an ascending series of ecclesiastical governing bodies. To the extent that the gradational view makes the connection of 1 Corinthians 11:3 to male-female relationships in general, it also tends to hold that positions of authority, whether teaching or ruling, are to be held only by men.

Adherents to the equivalence view have given less attention to the implications of their view of intratrinitarian relationships for the questions of church government. To the extent that one can draw analogies here, it would seem that this view would accord more closely with a congregational form of government or, to a lesser extent, a presbyterial form. Here, the priesthood of all believers is more strongly emphasized, and authority tends to be vested more in the individual members of the congregation. They have elected leaders to which the decision-making authority is delegated; but the point is that it is delegated upward, as it were, and in many congregational structures the congregational members have the power of ratifying or even overriding the decisions of the leaders. Ironically, Ware, like Grudem, is a Baptist, a denomination that has traditionally practiced a more congregational form of government, while Giles is an Anglican, a group operating under an episcopal form of government.

Many variations of each type of government can be found. In some elder governments, the elders are elected by the congregation; whereas in others, the elder board is self-perpetuating, choosing their own members and successors. The areas of authority also vary greatly. In some congregations, all ministers are called by congregational vote; whereas in others, only the senior pastor is voted into office by the congregation, all other positions being filled by the elder board. And in some cases, even the senior pastor is chosen by the elder board.[32]

---

32. If care is not taken in the construction of a constitution and bylaws, churches can find themselves in surprising straits. In one church, the senior pastor was called by the elder board, such a call had to be by unanimous vote, and the associate pastor

To the extent that these governmental structures are logically implied by a given view of the Trinity, they might provide us with checks on congruency of that view of the Trinity to the Scripture, if other Scriptures address the issue of government involved. This would be similar to the evaluation we made earlier of Ware's view of prayer. However, this does not appear to be as potentially fruitful as that case was.

We may note that Jesus spoke negatively about those who love to have positions of authority and honor and told his disciples, "But you are not to be called 'Rabbi,' for you have only one Master and you are all brothers" (Matt. 23:8). He rebuked the disciples for their contention over who was the greatest among them (Mark 9:33–37; Luke 9:46–48). These could be claimed by either side, however. One might argue that since they were not to consider themselves greater than each other, there should not be levels of authority, favoring the equivalence view. On the other hand, one could claim that those in authority are chosen by God himself, favoring the gradationist view. It seems unlikely that the truth of the competing views of the Trinity can be measured by the practical implications in the area of church government. Whatever the form of government, however, the lesson is the same: gentleness and humility should be present in those who exercise authority, just as Jesus modeled (Phil. 2:5) and contrasted, in his teaching, with the way the Gentile leaders ruled (Matt. 20:25; Luke 22:25). Jesus, the Lord, was the one who washed the feet of his disciples, who were unwilling to wash one another's feet.

There is one point in respect to which the equivalence view may have implications that give it something of an advantage in a postmodern age, although in light of the evaluation we might give of this aspect of postmodernity, this might not be deemed a desirable quality.

---

was a member of the elder board. Knowing that a particular candidate for senior pastor did not wish to retain him on staff, the associate was able single-handedly to veto the call of the candidate, thereby preserving his own job. Another church considered adopting a constitution under which the only provision for removal from office of an elder was by unanimous vote of the board, of which of course he was a member. This provision, which ultimately was not adopted, would have made it functionally impossible to remove a dissenting elder from office.

Because of postmodernism's hostility to metanarratives and single authoritative teachings, and its emphasis on each individual's contribution to the truth, it will be less receptive to a structure where authority generates from above. Of course, in this respect, it may be hostile even to an approach in which God is the source and definer of truth and the one who possesses and exercises authority and power. The same is true of one of the megatrends that John Naisbitt pointed out as early as a quarter century ago. He noted that in both industry and government the movement has been away from the model where authority is concentrated at the top and more toward a model where authority is distributed on several levels and tends to generate from the bottom up, rather than from the top down.[33]

Again, this trend might represent a growing hostility to authority in general and thus opposition to the lordship of God. Focusing upon the interhuman relationships alone, however, such relationships need to be related to the teachings in Scripture of the value of every human, in light of emphasis on all being in the image of God (Gen. 9:6), of God not showing favoritism (Acts 10:34), of the Shepherd seeking the one missing sheep out of one hundred (Luke 15:3–7), and of his knowing and caring about everyone, just as he cares about the fate of a single bird (Matt. 10:29–31).

In practical terms, since everyone is important to God, we should be interested in and concerned about and value everyone. Even conversations should try to involve everyone, rather than being dominated by one or a few. Persons should be more interested in asking others about themselves, rather than regarding them as audiences for talk about oneself. It may not be insignificant that Jesus associated with some of the lesser-regarded members of society (Luke 5:30–32; 7:34–50; 19:1–10) and that James (James 2:1–9) rebuked the tendency to treat with greater respect those of higher social status. If the gradational view might encourage any sort of elitism in practice, it is less in harmony with the picture depicted in these other teachings of Scripture.

---

33. John Naisbitt, *Megatrends: Ten New Directions Transforming Our Lives* (New York: Warner, 1982), 189–205.

So Who's Right?

We have examined at some length the two views of the relative authority of the persons of the Trinity and the arguments advanced by each of the parties to this debate. We have seen that the first group, the gradationists, maintain that the Father is eternally the supreme member of the Trinity and the Son and the Holy Spirit are eternally subordinate in authority to him but are equally God in their being. The equivalentists, on the other hand, contend that the subordination of the Son and the Spirit is temporary and functional, for the period and purpose of their special ministry in the accomplishment and application of salvation to the human race. We must now summarize our findings and make a judgment regarding the relative merit of the two views.

Biblical

The gradational view appeals to texts that suggest the Father's initiative in predestining some to salvation, in sending his Son into the world, and in the giving of gifts. These texts describe the relationship of the Father to the Son, not only during the time of the Son's earthly ministry, but also in times past and in the future eternity. Especially impressive is 1 Corinthians 15:24–28, which seems to indicate that in the consummation, the Son will be subject to the Father. Gradationists also make much of the descriptions of the Son as sitting "at the right hand" of the Father, an indication of the Father's superior authority. The very names of the persons, designated as Father and Son, indicate that, just as with human fathers and sons, God the Father is in the position of supremacy with regard to God the Son. The compilation of such texts is impressive and taken alone would have to be judged to have established the gradational-authority view as true.

There are, however, texts that seem to support the equivalent-authority position. Some of these are general in nature, such as the meaning of the names Father and Son, the variability of order in the listing of the three, and the variations of names used for the three persons. Beyond that, however, there are texts that suggest the Son and the Spirit fill the same roles as the Father, such as choosing persons for salvation and for special positions. In addition, there are texts that speak of the joint actions of more than one person and texts that describe the unity of the persons. These considerations suggest that the Father's authority cannot be taken in isolation from the authority possessed by the Son and the Holy Spirit. The references to the Son sitting on the Father's right hand are countered by references to them sitting together on the throne and are not persuasive regarding the gradational view. The support for appeals to the use of the Greek term *kephalē* in 1 Corinthians 11:3 is similarly disputable and does not render a clear argument for either side.

On balance, then, we judge that the best interpretation of the full biblical revelation is that no action of any person of the Trinity is an action done in isolation from the other two persons, even though one is primary in that action. This means that the texts that speak of the Father commanding and the Son obeying are to be understood as referring to the time of the Son's earthly ministry. The Father's will, which the Son obeys, is actually the will of all three members of the Trinity, administered on their behalf by the Father. While some texts, such as the 1 Corinthians 15 passage, favor the gradational view, it is our judgment that overall, the equivalence view does a better job of explaining more of the biblical evidence and with less distortion of the texts.

Historical

In the period before the Council of Nicea, there were several theologians who held to the functional subordination of the Son. In most cases, this was related to the concept of the Father's eternal generation of the Son. Some, such as Origen, also held somewhat unusual views in other areas of doctrine. In Origen's case, this included belief in eternal creation of the universe. At the Council of Nicea, any sort of ontological subordination of the Son was clearly rejected, but the concept of eternal generation or begottenness was basically retained. In general, eternal generation was more characteristic of Eastern than of Western theology. It is notable, however, that the Father's commanding and the Son's obeying was not particularly emphasized at this time.

In Augustine's formulation of the Trinity, functional subordination was basically eliminated, and the concept of all divine actions being the work of all three persons came to the fore. This was also the case with Thomas Aquinas and the Reformers, although Luther, who had relatively little to say about the doctrine of the Trinity, held a more traditional view of generation. Calvin had little place for the idea of generation in this theology and basically followed Augustine on most points. Calvin contributed an interpretation of 1 Corinthians 15:24–28 that has been followed largely by Reformed theologians since: that it is Christ, as the God-man, turning authority over to the triune God, including the second person of the Trinity.

While the Eastern tradition continued to place the Son in second place to the Father, as illustrated by the rejection of the *filioque* clause, this has been less prominent in recent discussions.

Summarizing the historical considerations, then, it appears that one can find a considerable number of theologians, especially early and in the East, who held to the functional subordination of the Son to the Father, and this was frequently tied to the idea of eternal begetting. As the church moved to delineate more completely what it understood by the Trinity, it moved more in the direction of the equal authority of the three persons. This trend continued, particularly in the West, into the late nineteenth century. Thus, while one can find historical precedent for the gradational view, it is safe to say that the slope of the evidence has been increasingly in support of the equivalent-authority position.

Philosophical

We divided these considerations into what we termed metaphysical questions and logical or rhetorical questions. The weightiest of these is the distinction the gradationists make between being and function. They insist that the three persons are fully equal in their being or essence, or what they are, but that there is an eternal functional subordination of the Son and the Holy Spirit to the Father. This is a crucial distinction, for it is what prevents their view from slipping into some variety of Arianism or Semi-Arianism.

It appears, however, that this distinction is problematic to maintain. If the Father is eternally and necessarily supreme among the persons of the Trinity, and if the Son eternally is subordinated to him, an interesting consequence follows. The Son is not merely accidentally, but essentially, subordinate to the Father. That means that there is a difference of essence between the two—that the Father's essence includes supreme authority, while the Son's essence includes submission and subordination, everywhere and always. There is considerable vagueness of meaning in the gradationist view at this point, but until the distinction is given meaningful content, the difficulty remains. One possible refuge would be to follow functional philosophy into functional theology, as the biblical theology movement did a generation ago with respect to Christology. The problems of that approach, however, are well known and undoubtedly would be present in this area of doctrine as well.

The equivalence view also recognizes a functional subordination of the Son to the Father, and of the Holy Spirit to the Father and the Son but maintains that this is necessary, not contingent, and therefore an accidental, not an essential, subordination. This was a temporary subordination voluntarily accepted for the performance of a particular task of redemption. Being temporary, it was assumed and later relinquished. This does not appear to present the sort of philosophical difficulties that attach to eternal functional subordination.

A further metaphysical issue is related to the claim that eternal subordination is essential to different identities of the three members of the

Trinity. The gradationists claim that if the three persons do not perform different roles, then the Trinity would be destroyed. They even
extend it to the point of claiming that our own individual personal
identities are in jeopardy. However, this appears to be a case of begging
the question, of assuming a view of the Trinity that would then be
excluded by the lack of different roles. The question of personal human
identity also seems problematic, since identical individuals, such as
identical twins, do exist.

We also examined the idea of generation or begetting. From a
philosophical perspective, this concept generally has not been given
much content. It seems to come down to the idea that the Father is in
some sense the cause of the Son's being, although this idea is generally rejected by those who want to maintain the concept of generation.
Thus the concept either is meaningless or has a tendency to lead to
some variety of Arianism. The philosopher Paul Helm contends that
this doctrine arose as the result of theologians being influenced by
Neoplatonic philosophy. It is notable that for the most part the gradationists have rejected the idea of eternal generation, considering the
"begetting" references to apply to the Son's earthly birth. It appears to
me that the concept of eternal generation does not have biblical warrant
and does not make sense philosophically. As such, we should eliminate
it from theological discussions of the Trinity. It should, however, be
noted that those earlier theologians who are cited in support of the idea
of eternal functional subordination in most cases tied it to the concept
of eternal generation.

There also are significant logical issues involved in the debate. One
crucial issue is the gradationist argument that differentiation of persons
requires difference of role. However, they assume that difference of
role requires different ranking of the persons. It is not different roles to
which equivalentists object, but rather the idea that one person always
has a role that is superior to that of the other person. The idea that difference of role requires that one person have authority over the other
appears to be unsubstantiated, yet it is a principle crucial to the gradationist position.

We also noted the presence of suppressed premises, such as in the argument that one person sending another demonstrates the sender's authority over the one sent. In each case there are other possibilities that are ignored, particularly B. B. Warfield's suggestion that the Son's coming may have been the result of a covenant between the persons of the Trinity.

A certain amount of stipulative definition also was uncovered in the analysis of the discussions. This is present in the gradationists' co-opting of the term *complementarian*, even though strictly speaking it describes the position of many of their opponents as well. It also appears in the distinction drawn by Schemm between subordination and subordinationism.

We also noted the substitution of rhetorical expressions such as "clearly" and "obviously" for arguments supporting the conclusions. This is particularly found in the writings of the gradationists. But among the equivalentists, Giles tends to add his own interpretation to quotations from theologians he is citing.

In summary, it appears that the philosophical problems attached to the gradationist position as stated are considerably greater than those encountered by the equivalentists. This is especially true of the combination of eternal functional subordination with ontological equality, but it also occurs with respect to both other metaphysical concepts and logical argumentation. While these theologians would claim not to be dealing with philosophy, it is they who have ventured into these areas and thus can be held responsible for what they have said and done.

Theological

A number of theological issues also have arisen in our examination of the two positions. One concerns the status of Scripture. Some controversy has been generated by Kevin Giles's statement that a given passage of Scripture can be read in more than one way. He adds that we can decide which is the correct interpretation of a passage by examining how historic orthodoxy has interpreted the passage. The gradationists have taken this to mean that there is no one correct meaning of Scripture. In reality, what Giles is saying is demonstrated by the fact that he and the gradationists give different interpretations to some passages. He is not saying that there is no one best interpretation. Some additional ambiguity arises from his reference to the Spirit speaking through Scripture, which could be understood in a neo-orthodox sense. Calvin's view of the Spirit illuminating the objectively present meaning of the Scripture seems more in keeping with other aspects of Giles's view. In practice, the gradationists, by their appeal to the views of earlier Christian theologians, seem to be doing the same thing as Giles and thus, in effect, conceding the correctness of his point.

Giles has contended that the gradationists are implicitly in violation of the Evangelical Theological Society's doctrinal basis, which declares that the members of the Trinity are equal in power. He does this by contending that authority and power are to a considerable extent synonyms. It appears, however, that the distinction between the two is sufficiently well established to nullify his point.

Ware has criticized the equivalence view on the basis that it is unable to give any answer to the question of why the Son, rather than the Father, became incarnate. Apart from the fact that there are many theological questions that we are not currently able to answer and that may not need to be answered, his statement is not, strictly speaking, true. The equivalence answer can be that it was the result of a joint decision by the members of the Trinity that the second person should come to earth.

There is a problem with the gradationists' hesitation to speak of the Son's inferiority to the Father, although they speak of the Father as superior to the Son. Even if the distinction between role and being is granted, they do not wish to speak of the Son's role or order as inferior to that of the Father. There does seem to be something of a logical contradiction present in the gradational view, as stated by these representatives.

A more serious problem is the effect of the two views on the understanding of the Incarnation, the humiliation, and the glorification of the Son. It is notable that what the Son gave up and regained is less on the gradational than on the equivalence view, for on the former, he was never equal in authority with the Father. If, of course, this is how things were, then it is not proper to attempt to magnify the effect of the Incarnation, but it is worth noting that the significance of the Incarnation is different on the two views.

Kevin Giles has made much of the issue of whether each of the three persons of the Trinity has a separate will, or whether they have one collective will. The issue underlying this is whether a will is a characteristic of a nature or of a person. He believes that the gradational view of three wills leads to tritheism. It should be noted that the word *will* is somewhat ambiguous, and that tritheism can be avoided by a view in which there are three wills but the three, in the pattern known as perichoresis, always agree.

We observed that the gradationists made much of the designations "Father" and "Son" for the first two persons of the Trinity. They argue that these two names carry the same meaning when applied to the divine persons that they do when used of a human family relationship. This led us to the observation that the gradationists have not sufficiently developed a view of religious language, utilizing a rather literal view of language for God here that they criticize in their handling of open theist theology.

The gradationists contend that if there is not a difference in the roles of the persons of the Trinity, which they equate with differences in authority, the persons would not be distinguishable, and the Trinity would not exist. This, however, appears to be a case of stipulative definition, in which *Trinity* means not three persons but three persons of differing rank. In our judgment, this is an inconsequential argument.

A further problem attaches to the question of the Son's obedience. If it could not have been otherwise—if the Son must be the one to become incarnate—was his coming really a free act on the part of any member of the Trinity? With respect to this one action, was God free? This appears to be a problem for the gradational view.

The question of the status of the Holy Spirit is also problematic on the gradational view. Since he was subordinate to the Son as well as the Father, and since subordination is taken as being similar to that of human sons to human fathers, there is a perplexity that goes back as far as Gregory of Nazianzus's question to Athanasius. Is the Holy Spirit's relationship to the Father more like that of a second son, or is it more like that of a grandson, two steps removed in authority? It seems this is a question the gradationists have not considered.

Finally, we noted that on the equivalence view, in which each action of a member of the Trinity is actually an action of all three members, there is a benefit for the substitutionary-penal view of the atonement. This has sometimes been pictured as an injustice, because an innocent third party is punished for crimes he did not perform. On this interpretation, however, the one bearing the sins of humans is not an unwilling innocent but is actually the same person who sentences him to bear the consequences.

While there are advantages and difficulties generated in other areas of doctrine by each of these views, it is my judgment that the gradationist view encounters considerably more theological problems than does the equivalence view.

Practical

Perhaps the strongest area of practical implication of these two views is in the practice of prayer. Both on the basis of Jesus' teaching in the Lord's Prayer and the implications of a correct understanding of the Trinity, prayer should always be directed only to the Father, according to Ware. A major difficulty of this theory, however, is that it contradicts several instances in the New Testament of believers praying to the Son. While Grudem does not follow the same pattern as Ware here, it appears that the implications of his view should lead him to the same position. The prayers directed to Jesus, such as the *maranatha* prayer for his return, logically ought to be directed instead to the Father, on the gradational view. Since the Father sent the Son the first time, we should pray for him to send him the second time, rather than ask the Son to return. This seems to be a point at which a practical implication of the theological theory contradicts Scripture.

Similarly, with respect to praise and worship, the equivalence view has greater basis for praising the Son, for his incarnation involved a greater surrender of equality and was undertaken as the result of a decision in which he participated. Thus, unlike the gradational view, in which praise to the Son is only penultimate, here his praise is ultimate, as is that given to the Father.

One concept that plays a large part in the gradational view is the idea of *taxis*, or order. The gradationists contend that this implies the Father's priority of authority. This does not follow, however, since order can have several different meanings and does not necessarily imply some sort of priority of one member of the group.

The gradationists also have tried to argue from the greater authority of the Father over the Son for a similar authority structure in the family and the church. They do this in large part based on 1 Corinthians 11:1–3, and on the idea that *kephalē* there means superior to or having authority over. The word's meaning is sufficiently unclear, however, that this argument cannot carry great weight.

We also have observed that the gradational view, if applied to church government, would favor more concentration of authority at the top, while the equivalence view would be more in accord with authority generated from the individual members of the congregation. While we cannot go into this difference in exegetical and theological depth here, we should note that views that concentrate authority and power in the hands of a smaller number at the upper levels of a group run counter to powerful societal trends of the present time. Further, we should note that in the manner in which each theory is stated, the authority is not exercised in a domineering fashion.

Once again, in the practical area, the equivalence view seems to have a clear advantage over the gradational view. It fits the biblical and theological considerations more fully and with less distortion, and it encounters fewer problems than does the gradational view.

We have seen that the arguments for and against each of these views are complex and range over a large number of areas. Neither view has any single fatal difficulty, and neither is supported unambiguously by all of the evidence. Consequently, we must choose on the basis of the stronger consistency and coherence of the two views, the relative weight of the evidence supporting each, and the ability of each to deal with its problems and the objections raised to it. Without calculating any exact percentage, it is my judgment that the equivalence view is, on the basis of the criteria we have outlined, considerably the stronger of the two views and thus to be accepted over the gradational view. At the same time, we must be careful to keep our minds open to the evidence and to continue to investigate the relevant considerations, being prepared to change our minds if the balance of the argumentations shifts.

At this point, I would ordinarily terminate my discussion of a theological dispute. Although the two views are quite different from one another, each falls within the boundaries of traditional orthodoxy. Neither view has ever been condemned by an official body of the church. In general, the gradational view more closely resembles the traditional Eastern view of the Trinity, and the equivalence view is a variety of the Western approach to the doctrine. I have no concern that the gradationists who have written and spoken so forcefully in support of their view are not fully orthodox in their doctrine of the Trinity, as well as the other major doctrines of the Christian faith. I have no fear that any of them will, within their lifetimes, move beyond the boundaries of orthodoxy.

Having said this, however, I do have a concern, and a significant one. Although the stated doctrine of the gradationists is orthodox, I believe that it contains elements that logically imply an unorthodox dimension of the doctrine of the Trinity. I have in mind here the idea of ontological equality combined with the eternal and necessary supremacy of authority of the Father over the Son and the Holy Spirit. As I argued in the philosophical chapter, I believe this is an unstable position. For if one member always and everywhere is functionally superior to the other, then there must be an ontological basis for this difference. In other words, while explicitly rejecting the idea of ontological subordination, this view actually implies it and thus contains an implicit ontological subordination.

It is not likely that the present gradationists will make the move to draw this conclusion, and if they did, I believe they would modify their theory in such a way as to delete eternal functional superiority and subordination. The way they have argued leads me to expect this of them.

We might, of course, question how long this logical problem can continue without resolution. If a man says he believes that he has in his hands two apples and three oranges, and no other objects, can he continue to insist (and to do so sincerely) that he is not holding five pieces of fruit? My concern is for the next generation of theologians, the students of these gradationists. I suspect that they will see and draw the conclusion that is implied by the tenets held. It is then that a crisis may occur in which some will modify the gradational view but others will move on to a view of ontological superiority and subordination, which will constitute some species of Arianism. For reasons of both psychological tendency and logical implication, a second generation often goes further than those who precede them. For example, in the death of God theology, William Hamilton took the neo-orthodox idea of a god that can be known only when he initiates an encounter to the idea of a god that, because he does not seem to be encountered at all, is unreal. Another death of God theologian, Thomas J. J. Altizer, took Paul Tillich's doctrine of God as not a person but the ground of being and of personality a step further. To him, there was not only no person of God but no transcendent God at all.

If indeed, the next generation of theologians move to this idea of ontological subordination, then much of what present-day conservative Trinitarian theologians, both gradationists and equivalentists, have worked so hard to preserve will be threatened. I therefore echo Giles's plea to the gradationists, "Go back. You are going the wrong way."

I sincerely hope that I am wrong in this concern. It is not a prediction, simply an indication of where a segment of evangelical theology could go under certain conditions.

In the early 1990s I wrote a little book titled *Where Is Theology Going?* It was not intended to be a prophetic book in the sense of what would happen but rather a description of several possible outcomes, depending on what factors became dominant. About five years later I used the book as one of the textbooks in a Doctor of Ministry course on current theological issues. The students were unanimous in agreement with the semi-facetious charge expressed by one of them: "You required us to read this book to show us that you were right." I would have preferred if, on some of the more ominous predictions, I had been proven wrong.

I am concerned to preserve the orthodox tradition, in this case, with respect to the crucial doctrine of the Trinity. I issue this sincere plea to the gradationists: "Please think through the implications of your view, observe the body of evidence against it, and reconsider the idea of the eternal functional superiority of the Father over the Son and the Holy Spirit." There is no shame in modifying one's view when confronted with considerations one may have overlooked. In fact, it is a mark of strength to possess a continuing open mind. The church of our triune God will be strengthened thereby and our God glorified. It is my prayer that this entreaty will be taken seriously.

Name and Subject Index

Scripture Index